COYOTE SPIRIT

The Improbable Transformation from Minister to Clown

David John Mampel

Table of Contents

~.~

"A trickster (coyote) is a mischievous or roguish figure in myth or folklore who typically makes up for physical weakness with cunning and subversive humor. The trickster alternates between cleverness and stupidity, kindness and cruelty, deceiver and deceived, breaker of taboos and creator of culture."

--S. E. Schlosser

This book is dedicated to my parents, Arthur George Mampel and Jacqueline Louise Mampel, with gratitude for their love and support through all of my wild becoming.

Endorsements

"David Mampel's memoir brings to light the joy and the anguish of growing up in an America where Ozzie Nelson and Timothy Leary lived on the same street."

—STEVE GLAUBER, award-winning producer of CBS News' *60 Minutes*

"Dave Mampel's *Coyote Spirit* will touch your heart and awaken your spirit."

—TOM CATTON, author of *The Mindful Addict: A Memoir of the Awakening of a Spirit and May I Sit with You: A Simple Approach to Meditation*

Foreword

To have known the close constancy of living and watching our son evolve through all the important stages of life, through all the hurt and healing, the exalted and low moments, through those feisty, rebel teenage years, and to witness the occasional promise of maturity in early youth, for the surprise and change that comes with the resolve of a young man setting out to find his dream on a road with twists and abrupt turns, dead ends, and the many uncertainties that lie in wait like an ambush. Any decision that requires the undaunted and steadfast gall to go unswervingly forward--trusting in an ever-unfolding dream--is a brave decision. To step up and make the solemn decision, to gamble it all on a career in clowning, a career whose only guarantee was a belief in the sureness that possibilities come when we dare life to be limitless in vision and rewarding of risk.

I have just finished reading the manuscript. My pace was ten pages every day with comments, suggestions, and notations, which he happily requested. I realize now there were gaps in David's life that were only consummated for me when I read this history, lived in the absence of his family.

I wondered if I liked what David wrote in this autobiography, because it spoke to me in familiar references, in shared memories, and because David is our son. I tried to read it as someone dispassionate and estranged from the personal events of his saga, but it was a lost effort. I could not make a credible separation of critic and father. Still, I confess, it was a pleasurable exercise and one I think the reader will also enjoy, delighting in the joyous sauntering of a life cut loose from the safety and confines of what's expected, a life that risks it all on the faith and certainty that new ways will present and reveal themselves as he moves forward.

Some years back David and I attended a poetry reading at the Fifth Avenue Theater in downtown Seattle. The Russian poet Yevgeny Yevtushenko spent the evening reciting poems with a high-spirited appeal. I found in one of his longer poems, "Zima Junction," a passage I thought especially appropriate for our author and clown, Daffy Dave.

ZIMA JUNCTION
—Yevgeny Yevtushenko

And the voice of Zima Junction spoke to me
And this is what it said,
"I live quietly and crack nuts.
I gently steam with engines.
But not without reflection on these times,
These modern times, my loving meditation.
Don't worry. Yours is no unique condition,
Your type of search and conflict and construction,
Don't worry if you have no answer ready
To the lasting question.
Hold out, meditate, listen.
Explore. Explore. Travel the world over.
Count happiness connatural to the mind
More than truth is, and yet
No happiness to exist without it.
Walk with a cold pride
Utterly ahead
Wild attentive eyes
Head flicked by rain wet
Green needles of the pine,
Eyelashes that shine
With tears and with thunders.
Love people.
Love entertains its own discrimination.
Have me in mind, I shall be watching.
You can return to me.
Now. go."
I went and I am still going.

~.~

A.G. MAMPEL
January 2014

Introduction

I am living the life of my dreams, but it was not always so. This book is the story of how I followed my bliss and is an attempt to share what I have discovered for anyone else who might be struggling to do the same. It is a story of the difficult decisions that allowed me to climb out of the deep hole I dug for myself as a young man and the road I took to the life I live now, a life of contentment and sometimes even joy. In many ways, this story is the story of the soul's journey back to itself, back to lost innocence, to childhood. Along the way, I found the vocation that had been waiting for me all along. If you have an inkling that some life better than the one you are now living awaits you, perhaps the story of my journey will help you to make those difficult choices in your life, too. If not, my hope is that you'll be entertained, inspired, and maybe get a few laughs, too.

In 1990, I was twenty-eight years old and parish minister of the First Congregational Church in Idaho Falls, Idaho. I had been restless and discontented for some time. I knew I was in the wrong profession but I didn't know what to do about it. I was scared, and I risked disappointing people I cared about if I were to leave the life I had chosen and jump off into the unknown. What I wanted to be was an entertainer, preferably a rock star who made overflowing buckets full of money and had women throwing themselves at me, but I had no earthly idea how to go about achieving that. To complicate matters, I was smoking marijuana regularly. Yeah, that's right. A parish minister, scared and lonely, smoking weed to avoid thinking about and making a difficult life decision. Not a pretty picture, right? But that's what I did. I was growing more depressed by the day.

Today, I have a rich spiritual life and I run my own entertainment business. I am blessed with friends I love, a home of my own, and several weeks of vacation every year. A couple of years ago, I traveled to Europe and spent more than a month there visiting places I had always wanted to see and making friends wherever I went. My annual income for the last several years has sometimes been in the six-digit range. Best of all, I haven't used marijuana or alcohol or any other drug for many years, nor have I felt the need to do so. My needs are simple and I am content. I am a professional clown, a far cry from the internationally renowned rock star I thought I wanted to be, but I am happy. I was always a clown, anyway. Everyone around me knew that before I did. Today I know that some Divine Power has led me to this place in my life and continues to guide me still.

Dave Mampel
August 2013

Chapter One:
Parish Pastor in a Tight Suit

"Follow your bliss. If you do follow your bliss, you put yourself on a kind of track that has been there all the while waiting for you, and the life you ought to be living is the one you are living. When you can see that, you begin to meet people who are in the field of your bliss, and they open the doors to you. I say, follow your bliss and don't be afraid, and doors will open where you didn't know they were going to be. If you follow your bliss, doors will open for you that wouldn't have opened for anyone else."
-- Joseph Campbell

One icy cold winter night, as a young parish pastor in Idaho, ecstatic after playing music with some friends to a packed house at the Espresso Kitchen in Idaho Falls where I lived, I invited my new artistic musician friends over to my mobile home to relax and soak in my new wood-heated hot tub. I was thrilled when several of them enthusiastically accepted my invitation, and I thought this might be the beginning of my feeling more at home in Idaho. It's not easy to be friends with your parishioners and be their pastor, too, and I had been lonely for friendships longer than I cared to admit. I welcomed these new friends from outside of my church, people I hoped I could trust to share in my joys and concerns.

When my creative, fun friends came over, we chatted for a while, then we went out onto my newly constructed deck for a soak. It was a beautiful clear night, and stars twinkled around a bright moon. The conversation was lively, and the cold breeze danced around us. Steam rose off the hot water. In a quiet moment, someone held up a joint of marijuana. "Okay if I light up?" he asked. Immediately my blood quickened and my powers of reasoning fled. I must have had a puzzled and vulnerable look on my face, because that was how I felt, and he quickly apologized. "Oh, wait. I forgot you don't get high. Sorry, Dave, I'll put it away."

"No, no." I laughed a little nervously. "It's okay." I didn't stop to think things through. "It doesn't bother me," I said. "Go ahead. Light it up." And I knew at that moment that I would take a hit when the joint was passed to me. When my turn finally came--and it seemed as if it took a very long time in coming around to me--I paused. I held the joint for a moment, pretending to myself that I was about to pass it to the next person, and then, out loud, I said, "Oh, one little hit won't matter."

"Are you sure, Dave?" someone asked.

"Yeah," I answered. "As long as I just do a little, it will be okay."

The next thing I knew, we were all laughing and rolling around in the snow. We warmed up in the hot tub again, rolled in the snow again, warmed up in the hot tub again, and finally ended up in my living room, chatting and playing music.

My years of abstinence were over. It was done. I had relapsed. When my new friends left for the night, I was left with an empty, deflated feeling.

~.~

Things weren't supposed to go that way.

I was awarded a Master's of Divinity degree from United Theological Seminary in the spring of 1988. Mom was right when she wrote, "Accomplishing things is the best high in life." Earning that degree was a gratifying and soul-expanding experience. Even better, though, was the experience of being voted in to pastor my new congregation, First Congregational Church in Idaho Falls, Idaho. I preached a trial sermon to about a hundred members of that congregation, and then they voted on whether or not to accept me as their new pastor.

In the denomination I grew up in, and the one I was then actively involved in, the United Church of Christ, a pastor has to be "called" to a parish, or in other words, voted in by the congregation, before he or she can be ordained. Unlike some other denominations, ministers are not assigned to a parish by a bishop, but a democratic process comes into play instead. The notion of one person, one vote shaped American democracy in its earliest days, a concept that came to this country by way of the early Congregationalists. Once I had been "called" to my new congregation, I was ready to go through the ordination ceremony. The ceremony was held at my dad's church, my "home congregation," where I was a member at the time, the Beacon Avenue United Church of Christ in Seattle.

The day of the ordination service arrived, and the church filled with people, overwhelming me with an outpouring of love and support. As is the tradition in my church, I wore a minister's robe of unbleached muslin, a symbol of serving others in imitation of Christ. After the ceremony, church members gave me some colorful stoles to drape around the neck of my humble robe. The service lasted about three hours and focused on celebrating and encouraging my calling. At the end of the service came the laying on of hands, during which loving hands were placed on my head and the entire congregation joined hands. Prayers were said for my charge and guidance, and I was filled with an emotion I still can't describe. Pops reminds me, "Once ordained, always ordained," and I know his words are true. In many ways, my ordination is still with me, even though today I am a no longer a pastor but a professional clown.

People came to my ordination from many chapters of my life. There were other ministers; members of my home congregation; family members; the supervising minister from my last internship; the conference minister, our church's version of a kind of bishop. To my surprise, Larry Cloud-Morgan came, too, a big, loving teddy bear of a man. Larry and I had worked together on a number of social justice issues while I was interning at Clergy and Laity Concerned during my seminary days. He had recently been released from prison where he had served time for protesting in Kansas against nuclear bombs by destroying Minute Man II missiles with a jackhammer. Larry was a shaman and a spiritual leader for many, and I looked up to him. I was very touched that he flew out unannounced from Minneapolis to show up at my ordination. When Larry died a few years later, his obituary in the *Minneapolis Star Tribune* read in part, "He was a peace activist, a playwright, a counselor in shelters and hospitals, on city streets and on the White Earth Chippewa Reservation. He was a storyteller, a spiritual leader, a historian and a linguist who helped preserve the Ojibwe language on tape at Harvard University.

"He was a convicted felon who served time in a federal penitentiary for taking a jackhammer to a nuclear missile silo. He gently confronted white protesters who wanted to deny his people their traditional fishing rights. And he was a reformer who helped reshape tribal government on the White Earth Reservation where he lived in northwestern Minnesota."

I had had no idea that Larry was planning to come, and I felt as if his presence that day connected my new life to another part of me--the mystical, pantheistic side that, today, I know is more who I am spiritually. His presence signaled to me that something even deeper than my being ordained was going on, that my ordination was not simply about my being a pastor in a Christian church. No, there was much more to it than even that. I was reminded of my experience of participating in a Native American sweat lodge and of other Native American spiritual rituals I had learned about, and Larry's presence that day signaled to me that my spiritual river ran wide and deep, no matter how I might try to force it into a narrow channel.

On the day of my ordination, my mind was focused on all the new things I needed to learn. I felt overwhelmed with joy and gratitude, but I also felt some concern about what was next for me. I pushed aside any vague stirrings I felt about this pantheistic side of my spirituality. After Larry left, though, I went into the room at Dad's parsonage where Larry had stayed and found a symbolic arrangement of precious agates that he had left behind for me to find, and I felt a sudden strong connection to Mother Earth, to God-in-Everything, to my deeper calling to the Great Spirit that goes beyond organized religion.

The stones reminded me of the stones I had once collected from around Lake Superior as a child, a haunting token of my earliest childhood.

For about the first year and a half of my parish ministry in Idaho, I felt I was finding a good balance between the responsible, spiritual adult and the playful, childlike sides of me. Poetry and music were still a big part of my life. Besides my communal duties as a pastor--performing weddings, officiating at funerals, visiting shut-ins and people in the hospital, and attending endless church meetings--I wrote sermons every week, wrote poems for our church newsletter, wrote and performed songs for the Sunday school, and sometimes played my songs in church services and at youth camps I directed. I submitted some of my poems for publication, and some were even published in small magazines like *High Country News* and *The Father/Sun Journal*.

Despite all these creative release valves, however, the artist in me continued to grow restless. I felt increasingly constrained in my role as a pastor. At about this time, some coffee houses opened in our town and I started going there, bringing pen and paper so I could journal as I sipped on my coffee there. One thing led to another, and before I knew it, I was playing songs and reading poetry in those cafés on my nights off from being a pastor. I met other musicians in the process, and we formed duos, trios, and other musical groups. We began to attract attention, and Idaho Falls welcomed our live acoustic music. We were big fish in a small pond, and we had fun. On one of those nights, my friend and I collected sixty dollars each in tips, and that did it for me. I was hooked. I really felt confident about my music after that, and I quietly dreamed of transitioning into a being a full-time musician.

By that time, I was almost two years into my parish ministry, and a number of insights and events came together to inspire me further. I read the works of Joseph Campbell and was excited by his concept of "following your bliss." I found my bliss in playing music, entertaining, and writing. Where would life take me if I were to follow that? Mr. Campbell illustrated with myth and story the rewards to self and society when a person follows their bliss. I read Marsha Sinetar's *Do What You Love and the Money Will Follow* and other books in a similar vein.

I began to develop the faith that God and the universe would help me to live out my dreams if I were to follow my own bliss. I was convinced that human beings find purpose in life by living that way, and surely, I reasoned, God wants that for us. Why else would God give us those dreams? My own creative dreams reemerged with a passion, including my dreams of being a rock star or an entertainer of some kind, and it began to seem to me that the parish ministry limited my very life. I started to feel as if I were wearing a suit that was too small for me. My creative desires were frustrated not only by the limitations I felt but also because I just could not imagine how I could change. All I knew for sure was that the parish ministry just wasn't for me, but that knowing scared the dickens out of me.

Even worse, organized religion itself was becoming like a room too small for me to live in, as my spiritual awareness craved insights from other sources, other religions, philosophies that intrigued me. It was getting harder and harder to move in that tiny dwelling of organized religion, but I still had to do so because of my chosen profession as a pastor. It was an agonizing time for an eclectic spiritual mystic like me. I felt as if I had one foot in organized religion while the other foot was starting to walk outside of it. I did a self-portrait at about this time, an ink drawing of a figure in a half-destroyed chapel with a long, winding path leading out toward a rising sun.

One Sunday morning, I led a worship service at my church in which I had everybody laughing to the point of tears. After everybody had shaken my hand at the end of the service, our church organist came up to me and said, "Dave, I think you're more of an entertainer than a pastor." I swear to you, I literally, not figuratively, heard bells go off and saw about five little bright lights flash before my eyes. I knew then that I was going to leave the ministry, even if I didn't know how or when. Like so many others before me, I had to experience a lot of pain before I could change my life.

~.~

Around this time, one of the members of my church asked me if I would dress up like a clown and entertain at her little girl's birthday party. I was taken aback at first, but then something in me said yes. I felt strange putting on the cheap clown costume she rented for me, but I seemed to know what to do. I had not developed many clown skills at that point, but I was a hit nonetheless. The kids were two- and three-year-olds so I made my voice sound gentle and silly, played some songs, and pretended to do magic. They loved it. I did one magic trick where I threw an invisible ball into the air and "caught" it in a paper bag. The invisible ball landed in the bag with a papery plop, creating the illusion. When it was time to light the birthday candles, I said, "Wait! I can do it with my finger!" All the little kids and even the adults stood quietly and watched in awe as I approached the cake with my finger extended. Everyone was completely still and quiet. At the last second, I pulled my finger away and said, "Just kidding! I can't do it," and they all laughed. That was one of my first experiences of creating a comedic magic routine, without the magic. I have since learned a way to light candles magically with my finger, but this was after years of practicing magic. I still love the "fooling around" comical parts of magic, even magic I don't know how to do. What arises then is true magic, the magic of laughter. Comedy, in many ways, is more important than the magic I perform in my show, but I now do both as Daffy Dave.

The woman from my church who asked me to be the clown at her daughter's party was so touched and appreciative that she wrote a poem about my performance for our church's newsletter in which she compared being a clown to being Jesus. Her poem reminded me of the part in Monty Python's Life of Brian where the crucified Christ sings, "Always Look on the Bright Side of Life." That mom's appreciation turned out to be a precursor for more praise in the years to come from grateful parents and organizers who hire me to perform my Daffy Dave shows. Over time, my skills have improved, and now I know how to keep young audiences mesmerized and laughing, sometimes to the point of tears, occasionally even peeing in their pants, and now and then falling over onto the ground doubled over with belly laughter.

Something clicked into place with that birthday party experience, but I was still working it out in my mind and my heart. It began to seem to me that everybody around me knew I was a clown before I did. I took my new "act" to the Eastern Idaho Regional Medical Center and clowned around with the patients there. I was an official hospital chaplain at the time, so clowning for the patients seemed a natural extension of my duties there. I had a great deal of fun doing it, even though I was nervous at times because I wasn't sure how helpful I was being or if I was being "pastoral" enough.

~.~

The mystical stream that wove in and out of my life during this time showed up in a number of ways. Recently, a former parishioner confessed to me all these years later that some of these mystical pursuits of mine were disconcerting for some people in my congregation. I once played Gregorian chants in the darkened sanctuary lit only with candles; I started a Wednesday night meditation service; I led a small eclectic group in a study of the Gnostic gospels. I didn't realize it at the time, but I now know that a good many of the members of my congregation found these practices unconventional and a little unnerving.

My mystical bent provided something important in my ministry, though, in my duties as hospice chaplain. It seemed natural to me to help people "let go" of their bodies at the moment of death. I made it a practice to visit terminally ill patients in the weeks and months before they died, getting to know them, joking and laughing with them, offering compassion, and praying with them. When the moment was right, I lovingly asked them the tough questions about dying. "Does your faith help you with letting go of life?" I would ask. "I'm just here to irritate you with tough questions like this," I would tell them, and maybe they would laugh a little. I counseled family members and prayed with them, and when the time came for their loved one to die, I was there. At least once, one of those patients actually waited for me to arrive before she allowed herself to die.

During that sacred moment just before death, I would ask everyone present to hold hands with each other and with the dying person. With the family gathered around, we would pray together. I would say a prayer to ask that all of us gathered together would be a calming presence for their dying loved one, that we would hold a space for death to be all right, to be just a birth, another part of life itself. Several times I witnessed a misty, softly lit presence rising up out of the person at the moment of their final breath. I know that my out-of-body visions, my other mystical experiences, and even my dad's afterlife experience prepared me to understand, accept, and help people die in peace. I was privileged to assist ten souls in leaving their bodies during this time in my life. However, despite all my experiences in this area, all these confirmations of another dimension, of an afterlife beyond the sensory realm, I still have no absolute, tangible proof of life after death. As my father's friend Dr. Tom Tredway likes to say, "I've never received a post card from the other side."

~.~

Cunning, baffling, and powerful, my addiction reclaimed my life ever so slowly. I was about two years into my parish ministry, and I was starting to enjoy playing music with other creative musicians at the local café scene in Idaho Falls. On the other hand, I was feeling lonely and trapped in Idaho, and I longed for more cultural stimulation. I continued to dream of living life as some kind of artist, dreams which were starting to come to a boil on the back burners. In 1986, before I returned to seminary to complete my studies for my master's degree, I had gone back to Twelve Step fellowships in Seattle. I accepted then that I am an addict and will always be an addict, no matter how long I have been clean, and that acceptance kept me abstinent during the years I was in seminary and the first couple of years when I served as a pastor in Idaho. Once I was ordained and had become a practicing minister, I failed to account for the fact that merely staying clean is not active, ongoing recovery from addiction. Accepting the problem is the first step to freedom, but it's not enough. I had stopped going to meetings; I didn't have a sponsor; I didn't work the Twelve Steps and practice the spiritual principles they embody; I wasn't in service to other addicts. As a matter of fact, I wasn't active in Twelve Step recovery at all. I wasn't living in the solution for my problem, as we say in those fellowships.

I made the mistake of thinking that being a church member was enough. I thought that because I was a pastor and had a spiritual life I would be able to keep myself from using drugs and alcohol, simply because I chose not to use any mind- and mood-altering substances. But willpower alone is not enough. The church is a place of corporate worship of the Divine with some forms of outreach into the community; it is not intended for or designed to be a program where addicts can identify with and help each other. Many churches, to their credit, open their doors to allow non-profit Twelve Step groups to rent meeting space for a nominal fee, and that is a very helpful contribution to the growth and success of Twelve Step fellowships around the world, saving numerous lives. Church folks may have sympathy for addicts, but they don't necessarily feel empathy, especially since most church members, in my experience, are not hard-core drug addicts.

I'm not the only addict who has made the same mistake. I know a number of recovering addicts today who tell about experiencing this same hard lesson: Simple abstinence is not sufficient for recovery from addiction. Most recovering addicts I know need not only to be in heartfelt acceptance of their problem, but also vigilantly dedicated to the solution. I have learned that Twelve Step fellowships and a rigorous, ongoing program of recovery are what I require to remain free from drugs and continue to live a new, spiritual way of life without drugs.

At first, my addiction expressed itself only as an occasional passing thought, a quick, romanticized memory of smoking marijuana, of laughing and feeling euphoric. Quick memories of the fun parts of getting high flashed through my mind now and then, with no recollection of all the negative consequences of drug use. I conveniently forgot about the emotional and spiritual numbness, the reckless and dangerous behaviors, the social isolation, the lack of responsibility, the apathy. I didn't think about the damage to my lungs, my brain, my body.

~.~

I had started to expand how I was doing ministry in Idaho by starting the Community Youth Center with other local churches, including Mormon representatives. There was a lot of tension in Idaho Falls between Mormons and non-Mormon Christians, especially from the non-Mormon Christian side. The Christians in Idaho Falls were outnumbered by the Mormons, and I guess some of them felt a little defensive about that. I wanted to help bridge the gap between the two groups, and it seemed to me that a youth center was a good place to start. Besides, young people of all faiths in Idaho Falls needed a cool place to hang out, socialize, and dance. In addition, they would be able to receive services such as a homework hotline. I wrote and obtained grants to get the project started, and it was exciting, especially when I experienced some initial success. Before too long, though, the other board members and I realized that we didn't have enough resources to cover our expenses. Additionally, the Mormon churches already had a strong youth program, and their teens had little need for a center like the one we were trying to establish. As if that weren't enough, members of my congregation began to resent the time I spent on that project because I wasn't available to minister to our church's own members.

The homework hotline survived for a little while after the program collapsed, but soon that, too, was gone. In a post-mortem board meeting, we reflected that we should have started small and built the program slowly. I take this hard-won lesson seriously today, and have taken pains to build my own business as Daffy Dave slowly, leveraging my success as I go, adding and diversifying a little at a time, delegating to vendors, and reinvesting profits back into new projects. These days, with my debts paid down, I am actually able to save a little money and even have some small financial investments; I enjoy some passive income from my Daffy Dave music recordings on YouTube, iTunes, and Spotify. I try not to take on too much too fast, and my business grows steadily. Like the third little pig in the fairytale, I take my time to build a solid brick house on a sturdy foundation.

While these activities were swirling around me, I was painfully and soulfully questioning my ministry and longing for more creative stimulation. One summer day in my church office, I was daydreaming about smoking marijuana. My dog Woody lay sleeping on the floor next to my chair. Just thinking about it, I almost felt high again. Resolutely, I brushed those memories aside. Months later, I found myself thinking about smoking pot again. Again, I tried to suppress the desire to use.

I didn't get high again for several months after that fateful evening when I smoked a joint in my hot tub with my new musician friends, but as time went on, I found ways to show up at parties where I knew there would be marijuana, and I would take a toke here and there. Before long, I was growing pot in my garage and hanging out with other people who smoked pot, even if I didn't like them. I started neglecting my responsibilities as a minister and acting inappropriately. I missed office hours, changed the message on my answering machine so that it sounded silly, and did other stupid, careless things. I am ever so grateful that I never ended up in legal trouble, but I was terrified that I would be found out. I lived in a state of paranoia punctuated by brief moments of being loaded, and the guilt and shame mounted with each passing day until my feelings were almost unbearable. Then, something happened that really woke me up.

I had just returned from directing a high school church camp in McCall, Idaho, and was completely sleep deprived. Have you ever tried to sleep in a rustic cabin while playful teenagers laughed and talked all night long? Late into the night, I had finally resorted to tricking them into going to sleep. "Hey, guys," I said. "I know hypnosis and could easily put you all into a trance." Eager for a new experience, as youth will be, they egged me on to try. Acting coy, I answered, "Nah. It's dangerous. I'd better not do it," which of course was all they needed to hear to make them want it even more. Finally, after much pleading and begging from my young charges, I diffidently acquiesced. "Lie in your bunks," I told them, "so I can prepare you to 'go under.'" I led them through some breathing exercises and guided meditations, and soon they were all asleep. All the same, I knew I needed to sleep very lightly myself, as there was always some kid who insisted on waking up and wandering off alone into the night and finding some way of getting into trouble. The other counselors and I were constantly on our guard.

When I got back to Idaho Falls, I went immediately to bed and slept soundly all night. The next morning I awoke with a piercing headache like nothing I had ever felt before. My body was electric with pain and I could barely breathe. I panicked and called one of my friends and asked him to come over and drive me to the hospital. "What's going on?" he asked.

"I don't know," I told him, "but I'm in extreme pain and can hardly breathe."

"I'll be right over, Dave!" he said. "Hold on!" I stumbled out the door of my mobile home when my friend drove up. He helped me get into his car and took off for the hospital.

As he drove, the pain got worse and worse, so bad I started to cry. "I do too much!" I cried. "I've got to slow down and not do so many things." My buddy didn't know what to say, but he patted me on the shoulder and drove as fast as he dared.

When finally I was in the emergency room, the pain became unbearable and I started hyperventilating. One of the nurses handed me a paper bag and told me to breathe into it. A team of doctors and nurses huddled nearby, consulting with each other about what to do to help me. At that moment, I saw and sensed a golden face with almond-shaped eyes float out of my chest and up to the ceiling in a corner across from me. It stared at me and communicated to me telepathically that it was the eternal part of me and that no human pain could touch it. Then it floated back inside my chest. I noticed that no one saw the face but me. I began to breathe more easily as I inhaled and exhaled into the paper bag.

The doctors gave me a CAT scan and ordered other tests. They gave me Demerol, which made me vomit, but it stopped the pain. After I was wheeled into a hospital room, I went to sleep, but not for long. I awoke from a horrific and vivid nightmare about a bunch of nurses who came into my room, took off their clothes to seduce me then stabbed me with knives. I vomited again and didn't want to go back to sleep after that, but I couldn't help myself.

The next morning, my doctors came into my room to see me and I realized they were both members of my congregation. They closed the door and asked me how I felt. Then one of them told me I had somehow contracted both spinal meningitis and viral encephalitis. "You could have died," one of them told me gravely. They went on to gently inform me they had found traces of cocaine and tetrahydrocannabinol, the active ingredient in marijuana, in my blood. "Do you have a problem with drugs?" asked one of the doctors.

"Oh, it's nothing serious," I said. "I took a little at a party, that's all." I looked down at my hands and tried to breathe normally. I felt sickened and ashamed.

They glanced awkwardly at each other, and then one of them said, "Okay. Well, you will need to take time off for a few weeks." He paused. "When you do go back to work," he continued, "you'll need to rest for fifteen minutes five times a day or your head will start to pound again." I had wanted to slow down, but this was more than I had in mind. "You may have to continue this regimen for a few months, but it looks like you will be okay." I was so relieved to hear I was not going to die that I almost forgot about my shame.

~.~

At one point during my hospital stay, I turned on the television and discovered that my favorite childhood movie, *My Side of the Mountain*, was playing. The film is about a young boy who goes out to the Catskill Mountains to live like Thoreau. I felt that seeing that movie then was a message, as if something from my childhood were whispering to me to follow my dreams the way that boy did.

Somehow, during the pain and the panic of the previous day, I had managed to call Dad. When I reached him, he was wrapping up a visit with his dear friends Bruce Carlson and Tom Tredway in Minneapolis. Instead of driving home to Seattle, he drove straight to Idaho Falls when he heard what was going on with me, a nine-hundred-mile trip. It all gets a little blurry here, and I don't remember if he came to see me while I was still in the hospital or if he came to my home the following morning. No matter. Dad arrived. His very presence calmed me.

I felt relieved not to have to attend to my pastoral duties for a while. I had some time to rest and reflect on my life. Before this near-death incident, I had been assembling a large collage of my life story up to that point. I walked into the garage and studied my collage. I reflected on all the phases of my life represented by various colors, symbols, knickknacks, and photographs taken at different times. I gazed at these representations of my life, this artistic expression on the giant canvas, and wondered what had gone wrong. Where and why had I gone astray? These were troubling questions, but I felt detached and even peaceful as I asked them. How could I untangle the dilemma I found myself in, I wondered, this yearning to be something other than a pastor? What was that strange vision I had had in the hospital? And what should I do about my recurring problem with drugs?

It took me a couple of months to get around to it, but eventually, I confessed my drug use to Pam, my official liaison with the congregation. When I told her, Pam's face contorted with pain. She was compassionate and supportive and encouraged me to get help, and I tried to do that. I returned to the rooms of Twelve Step recovery and sought counseling for my unresolved childhood issues. I managed to stay away from drugs for about a year, but I did not lose the urge to use during that time, and by October of the following year, I was smoking marijuana regularly again. When she found out I was using again, Pam confronted me about it. By then, practically everyone in my congregation was aware of my drug use. It was a horribly painful time for Pam, for that little congregation, and for me. I was scared and humiliated, and I had nowhere to turn. My life was crumbling to pieces around me. Eventually, I turned in my resignation and was given two months to wind up my assignment, with a couple of people assigned to monitor the process and usher me out. Later, I did my best to tie up loose ends and even tried to explain myself in one of my sermons. But I was not in good shape. The most generous people in that congregation tried to understand, but there were lots of hurt feelings and a good deal of anger. I continued to use drugs throughout that ordeal, making things even worse for myself and others.

It would be another six years before I wholeheartedly accepted both the fact of my addiction and the solution of recovery. That was on February 1, 1998. As of this writing, I have been drug- and alcohol-free and in an active program of recovery in a Twelve Step program since that date. I returned to Idaho Falls several years after my "clean date," as we call it in recovery programs, and did my best, with the help of my Twelve Step sponsor, to make amends to my old congregation. I telephoned the individuals I had hurt and not only apologized but asked each person what I could do to make things right for them. Some people were willing to forgive me, and some were not. It was not an easy process, but I had to do it, and I am grateful to my Higher Power for giving me the courage to see it through. Some of the shame and guilt fell away then, and I continue to work on the rest. My deepest hope is that my attempts at making amends helped the people in my old congregation. All I could do in most cases was apologize and admit I was wrong, but deep wounds remain. With this writing, I continue to further the process of making my amends, and I pray for healing for everyone I hurt. At this point in my life and in my recovery, all I can do is turn the outcome over to a loving, caring Higher Power and pray for healing for everyone involved. I am grateful when, by grace and in quiet moments, the freedom of forgiveness washes through my soul.

Chapter Two: Beginnings

"Truly, I say to you, unless you turn and become like
children, you will never enter the kingdom of heaven."
--Matthew 18:3

A misty memory comes to me: I am very young, holding
someone's hand and walking down a long series of
creaky wooden stairs. I realize now they are the stairs that lead
down to Gull Lake, where some friends of my parents lived.
It's a dreamy spring day and pine-scented wind laced with
the fragrance of fresh water purifies my senses and awakens
my mind. Whitecaps out in the lake look like hundreds of eyes
twinkling on a dark blue face, and I stare at the lake creature
for a few moments. A motorboat is tied to the dock far below
and trees sway along the distant shore. I am in the land of Paul
Bunyan, the ancient lands of birch-filled whispers, of Ojibwa
Indians living close to Mother Earth and Father Sky.

Another cabin comes to me in my reverie. I am with Mom
and Dad and we're vacationing for a few days near one of the
Great Lakes, probably Lake Superior, near Duluth, Minnesota.
We stop at a lodge on our way to the cabin where I wander
through a native arts gift shop and become fascinated by deer-
skin moccasins. At the rustic cabin, weather is stormy and skies
dark. Wintry waves splash in oceanic splendor onto agate-lined
shores below jagged cliffs. I am thrilled and a little scared, but
I feel safe and cozy with my loving parents inside the cabin.
Comforting flames in the fireplace warm my body. A hatchet
for chopping firewood leans against the stone hearth. Mother
warns me to be careful, not to touch the sharp blade or I could
bleed.

When the stormy weather passes, Mom takes me out to
the pine forest that surrounds us. It seems enchanted to me, like
something out of a fairytale. She holds my little hand. We walk

to a moss-covered cliff above the water. We find some green moss growing under the trees there, and she helps me pick some. Together we craft little houses out of the squishy stuff.

Northern breezes echo mysterious loon songs at sunrise. At sunset, their mournful cries awaken otherworldly longings in the human soul. Early evening steam rises from ten thousand lakes to transmute soft yellow twilight toward a friendly Milky Way. Clear skies surrender the northern lights, alien spirits visiting from outer space. Circling high and broad at the North Pole, solar winds whip up a frenzy of haunting green lasers, their strange swooshing sounds dipping toward earth, hovering and spinning all the way to Brainerd.

~.~

On November 24, 1961, wintry winds danced over white-caps on Lake Michigan and blustered around busy Chicagoans rushing to take their lunches at 12:18pm. At that moment in a delivery room across town at the Swedish Covenant Hospital, a doctor spanked a baby's bottom and the baby's startled cry reassured his parents that all was well. At that moment, in the middle of America, at the crossroads between the conventional fifties and the revolutionary sixties, in the shadows of a grim nuclear age and in the light of a hopeful new presidency, another human birth was recorded and celebrated. The happy parents, Art and Jackie Mampel, had their first kid, me, David John Mampel.

Art and Jackie hadn't been married very long. Art was a poet and seminarian at North Park Seminary, and Jackie was a registered nurse at the very hospital where I was born. I was named David because David was Dad's favorite character in the Old Testament, because he always put God first no matter how far he strayed; John became my middle name because John "the beloved" was Dad's favorite apostle in the New Testament.

1961 was also the year that the Swiss psychoanalyst Carl Jung died. In a filmed interview, Jung said we don't come into this life a "tabula rasa," which means "blank slate" in Latin;

we already have our character imprinted in our genes before we are born. Parents know this. They see the personality of the newborn right away. We come from the ongoing genetic code of our family tree, all of evolution, the elements, the stars, and from a mystery as deep as breath itself. Every life has a story that reveals the unique character we each are and can become, but as Jung also observed, many of us get stuck along the way or never fully actualize ourselves.

I was a preacher's kid, and like most preachers' kids, I possessed a natural innocence counterbalanced with rebelliousness. I'm the eldest of four children, a brother to three sisters: Jeanie, Sara, and Colette. When we were growing up, our dad was a parish minister. Approachable and easy-going, he grew up steeped in country western music and Christian Science. The members of his impoverished San Antonio family all had a paradoxical love of good literature running through their veins. An affable, even comical man, Dad has a passionate faith not unlike that of Tevye's in *Fiddler on the Roof*.

My mom is filled with music and a quiet pietism she inherited from a long line of well known Swedish Covenant ministers. The ideal minister's wife, she led the church choir, played piano, and taught Sunday school. Hers is a humble and loving presence balanced by a whimsical love of laughter. Both of my parents are caring people, passionate in their faith, open-minded, fun-loving spirits with lots of robust friendships and lively interests both inside and outside of their congregational life. They've now been married for more than fifty years and love each other dearly.

Right after I was born, one of my dad's buddies came to visit and arrived while my mother was giving me a bath. As he bent down to look at me in the bath, I peed and squirted him right on the nose. He looked at my dad and said, "Mampel, you need to enter this kid in a contest."

My dad still stays in touch with many of his college and seminary friends, and humor is a big part of their bond. It's hard to be arrogant around such folks. Humor has kept our family humble many times and made life fun. As Murray Burns said in *A Thousand Clowns*, "If most things aren't funny then they're only exactly what they are. Then it's just one long dental appointment interrupted occasionally by something exciting like waiting or falling asleep. What's the point if I leave things just as I find them? Then I'm just adding to the noise. I'm just taking up some room on the subway."

When I was about a year old, my father became pastor at his first church in Brainerd, Minnesota. While he was interviewing for that position, I ambled around the room and gave everyone there a big hug. My dad gives me credit for his getting that job. He says I was so cute they had to hire him. I would have done anything to help my dad get ahead and put baby food on the table. Did I sense trouble and put on a little act to sway the vote, or was I just a love bug? Maybe it was a little of both.

I don't know many people who can remember their lives as toddlers, but I do have an eerie memory of looking at my dad's face when I was very young and seeing it turn blue. I now understand this to be a psychic foreshadowing of my dad's near-death accident that happened when I was eight years old and we were living in Minneapolis. That accident would leave me traumatized and become a pivotal point in my life.

~.~

After Mom and Dad had settled into that tiny Swedish Covenant congregation in Brainerd, my sister Jeanie was born. When she had learned to walk, sometimes she would follow me around. My dad tells the story of how I was giving her a tour of the church once, and he popped out of his office to watch me work.

"Now, Jeanie, these are the hymnals and these are the pews," I proclaimed.

"But where's Jesus?" Jeanie asked.

"And this is the pulpit and this is the altar," I continued.

"But where's Jesus?" she asked again.

"And these are the offering plates and candles," I said.

"But where's Jesus?" she insisted.

Impatient and feeling pestered, I pointed up at Warner Sallman's famous painting of Christ hanging in the narthex and exclaimed, "Oh, Jeanie, don't you know? He's hanging up there!"

Afterward, Dad used that story in his sermons to illustrate how easy it is to get caught up in the business of the church and forget about the main message. He even reiterated it at my ordination service many years later in Seattle, Washington.

I was a nice Christian boy--when I wasn't being the classic rebel preacher's kid. There's a black-and-white photo of Jeanie and me as kids that illustrates these two opposing sides of my personality. Jeanie is a toddler; she's sitting on a tricycle wearing a big smile, her blonde bangs awkwardly cut in the shape of an upside-down quarter moon, the stunning result of my best four-year-old barbering skills. I'm standing askew next to her in a Minnesota Twins sweatshirt, holding a huge bottle of Pepsi and looking like I had just come from happy hour. My dad says I was acting drunk, trying to drown my sorrows for botching my sister's bangs. My pops dubbed me "the mad scientist" after that incident. These days, I find myself spontaneously drawing on my childhood mad scientist character when I make up tall tales for kids at local schools and libraries in Northern California.

Growing into my childhood, I loved inventing all kinds of things: miniature fans with tiny motors, teeth cleaners, pyramids that turned milk into yogurt, go carts, bike jumps, tree houses, sailboats made out of huge surfboards, and lots of role-playing games and adventures in our backyard and beyond. My middle sister, Sara, once told me she became a dental hygienist because of my motorized teeth cleaner. I would sit my "patients" down in a comfortable chair, grab my battery-powered tooth polisher (a tiny motor with cotton taped to the tip of the shaft), dip it in a little plate of toothpaste and say, "Open wide." Toothpaste spattered everywhere and I had to constantly wipe off their faces, but it actually cleaned their teeth. Well, at least it seemed like it did. One of my favorite characterizations in my Daffy Dave clown shows today is this wacky inventor persona. My

"Clap-O-Meter" is the culmination of this madcap inventing, and the kids love it. Sometimes, when I bring it out from behind my magic prop box, I'll hear older boys in the back row say, "Oh yeah! I love this trick!" The louder the kids cheer, the higher the red mark on the meter rises. I warn them not to cheer too loud or it will explode. Of course, they do, and confetti blows out of the top of the contraption, decorating my hat with colorful rainbow hair, much to my mock chagrin and their outright belly laughter.

~.~

I cherish the sense of enchantment these memories of my childhood give me, and one of the highest aspirations in my adult life is to convey those wonderful feelings of awe wrapped in a mood of mystery to others. I'll often interject this mood into my clown shows. After a hearty round of uproarious slapstick, with hats falling off and socks accidentally coming out of my baggy pants, after the Clap-O-Meter has exploded, I'll stop and look around as if I'm cautiously surveying the scene to see if anyone is spying, take a deep breath, bend my knees, lower my voice, and ask the kids if they want me to do a scary magic trick. "Yes! Yeah!" they yell, at least most of them do.

But then I say, "Nah, I'd better not. You'll get too scared."

"No, we won't, Daffy Dave!" they cry.

"Yes, you will," I counter. I let the bantering go back and forth for a few more seconds and then I say, "Okay. You promise not to get scared?"

"Yes!" they shoot back.

"All right then. Everybody hold onto someone so you don't run away." The kids grab hold of each other, and I bend into the audience, become hushed, open my eyes wider, and--here's the essential part--I let go inside myself and become enchanted. I believe what I'm saying is true. The more I feel it, the more the audience does, too. The loud group becomes very quiet. The kids are under my spell, and sometimes the parents are, too. I'll softly begin to tell a strange tale, sometimes even a scary one. Occasionally, I use a magic trick to illustrate how fairies drop pixie dust from an invisible world to help create magic in the visible world. Other times I'll tell them how I walked through a graveyard at midnight and a ghost put a spell on my balloons. I'll show them one of these "ghost balloons," have them help me hypnotize it and then slowly stick a long needle through the "half-ghost, half-balloon" without popping it. Now and then I'll hear an audible "Wow!" or "Awesome!" as the eighteen-inch needle passes all the way through the balloon. I'll know, then, that in some small way, I've helped to inspire wonder in these kids. Like loud/soft dynamics in music, this enchantment portion of my show is a soft break from the loud laughs. The kids love it, the adults appreciate a brief return to quiet, and the clown gets rested so he can build up the big laughs again.

A few years after our cabin vacation on the cliffs of Lake Superior, I was sitting in the backseat of a beige 1960's Rambler and our family was moving from Brainerd to Minneapolis. It was a time of no seat belts and no car seats for kids. I was crawling around the moving car, and Mom and Dad were trying to keep me still, a little mad scientist loose in the Rambler. Probably because she thought she would have a better chance at keeping me safe, Mom said I could sit up front between her and Dad. I was thrilled. I looked up at my mom, then at my dad, and asked, "Am I four years old?"

"Yes," they both answered. The sun was pouring in through the windshield, blinding me, but I finally sat still and began to wonder what our new home in Minneapolis would be like. I don't remember my sister Jeanie being in the car with us, but she was probably in the backseat watching all her older brother's entertaining antics, learning what not to do in order to avoid reprimands, or just taking a nap.

~.~

We arrived later that day in Minneapolis from Brainerd, on a warm, late summer afternoon. Elms and maples gently swayed in the breeze beneath a sunny sky. Across and just down the street a short distance from our new home was a great big aquamarine wading pool at Hiawatha School. What a joyous moment it was when I first saw that pool. Water and other kids! Lots of other kids! I couldn't wait. I was so happy to be in a new town with kids all over the place. There must have been fifty of them in the pool already, swimming, splashing, shouting, and running around. I begged my mom to let me go in the water before we even began to settle into our new home and was delighted when she said yes. Since my swim trunks were packed away somewhere, she suggested I go swimming in my underwear. I didn't want to wait, so I agreed. Though I was still an uninhibited four-year-old, I remember feeling a bit awkward about wearing only my underwear as I approached that pool filled with a crowd of kids I didn't yet know, but soon I was having fun and forgot all about it. Thus began my comic relationship with underwear.

That first winter in Minneapolis I looked out the window one morning to see three feet of fresh snow on the ground. Excited, I ran out the door wearing only socks and underwear, Mom close on my heels, fetching me back in to dress properly. In my sophomore year at college, someone took a picture of me with my roommate, Drew Fountain. In the photo, he is lying on the top bunk in our dorm room in Carlsson Hall pretending to bite a Beatle's album like a sandwich. I am wearing underwear on my head, smiling maniacally and holding a pair of open scissors in one hand. During my first winter in Idaho Falls, Idaho, as pastor of First Congregational Church, our congregation went on a cross-country ski trip. I had over-dressed and got so hot that I stopped alone on the wilderness trail and took off my snow pants to cool down. I stuffed my snow pants into my backpack, continued on the trail, and forgot about my clothes change.

When I arrived at the skiers' cabin for lunch, I walked into the room of gathered parishioners and was greeted with hoots of laughter. I looked down and realized I had walked into the cabin wearing only long underwear, a sweater, and sunglasses. Everyone wanted to have their picture taken with Reverend "Long Underwear" Dave.

One of the parts of my clown show today that gets the most laughs is when my baggy clown pants "accidentally" drop to expose funny clown boxers while I pretend not to notice. I also have a bit in which I show the kids how to cook underwear that then blows up into giant-sized "thunder wear." I was once called "the underwear master" in a write-up in a local newspaper. And it all began when I was four years old and my mom allowed me to go swimming wearing only my whitey-tighties in Hiawatha Pool with all those other kids.

I grew to love the playground that served as the setting for that pool. Swings on sturdy chains that hung from big metal arches loomed large and lured me. Maroon-painted pavements wound softly through the park. We kids would lie on the pavement to warm up after swimming, filling the air with chlorinated steam that rose up from our bodies, until our skin dried and our flesh heated enough so that we wanted to jump back into the refreshing pool. A large gushing fountain spouted like a whale in a forty-five degree arc from one end of the pool. Kids would take turns blocking the stream to make it squirt in different directions. What a thrill that was! Jungle bars challenged us to climb like monkeys, and a sandbox enticed us to play. The sandbox had a large cement turtle sculpture under which I used to love hiding from my sister and Mom. The black-and-white photo on the cover of this book that shows me hanging upside down from the monkey bars on that playground with my sailor cap on the ground beneath me was taken by my dad's late friend Bruce Carlson, former director of the Schubert Club in Saint Paul. That picture seems to me to foreshadow the slapstick antics I use in my clown act today using a colorful porkpie hat.

In 1964, when the Beatles released their second album, *Meet the Beatles*, I was only three years old. Three years later, when I was six, my dad introduced me to that album, my first exposure to rock 'n' roll. The music of the Beatles, and this album in particular, sent shivers up and down my spine and inspired me with the electric mojo of rock. I mark this moment in my memory as the moment when my dreams and desires in life first awakened. That album so electrified me that I played it over and over again in the basement of our Minneapolis home.

While I was too young to have much awareness of world events, the sixties were a golden time, a time of social awakening, a time of great social unrest. Think of the momentous events of that era: the Vietnam War; the Civil Rights Movement; the assassinations of President Kennedy, Malcolm X, Martin Luther King, Jr., and Robert Kennedy. While I in my childish innocence was barely cognizant of these events, they shaped my life in ways I have only gradually come to realize over the years. My dad was involved with a clergy group that discussed the issues of the day, and they stood against the Vietnam War. Both of my parents were influenced by Dr. Martin Luther King, Jr. and the Kennedys and took on the mantle for peace and justice in society. In turn, they instilled these values in me, and I came to see the importance of standing up for these values in order to keep them alive in our world.

~.~

My dad remembers the turbulence of the 1960's as the "decade of death," when even the pop theology of the day declared that "God is dead." As I reflect now on that time, I am struck by the fact that my dad's own near-death experience occurred in 1969, a year that stood at the pinnacle of what the author Walker Percy called "the Thanatos syndrome," a phrase Percy also used as the title for one of his books, meaning that the twentieth century, as he saw it, was an "age of death."

When Dr. Martin Luther King, Jr., was shot, my father wrote a poem entitled "The King is Dead" which was published in an issue of the *Negro Digest* that had a photograph of Dr. King on the cover. My cousin Robin Duncan once submitted an assignment that included the use of my dad's poem to a teacher with a stern disposition and a reputation for being angry and strict. Appearing moved and touched, she approached Robin and said, "You should be very proud of your uncle." Here is that poem:

The King Is Dead!
--A.G. Mampel
Originally published in the *Negro Digest*, a Johnson Publication, August 1968

The King is dead!
In some black town
some white suburb
there is an influence in the air
as definite as his death.

Uncertainty fills the National Soul.
Black tears crystallize
from too many white wishes
Hearts are sore
from too much weeping.

The King will come again
reads an ancient oracle.

From the streets
of Bethlehem's quiet hostility
a word goes forth--
"He has and he was black."

~.~

I remember asking him at around this time, "Dad, where is God?"

"God is everywhere," he replied. We were standing together on the sidewalk outside of our home in Minneapolis near a beautiful maple tree that grew there. I looked at the maple tree and the green grass. I looked down the street at the other trees and the houses there, further down toward Hiawatha School where I was in second grade, the park where I loved to play. I looked up at the sky, the sun, and the clouds.

Bewildered, I thought to myself, "Where is everywhere?" It was a moment of spiritual expansion for me that most likely marked the early beginnings of my pantheistic and mystical understanding of God and the universe. My spiritual views now, as an adult, continue to be earth-centered, with an eclectic mix influenced by Zen and other forms of Buddhism, mystic Christianity, Sufism, Hinduism, the Kabbala, and even some aspects of Native American culture.

Minneapolis during the 1960's awakened me to my own life story, and south Minneapolis was my extended playground, our neighbors my extended family. Most moms in our neighborhood stayed at home back then, and parents weren't so scared about crazy traffic or kidnappings as they are these days. We kids were free to run around the neighborhood. There was a sense of community, adults keeping an eye out for other people's children, backyard cookouts, and chats over neighborhood fences. I don't remember my friends and me watching a whole lot of television, but I do remember watching a kids' show in the mornings before school called Casey and Roundhouse. Roger Awsumb, a local celebrity, played Casey Jones, and in one episode he cracked me up when he dressed in a trench coat and sang "Winchester Cathedral." Just for fun these days, I sing the same song in a kind of 1930's radio voice, like Roger as Casey did back then. On Saturday mornings, I watched cartoons and other kids' shows for an hour or two, and I especially liked Bugs Bunny and friends, Rocky and Bullwinkle, and The Archie Comedy Hour. The Monkees had a television show that always made me laugh, and their music, like the Beatles', made me squeal with delight. "Valerie" was my favorite song, and sometimes today, when I'm nostalgic or blue, I'll play and sing it while I drive down the freeway. It always lightens my mood.

~.~

My first vocational dreams came from listening to the Beatles and the Monkees, the Banana Splits, and the Archies. Like so many of us back then, I wanted to be a rock star. I also loved entertaining my friends, being the guy who made up the games, told the stories, and dreamed up the adventures. My mom, bless her, bought me a cheap drum set at Sears and I would tap out the rhythm and sing along while I listened to my favorites. Shudders ran up and down my spine and my scalp tingled with delight and ecstasy. I pored over the Sears catalog, dreaming of holding one of their cool sunburst electric guitars and playing it like John Lennon, George Harrison, or Michael Nesmith. Their music made me feel alive. I wanted to be like them.

I played my first guitar at about this time. My mom had bought herself a cheap Stella steel string guitar and was taking lessons with some of her women friends. She let me play it and taught me a few chords. The steel strings hurt my young, untried fingers, but I actually learned how to play and sing "Down in the Valley." It was not the exciting rock feeling that the Beatles and the Monkees gave me, but I got a start with my favorite instrument that I still play today. This experience taught me that music takes work and that sometimes it can be tedious, boring, and even painful to learn a new language such as playing guitar. It wasn't until I started playing the ukulele several years later, when I was in fourth grade at Koloa Elementary School on the island of Kauai, that the excitement of making music proficiently began for me. Then, when I took guitar lessons and played my first rock bar chords at an after-school program when I was in eighth grade, my confidence grew that I could play like the Beatles. The first rock song I learned how to play was "Proud Mary." I accompanied myself on guitar as I sang, and this song lit the fuse that exploded like fireworks inside me. I truly believed when I learned that song that I could become a rock and roller after that. It even made me feel more confident with girls, and soon after I learned to play that song I actually had my first real girlfriend.

My dad's sister Jeanne and her late husband Darrell lived in West Covina, near Los Angeles, in the mid to late 1960's. I was so inspired by their kids, my cousins Darrell Junior, Scott, Shelley, and Robin, who was my age. They had a country music band they called the Duncan Four, and they played on television with Buck Owens and Jimmy Dean. When we visited their family, I was completely enthralled and looked up to them as genuine stars. The thrill of meeting and getting to know them overshadowed even my very first trip to Disneyland, which also happened on that same trip. I was in love with them all and had a crush on both Robin and Shelley. They are such fun and funny cousins, and I'm still close with them and my Aunt Jeanne. The Duncan Four were about to become pretty famous, but my Uncle Darrell was concerned that his kids were growing up too fast and might not get properly educated, so he slowed things down. Shelley, in particular, wrote some really good songs, and I'm sure they would have gone far. I was inspired by seeing them play live music with electric instruments while wearing their cute uniforms; the experience fueled in me a real sense of confidence that I, too, could someday be like them.

My Uncle Darrell was a father figure for me. Once, when I was in college, I had to leave a family reunion early to catch a flight, because I needed to get back to work at my summer job at a grocery warehouse in Seattle. He came up to me as I was leaving and told me he was proud of me. He said, "Sometimes we just have to do things we don't want to do, but it's the right thing." I felt like such a man. Later on, when I became Daffy Dave, I loved that he laughed at my material. He made me laugh, too; he could tell the best jokes. Both he and Aunt Jeanne could tell stories like nobody's business. Their stories, funny, interesting, and even spiritual, were mostly about various family members. At the end of every Daffy Dave show I include a bit that was inspired by Aunt Jeanne, from something that happened when we visited their family on the night before we were going to go to Disneyland and we kids were too excited to go to sleep. I'll share more about that later in this book.

I knew that I loved to laugh and make others laugh in turn. One evening, I ran out the door laughing excitedly after watching Rich Little's impersonations on the Ed Sullivan Show. I saw a couple of my friends down the alley and ran up to them. I tried to make myself have a double chin, clasped my hands together, and did my best Ed Sullivan imitation. "Tonight, we're going to have a big shoe, a really big shoe," I intoned. They rewarded me with their laughter, and I loved it! I also loved the silliness of the Banana Splits and the Three Stooges. Bud Abbot and Lou Costello could have me rolling on the floor, and I found Jerry Lewis, in particular, side-splittingly funny.

As Jung and others have observed, we all have about twelve archetypes, or ancient universal patterns, latent or active in our souls that have emerged from the collective unconscious of all human development throughout time. We need to go through phases with each archetype in order to become whole, so perhaps it makes sense that as a kid I wanted to be so many things when I grew up. Depending on what our soul needs to learn at different phases on the journey, we may find ourselves living predominantly by the innocent archetype, or the orphan, the wanderer, the fool, the magician, the sage, and so on. After I entertained the idea of being a rock star and a comic, I then wanted to be an archeologist. I loved daydreaming about finding dinosaur bones, or maybe even precious gems, like the agates (which I considered jewels) that my friends found up at Lake Superior in northern Minnesota.

I still have many competing desires of what I want to be or do on any given day. I have gotten better with age at listening to and feeling deeply what M. Scott Peck calls "angel nudges" to discern what's best at each moment. If I get a feeling to call a friend, for example, I usually listen to the feeling and do it. Sometimes, when they've answered the phone, they tell me they had just been thinking of calling me. Or, if I wake up with a line of poetry that sounds good, I'll get out my pad and the poem will flow. Perhaps an idea for a new trick comes to me, or the earth is warm and calls for me to work in my garden. Whatever that gut feeling is, in most cases, when I listen to these urges and follow them, good results ensue. The intellect can help navigate, but the truth is beyond the rational and is discerned on an intuitive level. In my clown shows as Daffy Dave, I am what is known as a variety entertainer: I'm a clown, juggler, magician, musician, balloon artist, comedian, puppeteer, and storyteller all in one. I'm not just a clown; I'm a circus! During each show, I try to feel in my gut what is going on with the audience and adjust my character accordingly. For example, with small children, I'll generally let the innocent clown dominate with gentle, silly, colorful tricks. On the other hand, if the audience is eight-year-olds, it could be that the magician combined with a more jester-like clown character will dominate the delivery. Sometimes there are more adults than kids in the audience, and the stand-up comedian takes over, but I'll be sure to come down continuously to the level of the kids in the audience so I don't lose them, either.

~.~

In the sixties, we didn't have video games, smart phones, Netflix, or five hundred cable channels. We had never heard of ADHD, and most of our parents, especially our fathers, were employed, as the unemployment rate was around three percent. Rent and the cost of living were cheaper and we didn't need much to have fun. I hardly ever played with toys, preferring instead to build forts or snow castles, talk with my friends over can-string phones, make mud pies from scratch, or have a rousing fencing match with stick swords. We made up games, had sleepovers, and rode our bicycles with banana seats and sissy bars. The cool kids had five-speed stick shifts on their bikes; I loved my own red Schwinn with a silvery white banana seat. Sometimes I "bucked" a friend or one of my sisters on my bike, meaning they got to ride on the back of the banana seat.

When I was about seven, my friends and I would sometimes ride our bikes to the Mississippi River, which was only a few blocks away. We explored the sand caves near the river banks and fished for crawdads in Minnehaha Creek. My mother cringes now when I tell her that we climbed the arches of the Ford Bridge. We had no need for planned "play dates"; our play was more spontaneous than that. If someone suggested a good adventure, we just asked our moms for permission. They would say, "Okay, but be home by dinner," adding, "Did you ask Kevin's (or Johnny's) mom, too?" then we would walk down the alley to meet up.

My favorite game was Kick the Can, because if I could manage to be the last one tagged, I could rescue my friends by kicking the can to get them out of jail. I felt like a big-shot hero whenever I did that. Today, I teach kids how to play this game, and they love it, too. Other games were Hide and Seek and Trapped on a Desert Island. On weekend nights when our parents would let us stay outside long after dark, we played a game called "Twelve O'clock Midnight I Hope the Ghost Won't Get You Tonight," a game that was really just Hide and Seek in the dark, and oh, so scary. We loved it! It would make us scared, and it made us laugh like crazy. In the winter, we speed-skated on the ice rink at Hiawatha Park or sledded down "golf course hill" on the other side of town.

We caught butterflies; we played pick-up baseball games with whiffle bats and tennis balls. We built dams in the water that flowed by the street curbs when it rained and sailed stick boats down the current. We packed cantaloupes and sandwiches in rucksacks for picnics when we had our adventures. We stole green apples at night from neighbors' yards and ate them with salt; we raided gardens, swam naked or in our underwear in the creek or the wading pool, or at Lake Hiawatha and Lake Nokomis.

We used garbage can lids for shields, stabbed rotten apples from an elderly neighbor's yard with cut-off-broomstick swords, and had long, drawn-out apple fights in the alley that ended only when someone's parents came out and made us quit because a kid got whacked so hard he or she cried. We explored fields, climbed trees, made rope swings, played drums made of empty coffee cans, and played Ding Dong Ditch, a game sometimes called Ring and Run. I used to love ringing some old guy's doorbell, running down the street, hiding in the bushes, and watching him come out in his t-shirt looking confused. When he didn't see anyone, he'd start yelling, "You kids better go home if you know what's good for you!" and slam the door shut. We would laugh until our sides hurt. But the best ring and run ever was one when we tied a fishing line to this old guy's screen door and after he slammed it shut, we pulled the line and opened the door back up again. He came out to look again, this time a bit freaked out, then shut it again, only to have it mysteriously open when we slowly pulled the fishing line from where we lay hidden in the lilac bushes nearby. I wouldn't be surprised if kids today start playing tricks on me now, as I'm becoming that old guy. Some kind of practical joke karma awaits my twilight years, I'm absolutely certain of it.

At sunset, our parents would step out of the back door and yell for us to come home for dinner. It was only then that we would realize how hungry we were. Nonetheless, we would slowly and reluctantly walk toward our homes, and as we walked we played Hit the Dirt. The darker the evening, the better this game would be. Pretending to be army men on patrol, we would fall to the ground and yell, "Hit the dirt!" whenever a car came along. You were supposed to fall quickly, as soon as you saw the car's headlights, before the headlights shone on you. I would arrive at the dinner table with eyes wide and cheeks glowing, regaling my family with stories about what I'd done all day, playing down the street, in Breck Field, or on the banks of the Mississippi, and making everyone laugh with the funny stuff that happened. Finally, one of my parents would say, "Okay, Dave, now let your sisters talk."

I played with other boys for the most part, mainly Kevin and Brian Bauer, and my very first best friend was Kevin Bauer. But sometimes we kids played games that included both girls and boys. Crack the Whip was fun when you could get twenty or so kids to play. You stand in a line and hold hands, then the leader runs and pulls the line in curvy zigzags until the "whip cracks," which means the last person on the line goes flying off onto the grass.

One day, a couple of friends and I snuck inside the sanctuary of Minnehaha Congregational Church when my dad was the minister there. It was a hot, humid summer day and the church was dark and cool inside like some ancient mysterious cavern. I looked over at my friends and said, "Hey! Let's take off our clothes." With no hesitation, we all three took off our shorts and shirts and started running naked up and down the main aisle, laughing like crazy. I think God laughed with us that day. It was all so innocent and funny.

36

~.~

I had my first childhood crush on a cute blonde by the name of Bonnie Eikaas, or as I used to call her, "I kiss Bonnie." I would fantasize it was me singing to Bonnie whenever I heard the Archies' song "Sugar, Sugar" or "Valerie" by the Monkees. Bonnie lived with her family in what we kids called the "new section," a housing development a couple of blocks away that was a little newer than our neighborhood.

One fall day when I was walking home from Hiawatha Elementary School, a bunch of older girls surrounded me and asked, "Are you in love with Bonnie?" I was very intimidated and didn't answer and felt ashamed. After that, I felt I had to really watch it and hide my love for her. I still snuck over to her house and tried to meet with her without her sisters seeing me. One time, while I was waiting and hoping to see her, Bonnie actually did come out of her house; I was thrilled. I had a couple of younger friends with me, and Bonnie invited us all to come to her backyard where she and her friends were putting on a talent show, my first-ever exposure to live entertainment aside from church choirs on Sunday mornings.

Later in life, when I was in my early thirties and first getting started as Daffy Dave in the San Francisco Bay Area, I saw Bonnie again. I had heard through mutual friends that she had gotten divorced, and I flew to Minneapolis to visit her. I wanted to see if the old attraction was still there. She was the director of a children's theater in Minneapolis, having taken her love of directing backyard talent shows into her adult life. We had fun hanging out, went to a Renaissance fair together, visited her grandpa, and caught up with each other. Nothing romantic ever came of that visit, but it was a validation for me. I couldn't help but notice that each of us had built our careers by following dreams that started in our childhoods.

~.~

In his courses and seminars, Werner Erhard taught that nearly every human being has a "break in belonging" at some point in childhood, an experience that leaves us with the notion that we are on our own emotionally, separate from others, particularly our parents. For most human beings, this event is traumatic, but some of us are so young when it happens we don't have the capacity to remember it; others of us repress the memory in other ways. Whether or not we remember it, this event shapes us as human beings, leaving us feeling incomplete, broken somehow, unable to fit in anywhere we go.

Other traditions teach the concept of the "wounded healer." A shaman in such a tradition has experienced a powerful wounding in childhood that leaves him or her psychically sensitive and empathic to others' suffering. I was eight years old when this powerful wounding, this break, occurred for me; I now remember it vividly, and it shaped the course of my life, as it initiated my soul in ways beyond my knowing when it happened and has become increasingly meaningful for me over time.

Somebody is mowing a lawn across the street from where I live as I write this, and warm summer breezes waft into the living room where I sit. The sound of the lawnmower puts me in a kind of trance; it reminds me of spring and summer in Minneapolis. In May of 1969, when I was eight years old, my father tripped over a toy in the middle of the night and fell down the stairs of the parsonage in Minneapolis where we lived, tumbling all the way down from the second story landing to crash onto the first floor below. I heard the loud thumping as he fell down the steps, and it woke me up. I bolted out of bed and ran to the top of the stairs. Gripping the railing, I froze at what I saw. Mom ran past me to Dad's side where he lay on the floor in a pool of blood with his left eye blackened and swollen to what looked to me to be the size of a softball. My memories of what happened next are spotty at best.

I know from stories my dad and mom tell now that Dad suffered a severe concussion and was in a coma for a week. He was even clinically dead for a few minutes. When he awoke from that coma, I was allowed to visit him in the hospital. Mom had given me a book about Western birds, and I brought it with me to show him. I held Mom's hand, and we walked into the room together. I was shocked at the sight of him. Blood trickled from the wound around his eye. He wore a bathrobe and sat in a wheelchair; he smelled like medicine. What scared me most of all was how spacey he acted. He was happy, too happy, and he seemed not to know what was going on around him, although I think he tried to concentrate on my book when I showed it to him. His attention was scattered, and I backed away from him feeling sheepish and confused.

My childhood ended abruptly with that experience. I reacted to this event inside myself by becoming the "man of the family." The silly, whimsical kid I once had been descended like Persephone into the underworld and gave way to a child who was serious, even brooding. I had overheard one of my dad's doctors say to my mom that if he fell again, he could die, so I began to follow my father around after he came home from the hospital, as if by my attentiveness alone I could save him from another fall. My sense of security had fled, and I was suddenly very aware in a childish way of my father's mortality, perhaps even of my own. I no longer trusted Dad to take care of me, but I didn't want him to die. I tried to take care of him.

My sisters used to hate it when, in my self-imposed role as man of the house, I tried to boss them around. "You're not the parent, David!" they would yell. But in my mind, I was not only the parent but the entire family's caretaker. I felt misunderstood on all sides. My parents were dismayed and frustrated by my behavior, yet they couldn't see the deep inner wound that led to that behavior. Years later when I was in my teens, I decided that our family was watching too much television and not conversing enough, and I cut the cord to the television set so that we would spend more time talking to each other. "Stop playing God, David!" Dad shouted when he realized what I'd done.

"Well, start being a better parent!" I retorted angrily. When Dad patched the cord and plugged it back in, angry sparks flew out from beneath the electrical tape he had used. There was a shocked silence in the room. After a moment someone laughed, and then we all did. Relieved, our family tried to forget the angry words, but I was still aggrieved. I felt that everyone in the family continued to be angry with me.

Chapter Three:
Paradise Found and Lost

Our family moved to Koloa, Kauai, in August of 1970, a few months after Dad's accident, because his doctor advised a more peaceful environment for his recovery. A small church had an opening for a pastor there, and Dad felt he could resume his pastoral duties in that quiet setting. When our family's plane had a layover in Los Angeles on our way to Kauai, I suddenly disappeared from my mother's side. Mom was frantic until I emerged from the airport restroom with Dad, where I had followed him to make sure he wouldn't fall again.

Months before our move to Kauai, Dad sat us down and gave us the news. At first I was excited and happy because I loved playing Trapped on a Desert Island with my friends in our backyard and I imagined we would be living in grass shacks like they did on Gilligan's Island. But then I got pretty sad because I realized I would miss all my friends, especially my best friend, Kevin Bauer. My heart sank with the knowledge that I would be leaving Bonnie Eikaas behind. I was still madly in love with Bonnie, at least as madly in love as an eight-year-old boy can be. I was taking piano lessons at the time, and I played "My Bonnie Lies over the Ocean" over and over again for weeks after we arrived on Kauai. That song could have been renamed "My Bonnie Lies over and over and over the Ocean" in her honor.

We lived on Kauai for eight years, from 1970 to 1978. It was a magical, golden time to be there. There weren't so many hotels back then, and the sugar industry was still Hawaii's economic backbone. The local middle class was fairly strong. The local culture was more cohesive then and the drug and crime scene had not yet taken a stronghold. Today, some of my Hawaiian friends struggle to live where we all grew up in Koloa, but many have had to move away to find employment on the mainland.

The local get-togethers we had back then are a thing of the past, such as the meet-up every Sunday of the "pulehu gang" down at Kukuiula Harbor. The word "pulehu" means "cooking over fire." Families would get together to fish, snorkel, "talk story," swim, and eat. When the fishermen came back on their boats from the deep sea, everyone would help clean and cook the fish. We kids would swim for hours and play water games until dark. Today, my old gang has vanished. But Ernie Sueoka's get-togethers still happen with regularity, and locals still hang out in other ways. I've gone back over the years from time to time, and I am happy to see the local culture still fairly intact. Maybe it's simply re-discovering itself with a new generation, because the aloha spirit is eternal.

"Kokua," which means helping or assisting, is a big part of Hawaiian culture. Hawaiians love to gather for a "kaukau," to share food and "talk story" in pidgin English. As an expression of that spirit, neighbors and friends were always ready to help in many ways, often bringing food over to our house when we lived there, as we did to theirs. Kokua, this spirit of helping and assisting, fit in with our family naturally, as my dad and mom are naturally giving and generous spirits.

It was a wonderful, wholesome, free-spirited time in the 1970's when we lived on Kauai. I got to walk barefoot down Waikomo Road from the large missionary parsonage we lived in to Koloa Elementary School. There were usually toads hopping on the wet roads and sometimes gross dead ones squished by the few cars that had passed in the night. By the time I was in the fifth grade, I was wearing "slippas," or flipflops, as mainlanders called them, pretty much all of the time.

There were so many new customs and language differences to learn about, tropical plants to wonder at, rain falling while the sun shone, waterfalls, lush green mountains, humidity, crowing roosters, yapping mynah birds, trade winds, bright starry nights when we could even see the Milky Way, crystal-clear warm blue saltwater, colorful fish, sweet flower fragrances, strange new foods, surfers, hippies, swarthy skins, pidgin English, and a mishmash of cultures. So much newness kept me occupied and focused as I learned to adapt and fit in. It was overwhelming at first, but the fresh experiences helped me cope with missing my old friends back in Minneapolis.

~.~

On the other hand, I was a haole, which literally translates to "no life spirit." Haole is the derogatory term used by Hawaiian locals to address white mainland foreigners, and in my case, being called one added to the break in belonging I had experienced in Minneapolis during the time of my dad's accident. Sometimes I was picked on and even had to defend myself in fights. I already felt ashamed and insecure and separate from others, and when other kids called me a haole those feelings intensified. I started wanting my skin to be brown like the locals' so I could fit in, but my skin was so white the local kids called me "shark bait," and when my nose got sunburned, they called me "Rudolph." When my blond hair turned white from the hot Hawaiian sun, they called me "albino" or "old man."

I became far better accepted by the locals when I started learning to speak the local pidgin English; I learned fast and could speak pidgin almost right away. In time, too, our family became "kama'ainas," which even haoles can become simply by being residents, as the word means "child of the land." When I started playing sports, too, I felt more like I fit in. I also learned how to surf, but the locals despised haoles who took their waves. Body surfing and boogie boards were okay with the local toughs, though, and I could "shoot da tube" at Brennecke Beach, a perfect sandy beach back then, with no rocks like it has today. My love for fun and games helped, too. My natural enthusiasm for making up games with groups of kids migrated with me from Minneapolis to Kauai, and before long my new friends and I were having fun making spears, playing "Indian" (without the cowboys, or "paniolos"), endlessly playing tag and touch football, baseball, and other games.

At first, I found it easier to make friends with the other

local white kids, but as the years went by, my friends included Japanese, Filipino, Chinese, Hawaiian, Korean, and a mix of other ethnic groups, and it was my affinity for pidgin English that allowed me to do that. A sense of humor is also a big asset on the islands. My love for joking around was enhanced by my growing up on Kauai, and more than once it helped me to avoid trouble with tough locals. In time, gentle island humor helped me to become a less serious, brooding child. My love for fun and games, my sense of humor, and my penchant for inventing things were the gifts that helped me start to regain a sense of belonging. That nagging sense of shame and fear I felt about being a haole and a skinny kid who was only an average student and athlete never quite left me, but I became more of a fun kid again as a way to survive and fit in. My naturally fun spirit connected me with others, even those who teased me or picked on me.

~.~

The warm and generous congregation at Koloa Union Church welcomed us with flower leis when we arrived for our first night in the parsonage. Everyone there was friendly, and the love, the spirit of aloha, was vibrant. Our house was huge, or so it seemed to me then, and the ceilings were twelve feet high. I even had my own bedroom. There were mango trees in our yard, along with breadfruit, papaya, banana, guava, avocado, lime, plumeria, tamarind, and macadamia nut. A large Norfolk pine that grew there had a distinctive forked silhouette from a split in its trunk, making it a landmark used by sailors. From a distance, it looked like two fingers making a giant peace sign, and I loved that tree. I once climbed all the way up to the start of the split in its trunk, about a hundred feet, or about half the tree's full height. Sadly, that ancient tree was recently cut down, and in its honor I have planted a Norfolk pine in the front yard of my home in San Jose.

There was even a graveyard behind the parsonage, which seemed to me very strange and a little creepy. I could look out of the living room or guest room windows and see its broken wrought iron gate with arched white marble tombstones beyond. When my local friends visited me at night, they would run through the graveyard to come and knock on my bedroom window, saying in quick pidgin, "Ho! Dat graveyard spooky, no? Make scared." That always made me laugh. When my sisters and I explored the graveyard for the first time, we discovered old black-and-white photos on the white tombstones, most of them pictures of the children of missionaries who had died there in the 1800's. Today, I call on this graveyard scene as the spooky backdrop when I tell ghost stories to kids as Daffy Dave.

My dad built a basic platform for a tree house in the spreading tamarind tree near the graveyard, and that helped me make friends among the local kids. When I told a bunch of kids at Koloa School that I had a tree fort, the biggest kid, John "Oto" Redongo, wanted to see it and have a sleepover in it. Mom and Dad said we could spend the night up there, but we had a hard time sleeping; the floor was hard and sloped and mosquitoes pestered us all night. The next morning, we woke up late for school and dashed off. We couldn't wait to brag about our sleepover in the tree fort. But when we arrived breathless onto the long covered wraparound porch of the school, the other kids laughed when they saw us, calling out, "Chicken pox!" because of the bright red mosquito bites that covered us. Oto and I laughed, too, when we realized the cause of their mirth, and that was the beginning of a series of tree forts in that wonderful tamarind tree. Everyone wanted to come over to my house to work on the current tree fort.

The parsonage had a huge yard, perfect for playing tag and other games, and that attracted kids, too. Before long, my new friends and I--Greg, Guy, Neal, Nelson, Eddie Hamamura, and others--regularly rode our bikes to Waita Reservoir to fish for bass. Or we would explore and fish or slide down the red volcanic mud at the little falls near there. At an old abandoned airfield behind my dad's church we found ruins of old camps that set our young imaginations soaring, and nearby we discovered some old bottles sticking up from the ground in rows among orange trees and other fruit trees. It seemed to us the place was haunted and mysterious.

One of my favorite adventures from this time was when one of my best buddies, Nelson "Rice Man" Inouye, and I packed some food and a tent and hiked to the top of Red Hill above Waita Reservoir. The town of Koloa twinkled below us, and the moon and the Milky Way shimmered comfortingly above us. The Koloa Sugar Mill, now closed, was lit up and humming away, and the sweet, pungent smell of molasses wafted up to us through the silky breezes with a clean, intoxicating fragrance. Mount Haupu, lush and green, stood between us and the moonlit sea at Mahaulepu. The air was warm and sultry, but cool trade winds enlivened it every now and then. We lit a fire and cooked saimin and Vienna sausages, "talked story," and joked until we fell asleep. The next morning we hiked back down to Koloa. On our way down, we heard loud sirens and saw fire trucks heading toward Waita. We looked up and noticed Red Hill was on fire, and we thought it was most likely because we had not extinguished our fire completely. We were scared and didn't tell a soul because we didn't want to go to jail.

We called Nelson "Rice Man" because his last name, "Inouye" sounded like "Hinode," a popular brand of rice on the islands. There was Neal the Eel, Eddie Spaghetti, Guy the Fly, and so on. My nickname was "Old Fut" because my blonde hair was bleached white from the Hawaiian sun and I looked like an old man.

Nelson and I loved to fish and look for old bottles, but the places where we loved to fish and explore are closed today. Back then, they were our free-wheelin' playground. We fished in the local fresh water streams, using scoop nets to catch medakas, little Japanese rice fish that look like guppies. We caught freshwater prawns, called "opae" or "little red shrimp," in Waikomo Stream, just up the way from our house on Waikomo Road.

One winter it rained so hard the stream overflowed, poured down the street, and ran through our back yard. I woke up in the morning to see my two chickens floating in their coop past my bedroom window and squawking for help. I ran out into the flood, grabbed the chicken coop, and opened its little door. Out scrambled my rooster and hen, flying in their panic to the top of the breadfruit tree. I trudged out toward them through the swirling water, climbed to the top of the breadfruit tree, and shooed them safely back into their coop. Flash floods like that tend to happen every now and then in Hawaii which is why most houses are built on pylons or stilts. My friends and I had just built a split-level club house, and it got flooded out, too. We had to drag out all the muddy carpets to clean and restore it. Soon after that, we built a much better club house, on stilts.

~.~

A local parishioner gave me her son's old "Blue Tanker," a very large and heavy surf board. It was too big and bulky for a kid like me to surf with, so I came up with an idea for another way to use it. I rounded up my neighbor friends, Neal Iseri, Greg Kobashigawa, and Guy Yoshimori, and we carried it through Greg's yard behind our house, down the road to Neal's house, and plopped it into the stream. We made paddles out of broomsticks and scrap wood. We even tried making a sail for it, but that didn't work. We forgot to account for the fact there would be no wind on a jungle-covered stream, but we had fun on it anyway. Our next-door neighbor, Lisa Liberato, and my sisters Jeanie, Sara, and Colette used to love paddling up the "river" on it, and so did I. We explored the jungles, pretended to be pirates, or just watched fish swimming in the water. Today, when I tell kids stories, this is another scene I summon as the setting for adventure plots. Whenever I go back to visit Kauai now, all my old friends and I love talking about the "blue tanka surf boat," the tree forts we built and rebuilt, and all the good fun we had during "small kid time."

Other memories include packing up rucksacks with my friends and cooking saimin, pork and beans, and Vienna sausages over small fires we made along the irrigation ditches for the cane fields behind my dad's church. We made go carts and rode them down the big hill there, called "Airfield" because there used to be a landing strip for small planes at the top of it. We snorkeled, went night fishing off the cliffs at Mahaulepu Beach where the Grand Hyatt sits today near Poipu, dug up old blob-top soda bottles, looked for washed-up Japanese glass floats on the beach, rode our bikes for miles and miles on the cane field roads, hiked the mountains, picked guavas and mangoes, hung out at Yamamoto store and joked around, and performed daredevil stunts. We made bike jumps; we swung on the rope swing in the backyard, letting go of the rope at the swing's apex and reaching for the branches of the tamarind tree. We got pretty good at grabbing a branch then turning quickly again to grab the returning rope and swing back up to the tree fort, like flying trapeze circus performers, little monkey daredevils.

As I learned to merge with the local culture, I began to drift away from my haole friends. I was afraid that if I hung out with them, the darker-skinned locals wouldn't think I was cool. I was torn inside by my fears, but I suppressed them all the same, flitting like a butterfly from one group to another. I hung out with my white friends at Cub Scouts and later Boy Scouts meetings and at church; then I hung out with my local friends around town, at school and on sports teams, or having adventures at the beach, or going fishing and exploring the island.

That pattern continued for me until I met Fred Oluf Joseph Johannessen. Fred showed up at Koloa School when we were both in the fifth grade, standing about a foot taller than everyone else. He had a nice smile, curly hair, and a certain feistiness about him. Little bursts of titters and gasps eddied through the school room as he entered and sat down on that first day. Obviously, the local boys wouldn't want to mess with this giant, and I decided he would be cool to hang out with, by virtue of his size alone. Plus, he was funny and self-confident. When he joined Little League later, no one wanted to bat when he pitched. He threw a mean fast ball, but it was wild and had a reputation for beaning the batter. Even the catchers behind the plate feared his pitches. And you just couldn't beat him at basketball.

Fred's family attended our church and my folks became friends with his parents, Gloria and Oluf, and I got to know Fred's younger brother, Gorm. Gloria, originally from Guatemala, was animated, intelligent, and very funny, with a personality reminiscent of Charo's. Olaf, a reserved engineer from Denmark, balanced her exuberance. He was a good father and husband, with eyes that were often squinted in a good-natured smile.

When our families got together for dinners Fred introduced me to Monty Python. I was taken aback by the naked ladies and couldn't believe such a thing could be allowed on television. I didn't get the humor until much later, but now Monty Python is one of my favorite comedy teams and I adore their offbeat, absurd comedy. Fred also influenced my love of playing with language. We would think of a word together and twist it around to make it sound funny. I would say something like "tilapia," and Fred would hurl back, "zephyalipod," and we would both laugh hysterically. We'd record really long fart sounds on a tape recorder, then play them back for my sisters and Lisa Liberato to enjoy. Fred taught me how to put both hands on my mouth and push air out hard to make the loudest fart sound I had ever heard. Mom hated it, of course, but Fred and I found it hilarious. In time, Fred became one of my best friends. Today, I play around with words in my Daffy Dave shows as Fred and I used to do. Pidgin English, poetry, and word play are all fair game.

Life on Kauai taught me so much, and the laid back, hang-loose attitude is still part of my temperament today. While living there, I acquired a love for different cultures and foods, joking around, the poetry of pidgin English, and spooky stories, like the stories of the Hawaiian Night Marchers and Madame Pele, goddess of the volcano. All of these influences went deep inside of me and today influence my rhythm, my writing, and my comic delivery on stage as Daffy Dave. My appreciation for plants first started on Kauai, too. Today I grow birds of paradise, hibiscus, and other plants that surrounded me as I grew up on Kauai; they help to remind me of the velvet breezes, pure air, crystal-clear water, and brilliant starry nights of my island past.

~.~

Paradise can have a dark underbelly, however, and Kauai is no exception. Our family would get "island fever" occasionally and yearn for the mainland. On a couple of summers my dad exchanged pulpits with mainland ministers in Minnesota so that we could have a break from the confines of island living. Kauai, after all, is only thirty-three miles long and twenty-five miles across; the road around its perimeter doesn't even complete its circumnavigation of the island. My parents and my sisters and I sometimes grew weary of the provincial attitudes that can come from living in an isolated rural community. For example, most of my classmates found it odd that I wanted to go to college after high school. Then there was the small-mindedness we encountered and the animosity we got from some of the tough locals toward white folks like us.

After awhile, too, speaking broken English, as humorous and colorful as it is, can dumb down the brain. I still love to speak pidgin today and am proficient at it, but after a vacation these days on Kauai, speaking pidgin English almost the whole time, my brain starts to feel like mush. My local friends on Kauai tell me their kids speak pidgin less often than we did. Hawaii and its inhabitants have had to change, since tourism is the primary source of revenue these days.

Pidgin English evolved as a way for the various immigrant groups to communicate with each other back in the early days of the sugar plantations on the islands. The funny words and sentence constructions made me laugh when I was growing up there and still do today. Pidgin relaxes a serious tone in any conversation. If I'm talking with my sisters on the phone and they're stressed out about something, I'll use pidgin to reply to them; soon the voltage of any problem is neutralized and mountains are reduced to the size of molehills. My dad says the same is true for poetry and conversation: When you use a surprise word in conversation, people hear you better. If someone has constipation, for example, the locals will say you have "stuck shit." How can you not laugh at constipation after hearing that? Laughing at it makes the discomfort of constipation a bit more tolerable. If too many people are sitting on a bench, someone will request room to sit there by saying, "Ay, broke seat or what?" This will ease the social tension of a crowded bench, and everyone will laugh and make room so the new person can sit down, too. If you're out fishing and see a lot of fish, you say, "Ho! Only get choke fish, bra!"

If you don't want to say everyone's names when referring to a group of friends, you just say one person's name and then add "guys" at the end. For example, "Auntie guys going come to da party, too?" Everyone in Hawaii is either "auntie" or "uncle" or "cuz," as it's a very family-oriented culture and even childlike in many ways. I carry this attitude with me today; Daffy Dave is a big kid who loves kids and delightedly plays with words. In my clown shows today, I'll use malapropisms and puns throughout my show, much of which come from playing with language as a kid, listening to my dad's poetry and then writing poetry myself, but even more as a result of speaking pidgin English almost exclusively for eight years of my life in Hawaii.

~.~

My dad likes to say that it's our responsibility as adults to give kids good memories so that when they grow up and life gets difficult, they can look back and draw strength from those memories to face tough times and move forward. While I experienced some dark and troubling times as a kid, overall my childhood memories are positive. I draw strength from those happy memories all the time, even when I'm not consciously aware of it. The innocence and joy, the smiles and laughter, the love and care, the adventures and achievements of my childhood and adult life boost me and reassure me that life is worth living, especially when I face new difficulties as an adult today. These joyful experiences are deep in my cells now. My mom and dad provided my sisters and me with lots of helpful, positive memories as we grew up. The wonderful people on Kauai and in Minneapolis, in Seattle, and all through my life furthered the process. Today, when I perform my Daffy Dave shows and hear kids belly laugh, teach them to play games, regale them with stories, do yoga with them, meditate with them, or do any form of service in my life, I know I am continuing in this purposeful and positive direction. The beauty of life grows in me with these actions.

~.~

One of my all-time favorite memories of belonging to the human family, of fitting in and feeling loved and a part of a meaningful community, was when our church in Koloa sponsored a state-wide luau (or 'aha pa'aina) for all the churches in our denomination, and also included many other folks in the surrounding community. That's how it is in Hawaii. The spirit of aloha reaches out into the community and beyond and invites others, well beyond family, friends, and acquaintances. The actual cooking of the food took place in our backyard. On the morning before the day of the big event, a number of strong local men showed up in our backyard and dug a large hole for the "imu," the underground oven for the cooking of two large pigs. Earlier that same morning, my dad asked if I wanted to come along to watch the pigs being slaughtered. I don't remember exactly how he asked me, but I do remember feeling curious and afraid at the same time. I hopped in the back of an open pickup truck with a bunch of other boys and men, and we drove to one of the Filipino camps, a cluster of shacks left from the early days when the sugar industry brought in immigrants to work in the cane fields.

We quietly entered the stalls where the huge pigs were kept, and I watched as a skinny Filipino pig farmer shaved the pig's hair off, tied the pig to posts, and quickly shoved a long knife up its throat. The pig squealed loudly, piteously, and I recoiled in horror. Blood gushed into a bucket. I went out to catch my breath, feeling appalled and sickened. I recovered myself enough so that when it was time to load the slaughtered pigs onto long wooden boards I could help. We then lifted the pigs on the boards onto the back of a big flatbed truck. That was my first experience of watching a slaughter and I felt shocked and disturbed, but knew it was going to be our food, too. I was confused about how we have to kill in order to live.

I understand now why Native Americans thank the animal to be slaughtered and apologize to it. Witnessing this pig slaughter was probably one of my earliest experiences of life's ambiguity, and I puzzled for quite some time over how death and life exist alongside each other. In Saul Bellow's novel . *The Dean's December*, Albert Corde, the dean, puts it this way: "I imagine, sometimes, that if a film could be made of one's life, every other frame would be death. It goes so fast we're not aware of it. Destruction and resurrection in alternate beats of being, but speed makes it seem continuous.... With ordinary consciousness you can't even begin to know what's happening."

My dad's near-death accident illustrated this polarity for me, too, of life and death existing side by side. I was to face this ambiguity again in life as a young seminarian. At that juncture, I had to come up with my own spiritual philosophy about it. As I was being grilled by my professors during my oral examination for my master's degree, one of the questions was, "How will you deal with ambiguity in life and in the church? How will you live and respond to evil in the world?"

I have meditated and puzzled over the answers to these questions ever since, and in midlife, my answers have to do with faith and acceptance. My faith allows me to surrender to the horrors of life and move into acceptance of whatever is happening in each moment. I'm powerless over the existence of evil; I'm powerless over death and even ambiguity. Sometimes life is painful and sad, sometimes it's happy and fun. All of the multitudinous aspects of life exist at the same time. Life is messy. It's ambiguous. Life is mysterious and unknowable.

When we got back to the imu in the backyard of the parsonage, the local men from the congregation, led by the dashing and trim Kili, were building a fire at the bottom of the pits. Crumpled newspaper and kiawe, a hardwood similar to mesquite, were the fuel, with bottles of kerosene lobbed in for good measure. When the fire failed to light right away, some of the men went closer to check it, and one of them lit a piece of newspaper and tossed it in. The pit exploded with a loud boom followed by a brief instant of shocked quiet. Relieved laughter ensued once we were all sure no one had gotten hurt.

The fire was allowed to blaze until it became hot coals, and then Kili led the men in covering it with porous lava rock that would absorb and keep the heat in all night. Ordinary rocks would have exploded with the heat; only the porous lava rock would do. The lava rocks were covered with banana stalks and sacred Hawaiian ti leaves. After a while, the men pulled some of the red-hot lava rocks from the imu and placed them inside the gutted, carved-up pigs. They carried the pigs, which had been wrapped in wire meshing, over to the fire and laid them in the imu on top of the ti leaves. They placed more banana stalks and ti leaves on top of the pigs and covered the whole thing with dirt, then canvas. The canvas had a little escape hole they poured water into so that the imu became a kind of steamy oven. Then they covered the hole in the canvas and left the pigs to slowly steam roast all night long.

That night, I was allowed to stay out in the large make-shift canvas tent with the local boys and men to keep watch over the imu. We had to make sure that no steam came out. If we saw steam, someone quickly shoveled dirt over the leak. We kept ourselves awake by joking and telling stories and eating delicious Hawaiian foods. The men carved sticks to pass the time, and we all swatted at the mosquitoes when the mosquito punk smoke wasn't enough. I felt like one of the guys, warmed and nourished in my spirit.

Earlier that day, I had joined in the joyful activity at our church down the street, helping to prepare dishes for the upcoming feast. An army of volunteers took part, and at one point when I looked around, it seemed to me that everyone in the whole town had shown up to help with the preparations. One of my jobs was to scrape coconut meat from the shell for haupia, or coconut pudding. The Japanese ladies were cooking rice and fish and cutting up raw salmon for lomi lomi salmon, and the men were cutting up meat and cleaning fish. In an atmosphere of joyful activity and camaraderie, smiles and excitement were everywhere I looked.

When dawn broke and the long night of watching the imu was over, the pigs were uncovered, lifted from the imu, and delivered to the cafeteria at Koloa Elementary School for the 'aha pa'aina. So many people showed up when it was time to serve the meal. Because the feast was held in conjunction with the annual statewide church meeting, people came not only from all over the island but also from the other islands, too. And because the celebration that year took place on Kauai and purple is Kauai's color, the ladies of our church made leis of purple flowers for everyone who came.

Maybe for the adults the focus was on the church meeting, but for me it just seemed to be a big community party. I don't even remember the meeting. I just remember the most delicious, melt-in-your-mouth, smoky-flavored, shredded pig. It was the first time I had tasted kalua pig, but I hope it's not my last. It was amazing. I gained a real appreciation for the ancient Hawaiian way of cooking in the ground, and I was enchanted by the loving atmosphere and the feeling of community.

Every now and then during the festivities, some of the men would quietly slip away to sip from their bottles of Primo Beer, a popular island beer at that time. At one point, Dad's camera caught four of them sipping beer while sitting on a church pew that had been placed on the basketball court behind the church. When they noticed the camera, they laughed and turned away, embarrassed. Dad kept the camera focused on them until they noticed it again and burst out laughing. When he edited the film later, he reinserted this scene several times for laughs. When we all watched the movie afterward, everyone thought this was the funniest thing we had ever seen.

Several weeks later, the big pit was still in our backyard. After a good rain, I went to look in the imu hole. The water was muddy, but all the same I thought it looked like a pretty good swimming pool. I called my sisters out and showed them. I said, "Hey, let's make a slide that goes into the water!" I searched under the parsonage and among the pylons found a long, smooth plank, the seat from an abandoned church pew. We carried it over to the imu and slanted it into the hole at a forty-five-degree angle. Then we used a garden hose to fill up the hole some more. When it looked about right to us, we started sliding down the pew seat into the muddy water. When we landed in the muddy pool, we noticed there were tiny pig bones floating next to us. It was gross, but we just kept sliding anyway. That is, until my mom came out and told us to stop. "You kids get out of there! You're going to get splinters in your bottoms!" she yelled.

"But, Mom!" we protested.

"Now!" she insisted.

"Okay, we're coming."

~.~

One of Dad's friends introduced him to a new hobby, looking for old bottles on the island. I still remember the day he came home excited about some old embossed bottles they had dug up. I was fascinated by the bubbles in the dark green wine bottles, the crude, thick glass. My dad showed me how to tell if a bottle was an older one or not. The older bottles were "free-blown," he explained, and on those, the mold line didn't go all the way up to the lip. Held up to the light, the ocean blue glass of the soda bottles was particularly beautiful. One of the prettiest, an aquamarine bottle, was embossed with the words "Kauai Soda Works." It was from the late 1800's and it had a wire stopper still intact inside the "blob" top.

The old bottles were not only pretty; they were also worth some money. Dad bought some books that gave the going prices for old bottles, and that inspired me to want to find some bottles, too. Pops told me he would take me bottle-hunting and I was thrilled. I had been rebelling against my dad around this time, a situation made worse when other kids criticized me for swearing. They'd say to me, "You mean, your dad's a minister and you're swearing?" At Sunday school sometimes I would get into trouble and one of the church ladies would scold me, telling me that since I was the minister's son I should set an example for the other kids. I hated the pressure and resented being the son of a minister. It was already hard enough trying to fit in as a haole local. The last thing I needed was the unrealistic expectation that I should be a nice, perfect preacher's kid, too! Sometimes I got so angry when I was scolded about my behavior that I would swear even more or find a way to get into even more trouble, just to prove I was as human as all the other kids. Looking for old bottles together was a way for Dad and me to be father and son without all the labels and expectations of church and community.

Bottle hunting on Kauai kept our relationship together even when I was a teenager and things got really bad. The first few times he took me out, I didn't find anything and became discouraged. When he invited me to go with him to check the Waikomo Stream area, at first I didn't even want to go. Pops gave me a pep talk and told me I'd eventually find something. I just needed to keep searching and not give up. I was skeptical but grudgingly went along. Dad had an idea that if we looked down the hill near the stream maybe we could find some bottles that had rolled down that way over time. Contrariwise, I decided to look around on the top of the hill instead. Sure enough, before I had looked very far, I saw five rectangular olive green bottles sticking up out of the dirt. As it turned out, they were gin bottles from the early 1800's, worth about two hundred dollars apiece. I had just seen pictures of bottles like these in Dad's bottle book and knew right away what they were. I excitedly yelled for Dad to come look. Dad helped me dig them out, saying, "You see, I told you not to give up."

"Yeah! You were right, Dad!"

Dad patted me on the back, laughing. "You son of a gun," he said, "and here I was telling you to look down the hill. Boy, what a lucky find! Son, I'm so proud and happy for you."

For years after that lucky find, my friends and I would occasionally find a rare old bottle, and we unearthed lots of common ones. But it wasn't until just before our family moved to Seattle in 1978 that my good buddy Nelson Inouye and I had another lucky find. While we had spent lots of time over the years looking all over the island for rare old bottles, it wasn't until we poked around among the thick hau bushes that covered the old stone walls right across the street from the parsonage that we found our best treasure trove of old bottles. To this day, Nelson and I still look for old bottles whenever I visit Kauai.

As our collection of old bottles grew, Dad and I started filling up most of the book shelves in the guest room. There were dark brown beer bottles, tall frosty green champagne bottles, aquamarine blob top soda bottles, long-necked cobalt blue medicine bottles, triangular ink bottles, and even a brown cod liver oil bottle shaped like a fish and embossed with scales and eyes. When sunlight shone through the window, colors danced on the walls; the guest room was like the inside of a medieval chapel.

One day when I came home from school, I heard Top Forty music coming from inside the guest room. I looked inside and was enchanted to see a man on a ladder singing and dancing along with the music on the radio, to the extent one can dance while standing on a ladder. All the while he was painting a beautiful picture of a white whale on the wall above the bottles. His name was Jon Petri and he was an artist from New Zealand. My dad had hired him to paint Moby Dick on the wall in honor of the bottles we had recently found around the old Koloa Landing near Poipu Beach, an area where the whaling ships had once tossed their trash. "One man's trash is another man's treasure," my pops would say.

I couldn't keep my eyes off Jon as he worked. He was so animated and enthusiastic. I watched as he painted a dark brownish-grey harpoon stuck in Moby Dick's side and then carefully dabbed a bit of red paint to look like blood coming out of the wound. Under his nimble fingers, a frayed rope appeared, trailing from one of the many harpoons that were bristling out of the great whale. The leviathan leapt out of the waves, its tiny sharp teeth glistening. Jon painted a whaling ship in the distance, presumably Captain Ahab's, from which the whale had just made another narrow escape. I marveled for a long time over Jon's painting, wanting to do something creative and colorful like that. I could sketch a pretty good wave on the beach, or a dragster peeling out from the starting line, but my skills weren't anything like Jon's.

I was further inspired about painting a few years later when my cousin Brad Anderson took his brothers and me to the art museum in Minneapolis while Dad was on one of his pulpit exchanges there. As a young adult, during the time when I was a pastor and had begun to realize I wanted to leave the ministry, I did a few paintings and pastels, finding comfort in that activity. I gave one of my best paintings from that period to my sister Sara and Mike Greshock, her new husband at the time, and they still have it hanging in their guest room. It is an expressionistic rendering of a hazy green field and hillside with a sky of layered blues that blend upward toward a dark night with stars. I actually like most of the elements of that painting, but every time I look at it, I want to re-do the stars. Because Jon Petri opened up this beautiful world for me, I've now wandered through a good many art museums in both Europe and the United States, and now and then I still dabble with paints and pastels.

Recently, I fell into a reverie thinking back to the moment in my young life when I watched Jon Petri paint Moby Dick, and I penned these words in an attempt to capture the essence of what that moment meant to me:

Old Bottles
--David Mampel
February 18, 2013

One man's trash is
another man's treasure
he'd say
digging up old bottles
like archeologists
on a cliff side
castaway dump

red rusty earth
easily giving up
clumsy bubbled-glass
mirror images
of a free blown surf
frothing thunder blue
on jagged rocks below

Kilauea's Lighthouse
kept watch
enviously looking over
Pop's shoulder
sweat struggling down
dirt-encrusted faces
waterfalls from Mount Wai'ale'ale
hidden in the distant
Hawaiian sun
Our eyes popping like blowfish
glimpsing secret truth
tenderly birthing another
Kauai Soda Works blob top
the curvaceous wire stopper
still intact

I'd dig excitedly
to find such a prize
dimple bottomed
three mold black wines
frosty sun dappled
purple gins
flaring to stub tops
of pyramid mathematical beauty
the elusive Tahiti Soda
marble-cod stopper
we never did find

At home
I could lay for hours
in the parsonage guest room

shelves of colored glass
kaleidescoping
plumeria mornings
Jon Petri's fresh painting
of a harpooned Moby Dick
on twelve-foot-high walls

I once sat with scalp tingling
fascination
as he painted that scene
dancing to Casey Kasem's
top forty electric songs
teasing with fanciful brushstrokes
new ideas bathed
in balmy mango breezes
whispering brainwaves across
cheap gossamer curtains
Daydreaming with bottle books
and prices

I was a nineteenth-century whaler
at Koloa Landing
a dreamer of double-masted ships
an ancient metallurgist
smelting sand for Babylonian vases
colors of esoteric rainbow
scintillating light of creation
a new soul awakening
to parallel universes
a feather lost in trade winds
a map hidden in a tossed whiskey
floating to the shore

I was my father's son
once more

Chapter Four:
Sleeping on a Mountain

B esides my father, other men on Kauai, as in every place I've ever lived, provided mentoring for me. I feel fortunate to have had adults besides my parents to teach me how to navigate life. From them I learned how other adults responded to life situations, and as a result, I had more options when similar situations occurred in my own life. My views were broadened because of what I learned from these other adults, and I had a glimmer of an idea that there were more perspectives to choose from than just my own original ones. It truly does take a whole village to raise a clown.

My parents loved having lots of people visit our home. They often joked about how their friends visited them when we moved to Kauai because we were a free hotel in paradise. But every one of us loved it, whenever friends came to visit for a while.

One of our early visitors when we lived in Kauai was my dad's former professor, the late Henry Gustafson, who settled into our home as Kauai's theologian in residence. His visit happened to coincide with that of my Uncle Ed Mampel. One evening, Katherine Baldwin, a local artist renowned for her seascapes, invited the adults of the house--Uncle Ed, Henry and his wife Joyce, and my mom and dad--to her beautiful home on Brennecke Beach near Poipu. Mrs. Baldwin was well known on the island, and everyone was anxious to make a good impression. Everything went well, for a while. The conversation flowed smoothly, the meal was delicious. And then, in an effort to compliment the hostess, my dad commented, "That has to be the best fish I have ever tasted."

Taken aback, Mrs. Baldwin replied, "Why, it was chicken!" The erudite Henry tried to change the subject and quickly engaged Mrs. Baldwin in a new conversation.

A few minutes later, however, Uncle Ed chimed in. "Katherine," he asked, "have you ever tried finger painting?"

After a brief shocked silence broken only by an embarrassed titter or two, Henry threw up his hands and said, "That's it! I'm through trying to cover up for you Mampels. You're on your own!"

~.~

Among the stream of guests in our home were travelers who hailed from various locales all over the world. Dad met a couple of guys at the beach one afternoon, Garth from South Africa and Mike from Virginia, and was so taken by them that he invited them to come and stay at our place for a few days. At dinner that first evening, I was flattered that both young men attempted to engage me in conversation and actually seemed eager to hear what I had to say. A teenager at the time, I was just starting to awaken to esoteric teachings and explore my own brand of spirituality. When these young men expressed interest in my theories about pyramid power and my interpretation of the esoteric symbols on the back of the one-dollar bill, I went so far as to show them what I had written on those subjects. I felt intelligent and mature, and my conversations with them reinforced my love for philosophy at an early age.

Other mentors taught me how to play rock-and-roll guitar and encouraged me, even if only indirectly, to seek out my dreams in life and move forward on my path. My cousins Scott and Junior Duncan belong on this list, not only because I liked them a lot, but also because I looked up to them as musicians.

Years later when I was a seminarian, I read Robert Bly's *Iron John: A Book About Men*. The central message I took from that book and others like it was that older, unrelated male mentors are necessary to the process of a young man's emotional maturing. Older males' attentiveness, their validation of my ideas and pursuits, and their support of my dreams in life gave me the energetic push I needed to grow out of childhood, through the confusion of youth, and gradually into young adulthood. I find myself now, as an adult male, paying close attention to young men like my nephew Michael, as well as other young men I know who are pursuing their creative dreams and even trying to make a living with their art. Others I meet in the rooms of Twelve Step recovery, eager to find their way to a healthy way of life. Since from my own experience I know how important male mentors are for young men, I take pains to show these younger men that I do care. I encourage them and listen to them. I can see in their yearning faces how much such attention means to them. I live for the moment when I first see the spark in their eyes that tells me they feel the validation I am giving them. I truly care about their lives and their dreams. In this way, the gift that was given to me comes full circle. As we like to say in recovery fellowships, "You keep what you have only by giving it away."

~.~

Kauai is the oldest island in the Hawaiian island chain, and it is called "The Garden Island" because it is so lush and beautiful. It is still one of the least commercialized of all the islands, and its residents still struggle to control that kind of growth. From 1970 to 1978 Kauai's natural beauty seeped into my pores and has stayed with me all through my life. I adore colors and beautiful plants, art and music. It was Kauai's natural beauty and childlike culture that encouraged my love of natural beauty.

Kauai is mysterious, alive with something magical, a vibrant, otherworldly energy. Many people feel it right away, as soon as they set foot on the island for the first time. A lush island in the middle of the ocean, gently caressed by the purest air and bathed tenderly in the cleanest water on the planet, Kauai's culture naturally keeps artificial lighting at a minimum so that the Milky Way is clearly visible on cloudless nights. This gentle environment encourages a much slower pace of life and thereby a deeper connection with a Nature's spirituality. Overflowing with enchanting beauty, Kauai offers vast cosmic nights and warm, tranquil days, allowing intuition and natural psychic abilities to open in ways that simply are not possible in the midst of fast-paced city life.

In the film *The Milagro Beanfield War*, an old man is visited by angels. When he asks them why he can see them when no else can, they reply, "Because you have time for us." While I was growing up on Kauai, even though I was only a child and a youth there, my life slowed down and I lived what is known as "island time." I remember my dad coming home from one of his first weddings there and remarking that everyone showed up about two hours after the wedding was supposed to have started with no sense that they were late. At first we were all simply amused about this aspect of island life, but we quickly grew to love this slower pace ourselves. It was a much easier way to live, but on the other hand, we were afraid of becoming too lazy. My pops calls this facet of island life "Polynesian paralysis." Even when they do get in their cars, most people who live there don't drive faster than thirty-five miles an hour. After all, there is only a single road, and that road doesn't even go all the way around the island, stopping as it does at the Na Pali Coast. And, by the way, if you've never been to Na Pali, you owe it to yourself to visit its cathedral-like cliffs, graced as they are by lush ferns splashed by waterfalls tumbling into a crystal blue sea. There are no buildings in sight, and the area is a luxuriant paradise. Mount Wai'ale'ale, looming nearby, has an average rainfall of more than four hundred eighty-three inches of rain per year, qualifying it as the wettest spot on earth.

I attribute much of my interest in mysticism and pantheism, the belief that God is in everything, to my eight years of living at a slower pace on beautiful, lush Kauai. Kauai's ambiance naturally opened the veil of my psyche and sensitized me to certain spiritual realities that are difficult to describe in words. Even though I was a regular kid--playing sports, building tree forts, surfing, going to school, and joking around with friends and family--I felt strange desires to go off into nature by myself.

Years later, when I was writing poetry in college and seminary, I remembered a time as a teen when I camped with Pepper, our black Labrador Retriever, in the forests of Koke'e.

I felt an intuitive need for a vision quest like those that many Native American tribes and other earth-centered spiritual cultures provide for their older children. What happens to our souls when our bodies change in youth? What happens to a girl when she has her first period or a boy when he has his first wet dream? Puberty shifts something deep inside of us, and that shift demands some kind of ritual to acknowledge the process and integrate the bewildering changes that occur when a person grows from being a child into a young adult. Dad seemed to know I needed this time and gave his permission easily, although he insisted on staying in an isolated cabin near where I camped by myself. I loaded up a backpack with a pup tent, food, and water and hiked off into the forest. Pepper was my animal guide as I faced my fears of being alone in the wilds, an apt metaphor for my fears about leaving childhood behind and becoming a teen. I wrote a poem about this adventure later in my life:

Sleeping on a Mountain
--Dave Mampel

With only
a black dog
in still
mountain air
I lay down
by dark pines
that arc
like
strong hands
cupped over
a small fire

Chewing the cold
sparks
and smoke
swallow the wind
eating their way

toward a full moon
the camp fire
settles
like a beast
after dinner

Circling palms
over my stomach
the forest phantoms
disappear
I remember
my childhood theory
that stars
were holes
in a huge blanket
made by spirits
of the dead
breaking through
to heaven

Beneath stars swelling
on a black sheet
I fall asleep
as a twig
snaps
then slips
from logs
in the fire.

~.~

As we became true kama'aina, steeped in local culture and island time, my sister Jeanie and I began to have other-worldly experiences that seemed to us to be visitations from the spirit world, for lack of a better term. Even today, in my most quietly tuned-in moments, I can still sense and even see or feel these other-worldly realities.

One night a few years ago, when I went to stay with Aunt Jeanne because her husband, my dear Uncle Darrell, had passed away, I was about to go to sleep in one of the bedrooms in their home. As I said a little prayer and slipped under the covers, suddenly I felt the foot of my bed slump down as if someone had sat down there. I knew it was my Uncle Darrell's spirit visiting me as if to tell me he was okay. I was a bit frightened and let him know, and the sunken impression on the bed returned to normal and he was gone. The next morning, I told Aunt Jeanne about my experience, and she said she had felt his presence in the house that night, too.

I've heard stories like these from several members of our family as well as from others I know. The more I share stories about these occurrences with others, the more other people around me open up and reveal their similar experiences. At a recent ghost stories soiree at my home, people came because they were eager to share these unexplainable experiences in their lives. It was a fascinating party and everyone left feeling enchanted. People who came wanted to identify with each other and better understand what had happened to them; they wanted not to feel alone in their experiences, to know they were not crazy because they had had such encounters. For me and so many others on Kauai, these visions emerged perhaps because of the slower pace of life and because the entire culture was more attuned to this other world. It shows what can happen for anyone who slows down enough and becomes sensitized. We can make the time for the angels to find us and speak to us.

My dad wrote a poem when we lived on Kauai that captured how we were all starting to slow down and become affected in new ways by island time:

Mohihi Trail
--Arthur George Mampel
from *Makai and Mauka*, Copyright 1977

When I ease to slower pace
And step this path deliberately,
I measure with another face
The green tranquility.
To gather in from spreading day,

And from the covered, slinking trail
The ripe and fruit of a new way:
The growing slant, the soft detail,
The mounting brush of feathered flight,
The final hush of Nature's night.
Marking all with but mere vision;
Tiny sounds with a close ear,
I succumb to indecision;
Where I've wandered is not clear.

~.~

Our sister Jeanie tells the story of a ghostly visitation that happened for her when our family vacationed in a rustic cabin up in the mountains of Koke'e near Waimea Canyon. Called Waineke Lodge, the cabin had running water but no electricity and was heated only by a wood stove. Because my dad was a minister, we could rent it for only one dollar per night for the whole family, making it an ideal vacation spot for a pastor's family of modest means. This is the same cabin Dad stayed in when I went on my "vision quest" as a young teen. On my first visit back to the island after we moved in 1978, I found the old sign for Waineke Lodge buried in tall grass. Someone had put up a new sign next to the dirt road near the entrance. I was thrilled to have found the old discarded sign and brought it home with me, where it now hangs in my living room, a reminder of our family's special times at this simple cabin.

Whenever we stayed there, we kids would gather sticks and twigs and logs to make fires for heat and roasting marshmallows. Mom would make us simple, delicious dinners, and we'd sometimes have fresh blackberries we picked near Kalalau Lookout for dessert. We especially enjoyed them with milk and sugar. Pops would then gather us up by the fire and read aloud to us from *The Hobbit*. We all giggled when he made his voice sound lower as he dramatically uttered the phrase, "... and Bilbo went up THE MOUNTAIN." On a night I particularly remember, the moon was shining bright, and I had trouble sleeping, as I often do whenever the moon is full. We kids giggled in our sleeping bags until, "Hush!" Mom called from the other room, and "Go to sleep!" yelled Dad.

Years later, Jeanie told me that she woke up in the middle of the night that night and saw an old man in the rocking chair smoking a pipe. She just stared at him all night long as he peacefully rocked back and forth. He vanished at sunrise. The next morning she told our dad what she had seen. Pops was taken aback, as her description of the man she had seen fit the description of his father, who had passed away in 1966 from stomach cancer. When she told Dad about the pipe the man was smoking, my dad got the shivers. Only my pops and a few others knew that his dad, my grandpa, used to smoke a pipe in secret.

Another time Jeanie had one of these visions was when she and her friend, Cynthia Martin, also known as "Choch," were coming home late at night from an event at Kauai High School in Lihue. There had been some cooked pork left over after the event, and the girls had brought some home with them. They put it in the back seat and started out--but one important thing was missing. One of the local beliefs is that you never travel at night with pork unless it is wrapped in ti leaves because Hawaiians believe that the ti plant keeps away evil spirits. For this reason, pretty much everybody in Hawaii has ti plants around their house; even a number of hotels have ti plants around their property. But Jeanie and Choch ignored this local custom.

As they were driving through what was known as the "tree tunnel" on the way down to Koloa from Lihue, their car suddenly stopped in the middle of the tunnel. The lights went out. The engine died. It was pitch black. Out of nowhere they both saw a woman in a flowing dress walking toward them. Jeanie and Choch jumped out of the car and ran to hide in the bushes. The lady walked over to the quiet car, opened the back door, took something out, and walked away. As soon as the woman was out of sight, the car engine started back up and the headlights came back on. Choch and Jeanie crept back over to the car, got in, and drove away as quickly as they could.

When they got home, they looked in the back seat for the pork. It wasn't there. To this day, they both believe the woman they saw was Madame Pele.

~.~

Chris Town was our seventh- and eighth-grade science teacher at Koloa Elementary School. Mr. Town used to start every class with a minute of meditation. He and I have kept in touch over the years, and when he recently showed up at Poipu Beach for our reunion this past summer for family and Kauai friends, he laughingly shared with us that he instituted that morning meditation to "shut you kids up." We all "bust laugh" when he said that because we knew how rowdy we were back then. Everyone there from our old gang--among them Lisa Liberato, my sister Jeanie, Miriam Asuncion, and me--was so touched that he joined us at this reunion nearly forty years later.

Little did he know back then that those one-minute meditations planted the seed for me to practice meditation on a regular basis as an adult. In fact, following Mr. Town's example, I now use short meditations with my preschoolers at Twinkle Twinkle School in Los Altos, California, to help them settle down after playing games outside. A brief moment of quiet time helps them to transition their focus for story time. I'll ask them to see if they can hold their breath while I count to ten. I use my fingers to count the numbers, but at first my fingers will appear to get stuck, or my thumb will pop into my mouth like a baby's, and they will laugh. Eventually, though, I shift from the antics into breathing and counting, and it becomes more like a meditation practice, centering their scattered energies and helping them quiet down to listen for story time.

Mr. Town would turn the one-minute meditation into a contest. If no one talked for that entire minute, he'd award us all points; if the class had accumulated enough points by the end of the week, we would have a party on Friday. Of course, there was always some clown making a noise a few seconds before the minute was up, but pretty soon the class would turn on those jokers because they wanted the reward of the party.

We actually became pretty good at group meditation during that minute, as good as seventh- and eighth-graders can get.

One summer, when our church had a vacation Bible camp, Mr. Town helped Mom and Dad to run it. One of the things he did with us kids was to lead us in making a collage out of trash. First, we all went to Mahaulepu Beach to pick up trash. Using driftwood and rope, we made a "trash mobile" and used it to collect all the trash we could find on the beach. We hauled the trash back to the basketball court behind the church and, using a big piece of plywood as a base, proceeded to turn our trash into art. We had a lot of fun with our project, and a reporter from the *Garden Island Newspaper* came out to interview us and take our picture for the paper. Boy, did we ever feel cool! More than that, we knew had done something worthwhile, something that was good for our community, and we learned first-hand about the joy of service. I still love arts and crafts made from so-called trash. One of my favorite hobbies today is to find washed-up sea glass on the beaches of Santa Cruz near where I live; I use the broken glass, worn smooth by the ocean, as colorful glass jewels to decorate mirrors and candleholders to give as gifts to friends. It is art combined with service.

What a marvelous artist is Mother Ocean! She takes our broken glass and tumbles it in her waves and on her rocks to smooth away sharp edges. Pieces of glass in every color of the rainbow--red, blue, green, white, brown, purple, yellow, and orange--become jewels in her hands. We take them home and place them where Father Sun can shine through them till they dazzle our eyes with their translucent beauty. Chris Town showed us kids back then that not only is "one man's trash another man's treasure," but also that trash can become treasure.

Those years as a prepubescent and early teen were probably some of my happiest years on Kauai. I had so many fun, inspiring, and character-building events during that time. I became more confident and found myself becoming popular at school, even though I would always be a haole. There were dances at school and a dance at my house for one of my birthdays that led to a whole series of dances at other kids' homes. I had my first real girlfriends during this time, and of course, I fell in love and had my heart broken more than once. Pops reminded me that it was better to have loved and gotten hurt than to have never loved at all or some such fatherly reassurance. He told me stories about his first loves, and when he shared with me about his break-ups, too, I was better able to cope with the tumultuous feelings. But once, when I felt my heart would break, I scratched up my arms with a rock, partly to make the pain visible to others so I could get sympathy. I was (and still am) such a dramatic personality. No wonder I'm a performer today. I sometimes don't know where life ends and the stage begins.

I hadn't yet, at that point, started dissipating my spirit by using drugs; that wouldn't begin until I was about fourteen. When drugs began to cloud up my young life, the golden time of my early teens provided strength I could draw upon. I had memories of joy and accomplishment; I remembered love and a deep awareness that God is in everything.

~.~

May Day is a big event in Hawaii. The celebration has become a blend of ancient Hawaiian traditions along with those from the many cultures now living on the islands. In the seventies, when I was there, the week before May Day was spent getting ready for the big day. At school, we practiced hula dances, prepared the May Pole with colorful ribbons, sewed leis, and rehearsed for the reenactment of the Hawaiian royal court. One year, the boys in my fourth-grade class wore grass skirts and learned a lively Tahitian dance. I could never get the moves down quite right; on a home movie Dad took, my hands were always pointing in the wrong direction, out of sync with the other boys'.

One of my favorite pictures of myself at this time shows me standing in our big backyard holding the string of a kite. The kite, clearly visible behind me, has crashed to the ground, but I'm looking up at the sky as if I'm wondering where the kite has disappeared to. In another shot I'm dressed in my red-and-white Koloa Phillies Little League uniform, posing like a tough, professional baseball player, but my cool batting stance looks ridiculous because I'm holding a miniature bat the size of a wooden mixing spoon. So many times in life, as in these snap-shots, I find myself being just a little out of step with reality.

~.~

During this golden time in my life, my dad became fasci-nated with old Model A Fords. His dad, Alvin, was a very good mechanic during the Great Depression. The family remained poor, though, because so often he couldn't bring himself to accept payment for his work when others were going through even tougher times. He even designed a rotary engine for which a big company was willing to pay him good money, but claim-ing that he didn't want to be corrupted by money, he turned them down. Family lore says that Grandma left him because of his attitudes about money, although she still loved him, because she had kids to feed, after all.

Pops was never all that mechanically inclined. When Dad was about twelve, he tried to help my grandpa fix some old ball-bearing brakes, losing washer after washer as he tried to put them back into position. He looked up at his father with admiration and said: "Dad, I'm going to be a mechanic like you!"

Grandpa Al took another sip of his blackberry brandy and, with an amused expression on his face, rubbed his greasy hands through his son's sunny hair. "Lad," he said, "you will be many things in life, but a mechanic should not be one of your choices." His statement turned out to be a prophetic one, never mind the alcohol. Pops worked a series of labor-intensive jobs to put himself through college and seminary, along the way earning a reputation for mishaps, once crashing through the rooftop of a greenhouse he was painting and another time breaking out with hives from overworking himself with too many such jobs.

But on Kauai in 1973, Dad became nostalgic for the days

of his youth in San Antonio when he noticed someone driving an old Model A truck around the island. Dreaming of rumble seats and chocolate malts on hot San Antonio summer days, he approached the owner and offered to buy it. He was thrilled when the young man agreed to sell it for only four hundred dollars and purchased it right then, on the spot. He drove it home and went to work fixing it up. I spent hours with him, helping to remove the old paint and sand down the fenders by hand. It took months, but eventually the old thing dazzled, sporting a fresh coat of shiny black paint, orange metal rails around the flatbed, and red spokes on the tires. I was pretty sure Grandpa Al must have looked down and smiled. The truck's horn, with its distinctive "Aaoooga!" call, made us all smile and laugh when we heard it. We kids loved the ol' Model A, especially when Mom and Dad loaded our friends and us onto the black flatbed sometimes after dinner and drove us out to Spouting Horn, a natural hole in the lava rock shoreline on Kauai's south side that spouts seawater like a whale every time the waves crash into it. I learned how to drive in that old truck. Dad taught me how and let me drive it as long as I stayed in our big yard.

Dad's next project was a 1930 Model A Cabriolet, complete with rumble seat. He still owns the Cabriolet and has promised to pass it along to me when he dies. I hope that doesn't happen for a long, long time, but still sometimes I fantasize about how cool it would be to drive to my clown shows in a Model A. Our sister Jeanie learned how to drive in that car, with the same stipulation I had, to drive only in our big yard. Once, when she was driving Sara and Colette around the yard, she wanted to give them a roller coaster ride. Going fast over the bumps, she lost control and crashed into the banana trees, toppling fruit-laden stalks into the yard. No one was hurt and we all laugh about it now, but Jeanie was a bit shaken up at the time. Dad loved that car so much he even wrote a poem about it.

The Model A Cabriolet
--Arthur George Mampel
Copyright May 5, 2014

You are a poem!
in your suit of BronsonYellow
and Sealed Brown rumble rear

And your four black fender cuffs
smartly poised as shelter
to four wired wheels

rolling wild and topless
on a hot summer night
with the breeze stroking ease

of pumping pistons--with valves
that open and shut
with robot regularity

The stars and the moon beam
above the roofless view
of that Van Gogh evening

the still water mirrors it all!
a maiden vanity
a reflective mirage

a mysterious beautiful pose
cruising fast as the wind
down the Lake wooded way

of the quiet shore drive, the
cherry trees with
flowers--pinned on their

branches--like thick pink corsages
a courtship of fond and lasting
backward glances

~.~

One day when Dad was driving the Model A truck down toward Poipu, a handsome man in a fancy car waved him over. The man, Ken Wales, got out of his car and asked my dad if they could use his truck for a movie he was filming. The film was *Islands in the Stream*, starring George C. Scott and based on the Hemingway novel, and Pops was beside himself when he learned about it. He is a great lover of Hemingway; he loves great literature of all kinds, and he loves movies. And when Ken told my dad they would pay him two thousand dollars for the privilege, he knew Mom could have the new piano she had been wanting.

The film was mostly shot at Kuikuiula Harbor, and Hollywood came to Kauai. Even Hemingway's widow Mary was on the island for the filming. Set directors turned the old harbor into a Cuban marina, and we all eagerly anticipated the arrival of the great Mr. Scott. Mom and Dad drove over to take a look at the set one day and were invited to be extras in the film. If you watch the film today, you can see my mom sitting on the porch in one of the early boardwalk scenes. Pops made a photo scrapbook of the whole event. He even got to meet George C. Scott.

Ken and dad hit it off and became friends. The whole cast came over to our house for dinner one evening and my mom prepared a great feast. One of the actors sat at mom's new piano that evening and played some rollicking tunes. Before long, Ken was attending my dad's Sunday services at the church. When our church hosted a celebration of the island's diverse ethnicities, Ken brought his makeup crew over to help. My sisters, Lisa Liberato, and a bunch of other kids, dressed in their Filipino, Japanese, Chinese, Swedish, Hawaiian, or Portuguese attire, all sported professional makeup that day. Ken was working with Sonny and Cher around this time, too, and he brought us pictures signed by the famous pop duo.

One of the Buddhist temples on the island burned during this period, and wood left from the set after the filming was used to rebuild it. Lots of people from every faith on the island came together to help tear down the set and deliver the wood to a local contractor's warehouse so that it could be used in the rebuilding of the temple.

Ken Wales and Dad have remained close friends, and they have kept in touch ever since that time. The heady thrill of having my folks be in the movie, along with the love and kindness I felt from Ken and his crew, impressed upon me a favorable perception of the performing arts, and I had a glimmer of a desire then to be a performer myself one day. I was learning how to play rock and roll guitar at this time, but it was still just for fun. I was trying out a lot of different activities and gave very little thought to what I would be as an adult. I was still just a kid, after all.

~.~

I became enthralled with Bruce Lee, as did pretty much all of my friends back then, and I covered my bedroom walls with his pictures. My friends and I made nunchuks from sawed-off broomstick handles, swivels, and dog chains. I painted mine black and got my hair cut in a style that I thought made me look like a rock star. My sisters hated my Bruce Lee phase because I would leap out in front of them, yelling "Waaaaaaa!" and proceed to flip the nunchuks over my shoulder and under my legs, finally attempting catch them under one armpit. Sometimes, I actually completed the whole maneuver, but several times I almost broke my elbow, and down I would go, writhing in pain. These days, I use the skills I gained back then to juggle clubs in my Daffy Dave clown act. During my act, I use three clubs, one of which knocks against my head on its way down. Kids love that part. That bit probably grew out of my nunchucks days when I was forever whacking my funny bone.

I learned how to ride a skateboard during this time, eventually learning to ride the length of a tennis court while doing a handstand on the board. This was a time of mini bikes, dirt bike tricks at Red Hill, "shooting the tube" and doing "three-sixties," which meant spinning in circles while boogie boarding down a wave at Brennecke Beach. I also played baseball and football and improved my tree fort and clubhouse building abilities. My friends and I got so good at building we even had a two-story tree fort at one time, complete with wall-to-wall carpet, television, radio, and a telephone made from garden hoses and funnels. We never managed to make a tree fort that we could stand up in, though. We had to crouch to get inside the structure and crawl around once we were in there.

~.~

That golden time started to fade for me when I graduated from the eighth grade and started my freshman year at Kauai High School. I'm not sure how it all happened, but I started to feel nervous inside and increasingly uncomfortable in my own skin. Part of it was my fear of growing up and attending high school. I had to catch the bus from Koloa to Lihue, first of all, and then I knew there would be lots of rough local kids that I didn't yet know. I was no stranger to anxiety, but that emotion intensified for me at this time. No longer was I able to ignore it by becoming absorbed with fun activities and sports.

That summer between eighth and ninth grades I started hanging out with some new friends, outside of my usual buddies. We went out to Nawiliwili Bay in someone's parents' car and I smoked my first marijuana. I knew what it was; I had smelled the stinky smell before when I hitchhiked down to Brennecke Beach from the town of Lawai and caught a ride in a VW bug with some hippies from Taylor Camp. The hippies lit up a joint while I was with them on that ride, but I was scared we would crash and didn't try it then. On that sunset ride out to Nawiliwili Bay a few months later, though, when my friend and his brother offered me a joint, I decided to try it. It didn't seem quite so scary then, because they seemed okay when they smoked it. They told me how cool it felt to them, but I didn't feel a thing. They told me it usually takes a few times before you feel high. So a few days later, I tried it again. That time the high kicked in. Suddenly, all that inner discomfort faded away. I felt relaxed and cool and found myself having lots of interesting thoughts and ideas. I felt euphoric; time stood still. I felt at ease and more sociable. And everything was funny! I was hooked.

At first it was fun, but before long I started feeling paranoid when I smoked marijuana. All the same, I continued smoking it, hoping I would feel those original euphoric feelings and have interesting thoughts again. Now and then a high would be fun, so I kept it up. Pretty soon other kids were smoking it, too, and the whole culture on Kauai seemed to change. The Vietnam War had just ended, and lots of disillusioned hippies and war veterans came to live on Kauai, searching for peace of mind. They brought with them all kinds of illicit drugs, including pot, and it wasn't long before lots of people I knew were growing pot and smoking it. It didn't seem like a big deal at first, but soon things turned ugly.

Marijuana became a lucrative crop, although it was illegal, and the island police began to raid growers' operations. People were even killed. Ignoring the dangers, I grew pot in a hidden place in our yard, too, and encouraged my friends to smoke it with me. During my freshman year, I skipped class whenever I felt like it, which happened with greater and greater frequency, and hung out with the other stoners off campus. Once I was so high in my pre-algebra class that I couldn't function. I told the teacher I was sick and went to the nurse's office. All of my grades plummeted.

There were times when smoking pot was fun again, but then I started hanging out with more unsavory characters. Together, we would go out looking for patches of marijuana plants to steal, bring the plants back to our tree fort, and dry them to smoke. Eventually I got into some trouble and, feeling guilty and remorseful, I went to my mom and dad and confessed to them. They were relieved when I told them, as they had suspected something was amiss and were worried. Together we took my stash box, my pipes, and the marijuana I had at the time and burned it in the backyard. Mom wrote me a note and left it on my bed. The words she wrote stayed with me and helped me in the years to come: "David," she wrote, "getting high on drugs is nothing compared to the high of accomplishing things." I quit smoking weed for about six months then and experienced a resurgence of esoteric interest. I had my first out-of-body experience during that six months of clean time and reawakened to the power of the Divine.

However, I was still confused and feeling anxious. Looking for some inner peace, I went to a yoga class offered by some hippies at the Koloa Community Center. I enjoyed the yogic breathing, the gentle stretches, and the quiet meditation at the end of the class. I felt at peace, with a kind of calm energy that was so much better than the high I experienced from drugs. However, I only went to that one class back then. Before long I was smoking marijuana again and this time I got into even more trouble. When I look back on it now, I can see that I was already an addict then, but I didn't yet know it, and I can see the progressive nature of my addiction.

Mom and Dad saw it, too, and decided it was time for the family to move. They found an open church in Seattle, and we packed up all our belongings. Our friends at church threw us a big going-away party that was both happy and sad. One of my gifts from that party that I really treasured was an empty journal to write in. The first thing I wrote in it was, "I feel like a famous author." Thus began my lifelong love of journal writing. I have kept a daily journal ever since that time. The book you're reading now is, in a way, a result of that gift, a gift that led to years of journaling.

Everyone in our family had mixed emotions when we said goodbye to Kauai; I welcomed the change for a number of reasons, even though I knew I would miss my friends and life on Kauai. I was looking forward to attending a school where I wasn't struggling as a haole to fit in. I was also starting to think about college, and most of my island friends planned on working for the county or finding a job with the sugar industry; they had no interest in higher education. But an even more compelling reason became apparent just before our family was scheduled to move.

On the day before we left Hawaii for good, I was wandering around in our big yard, wistfully admiring its lush greenery and thinking about how much I was going to miss my friends and island life in general. I watched idly as an old tan car, beat-up and dirty, drove up the road toward our house, stopping right in front of our driveway as if to block access and escape. The driver's side window rolled down, and a deep voice called out my name. "Ay, Mampels! Get ovah heah!" The pidgin English accent was so heavy that if I hadn't been used to hearing pidgin spoken regularly, I might have had difficulty understanding the words. As it was, I felt my gut knot up with fear. I approached the car. There were three big men inside it, two in the front and one in the back. All of them were dark and swarthy South Island types, with hair pulled back into greasy ponytails, and all much bigger than I was. "Ay, haole! Get ovah heah!" the driver boomed out again. "You been stealing my plants!"

Uh-oh! The locals didn't care if you stole the hippies' marijuana plants, which was what I thought I had done, but they didn't tolerate their plants being stolen. Had my nefarious friends and I wandered over onto the wrong plots? I swallowed hard and tried to breathe.

The guy on the passenger side pulled his sunglasses down on his nose just enough to peer at me over them. His upper arm was bigger than one of my thighs. "You betta bring 'em all back, Mampels," he said, "every last one." His voice was quietly menacing, and his pidgin accent even heavier than the driver's. Each word he spoke dripped venom.

I could hardly see the guy who was sitting in the back seat, not only because of the tinted windows, but also because I was so scared that I was hardly paying attention to anything but my own beating heart. Even so, I could feel him glaring furiously at me through the glass. These guys were really mad.

"Okay," I said, nodding vigorously to show them I would do whatever they wanted.

"If you don't," growled the driver, "we going come back heah tomorrow and kill you." And with that, the driver rammed the car into gear and roared off. With heart beating and palms sweating, I looked around quickly to see if anyone in my family had witnessed the incident. I was relieved to see that I was still alone in the yard. No neighbors, no one in my family was in sight. I escaped to my room and stayed there for the remainder of the day, willing time to pass more quickly than it could. I knew I had to get off the island, and fast. I hardly slept at all that night.

As I work my program of recovery these days, I wonder how best to make amends for what I did to those guys. We were all engaging in criminal behavior back then, so what should I do? For now, I tell this story in this book, to show my readers just how low a "good" boy can go when he's in the grip of addiction. Otherwise, I stay away from drugs and lend a hand to other recovering addicts whenever I can.

The next day at the airport, I started to feel the weight of imminent threat lifting as the time for our leaving approached. Lots of wonderful friends and people from our church gathered at Lihue Airport to see us off. To my surprise, a number of cute local girls lined up to kiss me good-bye, and boy, did I ever get kissed! Wow! As relieved as I was to escape with my life, it was hard to leave all that love and aloha spirit behind. Where had those pretty girls been hiding before? I boarded the plane in a daze.

Chapter Five:
The Emerald City

The first time Dad drove his Model A Cabriolet onto the driveway of our new church in Seattle, it backfired with a boom like a shotgun blast, and the elderly ladies chatting on the church's front lawn dove for cover. "Oh," said one, looking up to see what was happening, "I think that's just the new minister in his car."

What we didn't know before that moment was that Dad's new church--our new church--was located in a pretty tough neighborhood. The Holly Park housing project was just down the street, a hotbed of gun battles and crime. I once woke from a nap in the parsonage to the sound of gunfire and stepped outside, a near mistake. There was a gun battle raging just outside the parsonage between several men in separate cars.

Finishing high school in Seattle, sometimes referred to as the Emerald City, gave me focus and built my confidence. I still found ways to use marijuana from time to time but much less often than I had on Kauai. Living in the foreground of the snow-covered Olympic and Cascade mountains and breathing the piney saltwater air of the Pacific Northwest filled me with a new excitement for life. The wild beauty of Puget Sound and the vast serenity of Lake Washington reflected back to me my hope for a better life. On clear mornings, Mount Rainier hailed a lofty greeting through the windows of my second-story bedroom, a beacon of purity calling me to new heights.

I was well aware that I had narrowly escaped from Kauai with my life, and maybe that was why being in Seattle so quickened my blood. I was thankful just to be alive. With grateful open arms, I embraced all of the changes: from an island to a continent, from a provincial small town to a stimulating big city, from old friends to new ones, from warm tropics to the brisk Pacific Northwest. I was inspired to grow, to break free from regressive aimlessness. I focused on my classes at school and my grades improved. I agreed to chair the school's publicity committee and joined the high school track team, learning how to pole vault. I began to accomplish some of my goals and started feeling better about myself. Like Dorothy in the Emerald City, I was journeying toward maturity, toward adult responsibilities and the competence I would need to discover my dreams and live them out in my life.

~.~

My sisters Jeanie, Sara, and Colette were all changing during this time, too. Puberty was beginning to peak for all of us. I was not always the kindest of big brothers. I swung between my unconscious role as man of the family, a role I had taken on as a child after our father's accident, and the mean lone wolf. Sometimes, I would be the caring yet controlling older brother, and sometimes I just wanted to be on my own, far away from my self-imposed parental role. Of course, I had no understanding at this time of my inner motivations for my perceptions and behavior. Sometimes, I would taunt and tease them out of boredom or because I felt insecure and wanted to feel stronger than them. I felt outnumbered by the females in the household and tried to establish my identity as a rowdy boy. The dynamics of sibling rivalry and unconscious competition for the parents' blessing played their parts, too. And sometimes, we enjoyed each other's company and did caring things for one another. At the core, we loved each other then and we still do.

At some point, living there in Seattle, the tables turned. My sisters grew into more independence and I felt the changes in them. I was interested in girls and dating and curious about what they knew about the world from the female perspective, a perspective that seemed very strange to me. In some ways, I felt as if they were now parenting me, and at times, I thought they were just getting back at me for all the times when I had tried to parent them. If I wore clothes that weren't fashionable, my sister Colette would say, "You're never going to get a girlfriend if you dress like that!" I hated it when they ridiculed my self-righteous asceticism and emerging religious, political, or social beliefs. "You're so weird, David," one or the other of them would say. It was true, but nonetheless it hurt my feelings. On the other hand, their criticisms tempered my arrogance. I found myself asking them for advice on fashion and dating. I wouldn't always let them see it, but I secretly valued a good bit of what they had to say. I both feared and respected their new power as emerging young women. My sisters and Mom helped me respect women's struggles and issues. I learned a lot from them in our adolescent years and now realize how different we are in our personalities and perceptions. I have come to accept them for who they are instead of projecting a script of how I think they should be. Sometimes as adults we still clash, but we are bulldog loyal to each other and would do anything for one another. On a more practical level, Mom and my sisters taught me how to cook, do laundry, groom myself, keep a clean house, and pay some attention to fashion, however inadvertent. I observed how they communicated with their mates and realized that having disagreements in relationships is normal and not a threat to love. I benefitted as a man because my sisters and my mom sensitized me to uniquely feminine ways of feeling and experiencing life, even though women are still a great mystery to me that I'm sure I'll never fully fathom.

Our youngest sister, Colette, lights up any room with her naturally funny and entertaining presence. She can imitate almost anyone's gestures and accents, and she's been known to jump up on stage with the band, grab a microphone, and start singing along. She's the one who usually arranges our family reunions in the Cascade Mountains every winter or every other summer on Kauai. Once she joined my other sisters on a getaway trip to the kitsch Bavarian town of Leavenworth, Washington. When they had settled into their motel room, our sister Jeanie grabbed her video camera and started filming Colette making spontaneous, hilarious commentary about everything in the room, complete with a Bavarian accent and flamboyant physical gestures. She picked up a bottle of local beer called "Whistling Pig Wheat Beer" and, without missing a beat, she flailed her arms and bent her knees in a bizarre interpretive dance and sang a made-up-on-the-spot song in a German operatic voice, "Let's go out and get some Whistling Pig Wheat Beer. It's so whistling... and so wheaty." The sisters recount that earlier that day they visited a Bavarian chocolate store, and Colette started singing, "Bavarian styled chocolate! Bavarian styled chocolate!" Jeanie and Sara joined in the singing and together they sang Colette's ditty in perfect three-part harmony, right there in the store.

Another time my mom and dad met Colette's in-laws at the Bellevue Club, and all three of my sisters were there. At the end of the evening, the three sisters climbed up the huge staircase in the main hall and acted out the "So Long, Farewell" scene from *The Sound of Music* in which they nailed the harmonies again. Each sister would disappear and come out to sing her respective part. Everyone there looked on and laughed with delight.

Sara, our middle sister, will tell it like it is when no one else can admit the truth. She's a dental hygienist with the soul of an artist who makes enchanting scrapbooks for everyone in the family. When she was little she found Dad weeping and told him, "Dad, your tears look like wet stars."

Jeanie is like a second mom to Sara and Colette, and her cheerful positivity gleams like a powerful beacon when life gets difficult. On the day of Jeanie's wedding to Craig Swanson, I was standing at the front of the Augustana Chapel with the other groomsmen and I felt like I was losing my sister. I started sobbing, and before long all the other groomsmen and bridesmaids were crying, too. Crying and weeping spread throughout the entire congregation.

Jeanie is a registered nurse, like our mom, and she is known for her saintly patience in her care for others. She watches over her patients at Swedish Hospital with quiet tenaciousness, love, and good humor, and she listens to Sara and Colette like the caring, wise older sister that she is.

All of my sisters together are known for their funny scenes that make us all laugh. Our dad once came into the living room where the three of them were seated on the couch and heard Colette say to her sisters, "Who would have thought that we would become best friends?" I am so blessed to have sisters who are interesting, fun, funny, caring, and intelligent.

And we are all so blessed to have been raised by such loving parents. Pops is a naturally funny guy, and he was a beloved minister. He is just another human being in so many ways, but the people he served on Kauai and elsewhere looked up to him. He was a very caring, faithful pastor, and he is an exceptional poet.

Mom was the well loved minister's wife in all of the churches where Dad was pastor. She came from a long line of ministers herself, so that when I became ordained, I was a fifth-generation minister. Mom's great-grandfather was Nils Frykman, a legendary Pietist minister in the late 1800's who was expelled from Sweden because of his views about infant baptism. His life is celebrated every summer in the Swedish town of Sunne with a play about his life. He wrote more than seven hundred hymns that are still sung in the Swedish Covenant Church. When I traveled to Sweden a few years ago, I visited his monument near the town of Vasteras where my college friends, Kirk and Katarina, live. His cabin has been turned into a memorial, and I left some of my Daffy Dave CD's on his grave there. I wanted to pay homage to the music still coming through his progeny, even if through me it has taken the form of silly songs for kids.

~.~

I left Kauai High School at the end of my junior year and started the next term as a senior at Cleveland High on Seattle's south side. I was surprised to discover that once again I was in the minority as a white guy. As it happened, however, it turned out to be the perfect school for me. The year I showed up there turned out to be the year that school desegregation was mandated by the courts, and white kids and their parents from West Seattle were upset about having to be bused to the ethnic south side for high school. In order to ease the transition, the administration at Cleveland High scheduled an assembly, and another kid and I were asked to speak. The other kid was the fastest kid on the track team, handsome, funny, and kind. I really liked him. It just so happened that he was black as well. I felt honored to be asked to speak alongside him in front of the whole school. He spoke about his experiences as a black kid in a white culture, and I spoke about my experience of being in the minority on Kauai as a haole. What I had thought of as a negative experience became a positive quality that I could share to help my fellow students deal with racial tensions. I felt valued and accepted in my new school, and in addition I learned to accept my experience as a haole on Kauai. I began to realize that in God's sight, that experience had meaning and purpose. While the assembly did not end the racial tension at our school, things did ease up a bit after that. Overall our senior class pulled together and ended up being a fun graduating class.

At about this time, I made a decision on my own to dedicate my life to Christ. Mine was not only what some call a "born again" experience, though, as my beliefs even at that time were broader than that. I cringe now when I hear people identify themselves as born again, even though I too did so at that time; there are so many negative cultural stereotypes associated with that phrase. When I hear the phrase "born again" I think of closed-mindedness, hatred of different lifestyles, religions, and cultures. That was not what I aspired to. I had a mystical, esoteric vision of Divine Love that inspired my spirit and stabilized my turbulent teenage years. Mine was a comforting, lively, intimate faith coupled with hope for the future. I experienced a deeply personal sense that Jesus Christ was more than a spiritual teacher; He was an actual resurrected presence Who would lead me to become whole, or, in more traditional Christian parlance, saved. I made a decision to accept this belief as my own and tried to imitate Christ's example as I interpreted it from the New Testament. I felt my heart open up to a palpable sense of Christ's mystical divinity and tried to live the way I believed Jesus did in his time. This way of living became my first priority in every area of my life. I was still a member of my parents' church, the United Church of Christ, which is a more traditional Protestant, liberal, mainline church, but somehow choosing to believe I was born of the spirit made me feel closer to God. Many folks in the United Church of Christ believe as I did then that some aspects of being a born-again Christian seemed to be closer to how the early Christians lived, an almost hippy-like, socialist lifestyle, meaning they shared all they possessed in common. During my teen years, I identified with the characteristics of the born-again movement, because it seemed to me that it was more down-to-earth, not so concerned with ecclesiastical trappings, dogma, and organization. This was what I now consider to be a nascent, but significant, spiritual awakening for me. Though I don't now consider myself a Christian in any conventional or traditional sense of the term, my present eclectic faith and spiritual practice is deeply informed by the essential teachings of Christianity: "Love your enemies;" and "The Kingdom of God is within you;" and others. I now interpret Christian teachings in a non-exclusive, universal fashion. I don't reject Christianity or the Christian church, but rather adopt their core teachings as complementary to other spiritual philosophies I value and practice, such as Zen and other forms of Buddhism. I value this early emotional spiritual experience today primarily because it opened my heart and soul to a more passionate connection with the Divine and shaped my ethics in everyday life, such as being of service to those who need my help, practicing honesty with myself and with others as well as I can, and forgiving those who have harmed me.

I was getting better on guitar and became pretty popular at school. I even started having girlfriends again. I loved going to the Pilgrim Firs Youth Camp with other young people from our church. At camp, we all bonded in our common teen issues and fledgling faith. We enjoyed knowing our camp was the very same camp that Ann and Nancy Wilson of the rock group Heart had attended when they were our age; the duo had even written songs while they were there.

My dad was invited to give a poetry reading around one of the evening campfires. At first, I was a little embarrassed to have my dad do such a thing in front of all my cool teen friends, but when he recited his poems in his lilting, Richard Burton/ Dylan Thomas voice, all my friends, especially the girls, were blown away and thought he was awesome. This latter fact was not lost on me, and from that point on, I started thinking about writing my own poetry. Up until that point, I had had no significant interest in it, but if girls liked it, I thought poetry would be a worthwhile hobby. I didn't write poems immediately, but started picking my dad's brain about his poetry writing, and this brought us a little closer together again as father and son. We also got closer because I was getting ready to apply for colleges and needed his wisdom on that score. We had lots of late-night conversations at the old parsonage on Beacon Hill, and Pops really inspired me with his stories about how fun college could be. I also wanted to learn more and gave some thought to becoming a minister, especially since I had had a born-again experience.

Dad told me about his college friends who became his best friends all through life, and I realized I knew them all. I already loved Tom Tredway and Bruce Carlson. They were mentors to me in subtle ways. When Pops told me Tom Tredway was president of Augustana College in Rock Island, Illinois, I entertained the idea that "Augie" would be a good school for me. It was a fine liberal arts college with a strong emphasis on the humanities. My heart opened up and I felt a surge of enthusiasm to graduate high school and go to college.

One of the most encouraging experiences I had in high school was when I got to be the psychology class teacher for a day when we had student-teacher switch day. I loved leading the class and felt so mature as the "teacher." It was when I played the role of Sir Edward Ramsey in *The King and I*, though, that my fuse for the performing arts really got lit. It was so much fun to learn how to waltz on stage with the girl who played Anna, and the whole cast grew close during that production. I just knew I wanted more of that.

Right after I graduated from high school, I gave my first sermon ever, at Dad's church. I wrote in my journal that evening that I could feel my life starting to turn around. I felt confident, happy, and inspired to grow into an adult, become a minister, get married, and have kids. I was still struggling with smoking pot and drinking alcohol, but I managed to graduate with straight A's that year and was accepted at Augustana College. I was also working part time at Herfy's Hamburgers and earning my own money. I qualified for student Pell grants and received financial aid for college. Life was looking up.

Chapter Six:
Blessed Wound

"The only way out is through."
--Robert Frost

If only I could have articulated what was going on with me for all those years after my dad's accident, I would have told my parents, but I wasn't aware of what it was myself. I felt angry and hurt and confused and completely overwhelmed by the adult responsibilities I had fearfully and unconsciously taken upon myself. I swung between trying to be that overly responsible adult and being a fun and free kid or a wild rebel. It was confusing even to me, and it must have driven my family nuts. However, I was unable even to name those emotions which swirled within me. It wasn't until I was in my early twenties that I began to have some awareness of what had happened within my psyche. In my first year in seminary, I had nightmares nearly every night. I would wake in a cold sweat, crying, from dreams in which my father tumbled down the stairs and landed in a puddle of blood.

Was I trying to save my father by studying to be a minister as he had done? Was I trying to live his life for him? Was I trying to redeem him somehow? What about my own life? I had no answers to my questions. The questions themselves were only vague feelings in my adolescent soul.

I started writing at about this time. My first piece was a long treatise about pyramid power and my theories about Atlantis and the pyramid symbol on the back of a dollar bill. It was the sincere attempt of a young, awakening soul, very speculative in its ramblings. I laugh now thinking about it, and I wonder whatever became of it. I remember reading parts of it to kids on the bus as we rode to and from Kauai High School.

Some of them would become spooked by my ideas and would sit as far away from me as they could. I had mixed feelings about their reactions. On the one hand, I was a little sad to be considered weird in yet another way. But I also felt a sense of identity and power, especially since some of these kids were tough locals and I was a haole. Hawaii's culture is steeped with taboos and superstitions, so it made sense that some of the kids were afraid of my eerie-sounding revelations. My early mystical bent was starting to form a kind of unusual persona for me that, to this day, continues. After all, not many people are full-time clowns, and my profession can be seen as a kind of weirdness all its own.

At an earlier time, when I was about fourteen and we still lived on Kauai, I asked my Dad to take me to see *Beyond and Back*, a documentary about people who had near-death experiences. I had become fascinated with anything having to do with the occult and had been reading books about psychic phenomena, pyramid power, UFOs, Atlantis, mysterious aspects of the Bible, the Findhorn Community in Scotland, and one odd book about auras, colors, and sound and how each color and musical tone affects people's spirits in different ways. I had also had my first out-of-body experience at this time, and I was still trying to figure out what that was all about, too.

~.~

As Dad and I drove home to Koloa from the movie about near-death experiences, he opened up to me about his own near-death experience, which he described as an "afterlife" experience. My jaw dropped when he said that. Until that moment, I had no idea that my own dad had experienced such a thing. I felt a new appreciation for him, and he could tell I was eager to hear more, so he went on. "What I experienced was very similar to what the people in the movie described," he said as he drove.

"Did this happen while you were in that coma?" I asked.

"Yes." He nodded. "I suddenly became aware that I was

in a huge place, like a castle. There was a curtain that opened and people were on the other side of it beckoning me to join them." He smiled. "I'll tell you son, I felt more joy than any human word can describe. I wanted to go with them. Suddenly, I noticed a marble judge's bench. I admired it greatly and noticed that the judge sitting behind it was me! Or rather, it was my completed self. He had a wonderful smile and seemed to be playing with me. At that very moment, I realized that life is but the blinking of an eye. I told him: 'I want to go on! I want to go on!'"

I sat beside Dad in the car, in complete silence, my jaw and eyes wide open. "What happened next, Dad?"

"Well", he continued, "the judge or some part of me in the future told me, 'It's fifty-fifty; either you can go on or you can go back.'

"'Oh, I want to stay here! I feel such joy and peace.'

"The judge nodded and said, 'Well, you haven't really finished up your time yet and a lot of people still need you.'"

Dad continued. "I then saw my own body lying in the hospital, with your mother and you and your sisters concerned and sad."

Dad glanced over at me beside him in the car. "I wasn't worried about you, or your mother and sisters," he said. "I knew you would all be okay. But then I asked the being, 'What's the decision?' and shrugged my shoulders. The next thing I knew, I was back in my body. Immediately, I grabbed the doctor by his big white tie hanging out from the collar of his doctor's robe. In my euphoric state, I yanked the doctor close to me and said, 'Doctor! Doctor! What does critical mean?' The doctor replied, 'If you let go of my tie, I'll explain it to you.' I let go of his tie, and he told me, "Well, Mampel, it's another way of saying you have a fifty-fifty chance.'"

My dad's story about his afterlife experience affected me greatly, and I became even more interested in spirituality and God. I grew to understand that not only was God everywhere, but God was also beyond everywhere. I was aware of the grandeur of life and God, and my quest for my own spiritual understanding of life grew.

Trauma has a way of opening us up to the possibility of becoming empathic, a wounded healer. Eventually I came to see my early childhood trauma, this rending of my psychic fabric, as a gift which led me into varied vocations: a minister, a counselor, a poet, a clown, a teacher, a musician, a raconteur, and whatever else comes next for me. It has turned out to be a rich, multi-dimensional source of creativity and spiritual growth.

If you look up the etymology of the word "wound" you'll find it comes from the French word *blessure*, which also means blessing in French. A wounding experience can also be a blessing when it awakens a person to an appreciation for health, for life, for love, and to empathy for others who are suffering. I've read about Native American shamans who say that the reason they became shamans in their tribe is that they had a deeply traumatic experience in their childhoods that sensitized them to the spirit world. Their early emotional pain somehow opened up their psyches and increased their psychic abilities so that they could learn and help others with spiritual lessons and healing. They had experienced, in their early psychological traumas, a kind of spiritual initiation. It is well known that clowns and comedians are generally very sad people underneath their jokes.

I feel something similar happened to me, and I sometimes wonder if my supernatural out-of-body experiences occurred because of the psychological wounding I experienced around my dad's accident. I do think that my inner pain was intense during the moments just before each of my out-of-body experiences, and that my spirit was leaving, taking a respite of some kind. I could never will these out-of-body experiences to happen. They all occurred spontaneously and with no prescience or effort on my part. Did that early childhood trauma open up my psyche and sensitize me as the shamans' experiences sensitized them? Interestingly, many clowns in Native American tribes were also shamans. I really feel like I am both a clown and a mystic, and sometimes, a shaman, but not a clearly defined one. There have been times in my adulthood when I created and performed New Moon rituals with my friends or led groups with guided meditations, and when I have done these rituals, I feel very at home with performing them.

Dad's accident and my reactions to it affected me and my pursuit of my creative dreams in two basic ways. Initially, as I have already mentioned, I unconsciously formed a fear-based caretaker pattern in my personality as a way of coping with the pain and fear of very nearly losing the love and security of my father. Dad's afterlife story initiated a second effect in me, in that my awareness started to expand. I began to glimpse mysteries of which I had hitherto been unaware, caught sight of a Divine grandeur to life that I had been blind to before. I now see this traumatic event as a kind of soul initiation, a wounding that shocked me into a broader awareness of life, into a deeper experience of my own life, even though that awareness came slowly and caused me a great deal of pain as it emerged.

~.~

I swung back and forth after Dad's accident between being a serious caretaker and a wild rebel. When the internal pressure of taking on adult responsibilities became too much, I sought release by getting into trouble and acting silly. I loved the thrill of rock and roll music, the adrenalin rush of risk-taking behavior and dare-devil stunts, and the escape from life and responsibility afforded by intoxication from illicit drugs. My internal struggle outwardly demonstrated itself over and over again as I grew up, contributing to my confusion about choosing a vocational path. The caretaker was drawn to the ministry, maybe even as a way to redeem my father. The rebel was drawn to the arts and the life of a rock star. Thank God, the quiet, introverted aspect of my soul helped me to balance these two directions with journaling, meditation, poetry, prayer, and solitude.

In general, there is a dark and light side to each of these two tendencies, both the caretaker and the wild man. The caretaker can be a fearful manipulator who tries to fix people inappropriately, anxiously taking on their issues. When I do that, I alienate others and rob myself of healthy relationships, and in the process I squander my own precious energies. The light side of being a caretaker is that I am for the most part a responsible adult. I take care of my own needs, and I have learned how to help others in healthy ways. When I start a project, I generally complete it, too. The dark side of the wild man shows up in self-destructive habits, addiction, insensitivity, and selfishness. The light side manifests for me as a creative clown, a musician, an entrepreneur, and a joyous adventurer. It has taken me years of therapy and Twelve Step recovery work to understand these patterns in my personality and to find healthy, positive ways to live and express myself so that I'm more attuned to the lighter sides of these patterns. I've gotten better over time and with daily practice, but I still make mistakes and have to mend fences whenever I do.

When I was a seminary student, I was still suffering from the trauma of Dad's accident and I decided I needed help. I began to see a psychotherapist to help me root out the source of my inner suffering. Thus began many years of long, hard inner work that would finally allow me to come to terms with the unresolved trauma I was left with as an eight-year-old boy. Slowly, painfully, I began to recover my lost innocence.

After I had been in therapy for a while and was clean from addiction again after my relapse as a minister in Idaho, I began to understand that my struggle with remaining in the parish ministry was related to this childhood trauma. I started to see that I was still unconsciously trying to be the man of the family. My warped belief system, based on wounded memories and broken perceptions, led me to feel that I needed to take over my father's place as a minister and try to save our family. By becoming a pastor, I was reenacting the scared eight-year-old boy, still trying to save my dad from falling by taking his place in the pulpit. I was trying to be my own father, an impossible undertaking.

As I write these words, my friend Diane Karr is taking care of me while I recover from foot surgery, and she is in my living room watching the movie *Mental* with Toni Colette. In that film, Toni's character loses her mind and starts to believe her family should be like the Von Trapp family in *The Sound of Music*. I mention to Diane that Christopher Plummer plays the stern father Captain Von Trapp in that film. Just as I speak these words, I hear Captain Von Trapp in the background singing "Edelweiss."

Whenever I become very tuned into a novel, a film, or a story, life events pop up in a synchronistic fashion, reflecting what I am reading, watching, or writing. Now, it's happening again! A few minutes earlier, Diane asked me about the story of my dad's accident. I told her, and at the very moment I finished the story, my phone rang. It was my editor Carrol Strain, calling to discuss the progress of our manuscript, and I told her how much I liked the way she refined what I wrote about my dad's accident. As I hung up after that call with Carrol I suddenly remembered that I sob whenever I watch *The Sound of Music*. I now understand why I have this reaction. It seems to me that *The Sound of Music* is the story of a father who forgot how to be a father to his children because he was lost in his grief over the death of his wife. When Julie Andrews appears as Sister Maria, Captain Von Trapp is reawakened; it is as if an evil spell is lifted from him. He is softened by love and music and gradually becomes a loving father again. This story reminds me of how my father became my father again for me, and this is why *The Sound of Music* triggers these powerful feelings in me.

Later in life, about two years into my recovery from active addiction, I once again experienced dark emotions regarding my dad's accident. This was after I had been Daffy Dave for about nine years, around the year 2000. I became clinically depressed, returned to psychotherapy, and took anti-depressants for nine months in conjunction with the therapy. Even though my dad was, in reality, a wonderful dad, I still carried resentments toward him, stemming from his accident and my loss of trust in him. He was in no way to blame for my resentments; they were my own unresolved emotions, my own scars and unfinished healing from that trauma. After some therapy, I went home to share my truth about my feelings with my Dad so that I could release them and begin a new relationship with him. Mom was there, too. I couldn't talk without sobbing. I confessed that I had carried this resentment and distrust for years and I didn't want to do it anymore. Dad was ready to hear what I had to say. He hugged me and cried with me and said, "It's okay. I'm the father now. You can be the son again." Much healing began in that moment. My resentment lifted from me, and a huge weight was released. My father became a father to me again, just as Captain Von Trapp softened and became a father to his children again in *The Sound of Music*.

Later, Dad shared with me a poem he wrote about the time when we were lost to each other. Eerily, he wrote this poem long before either of us became consciously aware of this unresolved trauma in me or of the conflict hidden in our relationship. Poetry can do that. Poetry has a way of allowing deep, unseen things to surface even when we don't fully grasp their meaning at the time we write them:

Rescue
--Arthur George Mampel
from *Silk over Wood*, Copyright 1981
Used with permission.

I see my son first easy in the light floating air
Strong along the wooden rail then flung outward
cramped strained in the morning water blue
barely able to breathe in the shaken sea The turn
of his sun-dark shoulder in the wave the rubber
movement of his body as it fights down the dark
water to the earth-sunken weeds the pitch of the
moon-pulled sea rolling him like a fierce
ball heaved against the rock bottom base of creation

I go down into that dark direction down in the
ancient water where life is urgent and unborn
sure of my movement along the hard edge of
incrusted rocks I am over the green swaying

heaven undercut in the silky blue meaning
a mere shadow swept in the company of small
fish blurred hardly visible to my liquid sight
a movement broken a ghostly nod and I am
under his long waving arm bursting inside
reaching ever upward dying desperately
breaking the surface like Skywalker alone
in the universe

~.~

When after four years of being a pastor I left the ministry
and became a clown, I was in a very real sense trying to reclaim
my childhood and heal myself. I see now as I saw then that it
was absolutely necessary for me to leave the parish ministry. I
had to return to the child I had been before I shut down, before
I became a scared, overly serious eight-year-old child. I needed
to heal, to re-parent that traumatized little boy by reclaiming
my original, suppressed creative dreams in life. That was the
only path that would allow me to become true and whole in
myself again. The only way out was through.

I faced the pain and felt it deeply as I moved through it,
but I could now see the end of my suffering. My dreams of
who I wanted to be and what made me feel most alive in life
were to be my guide. Like Beatrice guiding Dante through the
inferno, cultivating my inner joy would take me to Paradise.
Seeking to live out the dreams that made me feel excited and
inspired would lead me through the twists and turns of life. All
I had to do was make the fundamental decision inside myself to
begin the journey, to pay attention to my best lights, ideas, and
hunches, and to be fully aware of the blessings that came to me
from heeding this authentic vocational path. I now know, after
having lived out my dreams these past twenty-one years as
Daffy Dave, that I have been truly blessed on this path. When I
decided to follow the bliss of doing what I was born to do and
being who I was born to be, my soul's blueprint began to direct
the construction of my authentic self, allowing me to begin ful-
filling my purpose in life.

I, too, wrote verse that described the healing that occurred between my dad and me. When I wrote the poem below, I had no idea of its deeper meaning. All I knew at the time was that I wanted to write an "adult song" for my fourth album, *Class Clown*, ostensibly for the parents to enjoy. But as I read it now, in light of the healing that has taken place between my father and me, it seems to be an unconscious poetic response to my dad's poem, "Rescue." My poem includes music I composed, and on the album it is accompanied by wonderful instrumentation added by my producer, Scotty Smith of White Rabbit Studios in Campbell, California.

Sailing Through the Storm
--Dave Mampel
from *Class Clown* Copyright 2006

Time it was when I lived on an island,
in the middle of the sea,
dreaming that I'd sail away one day,
to see how big the world could be.
Looking out the sun was setting low,
I wondered where the sun would go;
I'd like to sail right up and say hello.

A falling star across the sky,
the moon turned red and so did I.
I ran home, the clouds grew black.
I faced my fear
and turned right back.

I faced the thunder! I faced the lightning!
I faced the waves came crashing down
and how could it be,
a boat washed up to me.

I faced the wind blows! I faced the I don't knows!
I faced the whether I should goes.
But, the best way to learn how to sail

104

is when you sail right through the storm.

So I got in and sailed my little boat
to the end of the world.
The wind and stars pulled me on my way.
I said good-bye to the bay.
Out beyond where whales and dolphins play,
I think I saw something move.
A mermaid flashed her tail
and swam away.

A shooting star across the sky
the moon is new and so am I.
I'm sailing on, the sky is clear,
I know how to love,
I let go of fear.
I love the thunder! I love the lightning!
I love the waves come crashing down.
And, now I love to be
sailing in my boat
and I am free.
I love the wind blows! I love the I don't knows!
I love the whether I should goes.
Now I know the best way to sail
is when I sail right through the storm.

~.~

As I faced the computer screen and started to work on this book one recent morning, I felt a wave of emotional pain surge up in me, and I had to stop to meditate and pray first. I knew I needed the spaciousness that meditation provides in order to accept painful feelings and allow them to flow through me. After meditation I was able to write again. Meditation gave space for my feelings to exist in a neutral way, alongside strength from a Divine power. That power lifted me up and through the painful emotions, leaving me in a state of emotional tranquility that has become familiar, as these days I meditate every day. The poet William Wordsworth has said of poetry,

"Poetry is emotion recollected in tranquility," and meditation has a similar effect on me.

My meditation practice is a simple one. I simply sit and pay attention to my breathing for about a half hour every day. When I meditate at home, I sometimes burn incense and softly play a recording of the ringing of Tibetan bowls. I sit in a chair that I use only for meditation, and next to it a Himalayan salt lamp emits a rosy glow. The lamp sits on a lamp stand decorated with sea glass I collected on trips to the beach. I associate this peaceful spot in my home with inner peace.

I meditate with other people, too, on a regular basis, and I can meditate almost anywhere at any time. I actually prefer meditating with others, as our shared intention to surrender to the silence creates a kind of energy field that often brings me to that inner happy place faster and more deeply than I am able to achieve when I am by myself.

Meditation takes practice. Sometimes when I meditate I have an amazing experience of deep peace and joy. Sometimes I have a vision. Sometimes I feel bored or agitated by whirling thoughts in my mind, and I have a difficult time paying attention to my breath. I began meditation when I was about sixteen years old, and I established a regular, daily practice a number of years ago when I began my program of recovery from addiction. I've gotten better at meditating, especially since I helped to start some group meditation meetings and committed to a daily practice at home. I find that meditating in the morning works especially well for me. It helps me to better cope with life and find the peace and strength I need to face life on life's terms throughout each day.

Chapter Seven:
Slow Awakening

"I wake to sleep and take my waking slow.
I feel my fate in what I cannot fear.
We think by feeling; what is there to know?
I learn by going where I have to go."
--from *The Waking* by Theodore Roethke

Several of my clown character's traits and motivations are influenced by my dad's sense of humor. His sneaky "play dumb" innocence endears him to people and gets him out of sticky situations or allows him to gracefully decline doing things he doesn't want to do. At least, that's how I observe him. He hardly ever defends himself when someone criticizes him, a characteristic that throws his critics off balance. I use my Dad's non-defensive posture as a trait in my clowning and performing. If a kid says to me, "You're silly, Daffy Dave," I'll act overly flattered and sheepishly say, "Thank you very much." This lack of defensiveness particularly thwarts aggressive older kids who want to look cool in front of their friends at my expense. When one of them says to me, "You're weird!" I simply thank them in a sincere tone, acting calm and poised as if I've just received a huge compliment. They are left dumbfounded. I know they want me to feel ashamed, hurt, angry, or embarrassed, in order to look better than me in front of their friends. They say these things out of fear and a need to feel accepted and wanting a sense of power, but my calm and neutral posture softens their attack. Sometimes it even endears me to them, and they end up telling me my show was cool, and they want to know how I did my magic tricks.

As my dad's hairline receded over the years, he wore hats to hide his hair loss. When the wind blew his hat off, his desperate maneuvers to retrieve his cover always made us kids laugh. In my Daffy Dave Show today, I often include funny antics with hats. I have several routines in which my hat falls down to the floor and can't stay on my head. As I think about it now, I am my dad with his hat falling off and, instead of me and my sisters laughing at our pops, the families watching my show are now laughing at me.

At the beginning of most of my shows, I walk out, scan everyone's eyes, clasp my hands together, take a bow, and say, "I'm soooo excited to be here!" At that very moment, my hat flies off my head and lands in front of me, but I pretend I don't notice it. The kids start yelling to let me know it has fallen, but I act as if I can't hear them. Then, I suddenly look worried, glance around the room, and touch my head, feeling for my lost hat. I look behind me, up to the ceiling, to the sides, then finally react to what the kids have been trying to tell me all along. I see my fallen hat at my feet, jump back in surprise, and say, "Hey! What's my hat doing down there?"

"It fell off your head, Daffy Dave!" the kids shout back.

After I scold my hat for falling off, I ask it, "Do you want to take a timeout?" I attempt to put it back on, only to have it magically pop straight up in the air at the moment when I place it on my head. This happens a few more times, and each time I act more and more frustrated. The kids laugh at my frustration, and I pretend to try other ways to keep my hat on. Nothing works, of course. Sometimes, it "accidentally" covers my face. I'll sheepishly peek out around the side of it and say, "Hey! That was scary! It was dark in there." Then I'll hide behind the hat on purpose and look at the kids from the other side and say, "Peek a boo!"

After some other gags, I'll flip my hat up in the air and it will land perfectly on my head. When the audience applauds, I will act very proud of myself and take a bow. Of course, my hat then falls off my head onto the floor again, and more laughter ensues. I innocently play dumb like my dad does. I use this trait and at a number of points in my show or during improvisational street clowning. This clueless, innocent attitude always gets a lot of laughs, just as it did for my dad with his friends and all of us growing up with him. We Mampel men are natural clowns.

My show also includes plenty of wordplay, including puns, malapropisms, and playful mispronunciations of kids' names. If a little girl tells me her name is Sophie, I will unself-consciously and playfully pronounce it "Soapy." Or, if a boy says his name is Jacob, I will innocently call him "Hiccup." My feigned innocence makes me the butt of the joke, deflecting shame or self-consciousness from the child whose name I just flubbed up. It also makes everyone laugh in a positive, non-teasing atmosphere and provides an early experience for kids to start learning to laugh at themselves. They giggle at my mispronunciations of their names in an innocent, positive, and humorous way.

Other wordplays and goof-ups in my clowning include free associations with words, both onstage and offstage, in funny ways. A lover of words, my dad recites classic and original poems by heart. It's clear to me now that I absorbed my dad's love of poetry into my own consciousness over the years. In *The Smile at the Foot of the Ladder*, Henry Miller defines a clown as both a poet and an orangutan. My dad's love of poetry got mixed into my monkey-mischievous personality and morphed into part of the clown I am today. I didn't consciously create comedy routines with my dad in mind, but I'm pretty sure I put the off in offspring.

When my mom wasn't serious with music, she was silly with it. I used to love hearing her play a song called "Nola" on the piano. It's a very snappy tune, and she would become animated and joyful whenever she played it. My sister Jeanie says she, too, loved that song when we were kids and wanted to learn how to play it. Other times, my mom would make her voice sound funny as she walked around the house cleaning and singing at the same time, which I remember her mom doing as well. I now have a song about cleaning your room while singing and dancing that kids just love to hear and sing along to, called "My Name Is Daffy Dave." Some parents have told me that their kids will request this song to be played while they clean up their rooms. (Inspiring kids to clean their rooms? Mission accomplished!) Part of it goes like this:

"My name is Daffy Dave, and I will show you how
To sing a song and clean your room, your parents will say, 'Wow!'
So, get right down, and wipe away your frown.
My name is Daffy Dave. I'm a real clean clown."

~.~

My mom passed down her playfulness with music to me. As a kid, I loved changing the words in songs we sang during Sunday school and church, sometimes to my mother's chagrin, sometimes making her laugh. We sang a song in Sunday school called "I Cannot Come." It's about the New Testament story of the wedding at Cana. The verse I loved changing was this one:

"I cannot come to the banquet; don't trouble me now.
I have married a wife; I have bought me a cow.
I have fields and commitments that cost a pretty sum.
Pray, hold me excused. I cannot come."

I'd change the second line to: "I have married a cow; I have bought me a wife." Of course, all the kids sitting in the pews around me would laugh. Yes, I was an entertainer all along.

Unfortunately or fortunately, my predominant vocational fantasies were mostly about being a hip, slick, and cool kind of entertainer, a rock star, not the goofy clown I really was much of the time. It took me thirty years to gradually understand and accept this goofy clown and then figure out how to turn him into gold.

Once when I was about eleven or twelve years old, I made some kids laugh so hard in our Sunday school class with my imitation of a pompous, stiff-laced minister, they were falling out of their chairs with tears rolling down their cheeks. I remember being deeply gratified by their reaction. Still, I don't remember thinking to myself after these and similarly hilarious episodes, "Gee, I would make a great clown. I'm going to pursue that prestigious line of work!" No, I wanted to be Paul McCartney or Davey Jones. Or then again, maybe I would be an archeologist or a mountain man living by myself in the wilderness like Jeremiah Johnson.

~.~

Ah, but what early events led up to my fundamental decision to follow my bliss as a variety entertainer and self-employed entrepreneur? And how did those insights coalesce within me? It was a Hegelian dialectical progression. Hegel believed that one can overcome obstacles and contradictions in life by absorbing or integrating the contradictions or obstacles and preserving the whole, though he was speaking more about society and history than individuals per se. I like to understand this dialectical progression toward wholeness in terms of the psyche's development, more along the lines of Jung's idea of accepting one's shadow sides in order to be a whole and self-actualized person. Rather than seeing myself as going through phases, such as going from being a minister to being a clown, I feel the minister is still within my larger self, which now includes the clown, too. They have both been absorbed into the whole of my being. This way of thinking works better for me than rejecting the minister as I became Daffy Dave the clown.

I believe that the quieter, intellectual, more reflective aspect of me is the healthier part of why I was motivated to study diligently in school, pursue my education, and obtain the practical academic degrees that would help me survive in society. I wanted to have a creative profession, but I was also practical enough to know that I needed a higher education to develop my thinking, increase my knowledge of the world, and find a career path that would allow me to get paid using my creative energies. However, a more insidious, dysfunctional reason I wanted to be successful in school is related to my unconscious fear that I needed to be perfect, redeem my father, and save my family, as I mentioned earlier.

In my late teens, as I looked ahead to the world of adult responsibilities, I wondered if I would be able to actualize my creative dreams and still pay my bills and survive. Would I be able to get married and have kids if I were to try to make my living as an entertainer? The life of an artist-entrepreneur began to look unrealistic, and those dreams moved to the back burner. Graduating from high school, college, and seminary moved to the front burner.

Chapter Eight:
College and the Law of
Reversed Effort

Much of my understanding of humor, especially slapstick, irony, puns and absurdity, developed during my sophomore year at Augustana College, not so much because of the academics, but because of the free-spirited interactions with my eccentric, bohemian friends. Their names alone make me smile: Empty Sky, Mark Dugo, Greg Owcarz, Katarina Eskilsson, Joy Golisch, Kate Ague, Gregg Peterson, Liz Ready, John Watkins, Keith Davies, John Blommaert, a guy we called Bagel, and especially my roommate Kirk Chilton. Kirk was tall and lanky and sported a scraggly goatee. He was a superb violinist who read and maybe even understood James Joyce. He and I used to jam together, and we shared a love for poetry and literature. Kirk possesses a noble philosophical spirit offset by an absurd, ironic sense of humor. He still makes me laugh today. I've visited him and his wife, Katarina Eskilsson, and their kids Kyle and Miranda at different times over the years in their homes in Belgium and Sweden.

One of Kirk's antics that at times had me in stitches was when he would wrap one of his spindly arms over the top of his head to answer the phone on the opposite ear, like a contortion-ist answering calls on a radio talk show. That pose, contrasted against the serious tone of his voice, would have me laugh-ing so hard I couldn't breathe. Then, still holding the phone pretzel style, he would pick up "Angst," a clay bust sculpted by a mournful art student. Angst had a primitive face bearing a shocked and sorrowful expression reminiscent of Edvard Munch's painting "The Scream." Kirk used Angst as a puppet to mock the unsuspecting caller until even Kirk couldn't hold back the laughter anymore.

Kirk's philosophical explanations of slapstick comedy helped me see how the best humor releases us from the stress of taking life and our lives too seriously. His laughter drew me in. Together we laughed as we watched the Marx Brothers, the Three Stooges, and my all-time favorite movie, *A Thousand Clowns* with Jason Robards. From Kirk I learned that slapstick makes fun of human limitations and the human condition and makes light of the problems inherent in living in a body. Anything is fair game in slapstick, especially silly societal mores and expectations, status seeking, and ego and power trips.

Kirk loved my poetry and encouraged me to write, and I admired his erudition. He introduced me to a number of musical styles and a wide array of art, literature, and film. Even when he and I played music together, with him on solo violin and me singing and playing rhythm guitar, he would throw in some slapstick. We would sit side-by-side on the raggedy pink thrift-store couch we had in our off-campus living room, and while he was playing, he would make his bow go back and forth near my face just under my nose. I once caught a glimpse of the mustache effect on my face in a mirror across the room, and I laughed so hard in the middle of singing Van Morrison's "Moon Dance" that I fell over laughing.

Kirk and I shared our apartment with Karl. Once when Karl was preparing to walk down to the laundromat a few blocks away, Kirk and I hid an iron in the laundry bag with his clothes. When Karl came back from doing his laundry, he stood in the doorway and said, "Okay. Which one of you hid this iron in here?" Kirk and I bent over laughing, half-heartedly apologizing to Karl, but then laughing even more because Karl tried to act like he was above it all, until he started laughing with us.

Another time at Augustana, the joke was on me. In the middle of an icy winter, Kirk was bundling up to ride his bike across the Bettendorf Bridge to his job on the graveyard shift at a mental hospital in Davenport, Iowa. As he was leaving, I was sitting on that crummy pink couch of ours studying like crazy for midterms or finals. As much clowning around and partying as I did, I was still a very dedicated student. Kirk walked his bike to the door and turned to say good-bye. "Have a fun ride," I said, barely noticing what I was saying. About five minutes later, I had an eerie feeling that someone was watching me. I looked over at the front door, and saw that it was still slightly ajar. Then I saw one of Kirk's bright eyes peering in at me through the gap between the door and the doorframe. Apparently, he had been standing there, looking in and staring at me that whole five minutes. When he saw that I saw him, he giggled, and I laughed. He opened the door and, laughing, said, "Okay, Dave. See you later."

I laughed again and said, "You nut. Okay. See you," and went back to studying. Five minutes later, I looked up again and there he was, still staring at me from behind the door. I yelled, "Get out of here, you nut case!" We both laughed again.

"Okay. This time, I'm really leaving. Sorry, Dave. I couldn't help it." We both laughed and I went back to my book. About ten minutes later, I still had this sneaking suspicion Kirk was spying on me, but when I looked up at the door, it was shut and he wasn't there. Then I heard muffled laughter. I looked over at the bay windows, and there he stood outside in the snow. Again, Kirk's face stared in at me against a background of an icy, dark December. We both laughed, but I laughed so hard I peed my pants.

The next morning when I saw him I asked him about his bike ride across the bridge the previous night. As it turned out, he had ridden through a blizzard, and the wind-chill factor had been about fifty degrees below zero. His description of that snow-blown ride in the dark made me laugh even harder than I had the night before. By the time he got to Bettendorf Bridge, the snow had piled up as deep as twelve inches in some places, and an icy surface hid beneath all that white powdery profusion. The wind whipped up off the frozen Mississippi River like Thor's hammer, pounding Kirk's body with an icy Nordic retribution. The razor-sharp wind was so fierce that it blew his bike from one side of the bridge to the other, back and forth, as he struggled to peddle across the icy, snow-covered bridge, like Sisyphus endlessly trying to get up the hill only to fall back down time and again. It took him an hour to ride all the way across the bridge, and he just barely made it to his job on time. When he finally made it to work and stumbled, numb with cold, through the door of the mental ward, the first thing he saw was a patient trying to beat up a drinking fountain. His good-natured depiction of his struggles had me laughing harder than I had ever before laughed in my life.

My friendship with Kirk changed me forever. His light-hearted spirit seeped into my soul and taught me a new perspective, shaping my own sense of life and of humor. Because of Kirk, I can now laugh at anything, even in the darkest corners of my life. I have moments in my Daffy Dave Show where I know I am imitating his comic delivery style. Kirk and I remain close friends even now, though we rarely get to see each other in person, because he lives in Europe with his family and I have remained in the United States. But when we do get together, our friendship picks right up where we left off, and it's as wonderful and fun as it was during our college days.

My college friends and I used the opportunity of our career at Augustana to develop our philosophies of life. We often stayed up long into the night discussing playwrights, poets, artists, and musicians, trends in society, history, and life itself, with our late-night musings often including the works of Marx, Hegel, Yeats, Keats, Kant, and Kierkegaard. With exuberant good humor, we improvised skits that we acted out in the dormitory hallways, such as the one we called "The Old Testament Versus the New Testament." At one point, using candles as nails, we "nailed" one of our friends to the wall in the third-floor hallway Carlsson Dorm. At the very moment that our faux Jesus cried, "Father, screw them over for they know not what they do," a bunch of drunken fraternity types came stumbling into the hallway and threatened to beat us up for our blasphemy. Fortunately, our Jesus was a star linebacker for the football team, and his looming size and booming voice scared the drunk dudes away.

College was a time for experimentation. We tried on new ideas; we thought about what we believed and didn't believe and changed what no longer worked for us. I started college as a born-again Christian and left as a starry-eyed poet who dreamed of playing original folk music in the cafés of Minneapolis while writing novels and trying to publish my poetry. I had no inkling that I would later become a clown. Those roots were hidden far beneath the surface, and that plant wouldn't sprout and begin to grow for several years.

A unique chemistry developed among these friends of mine. These talented, artistic, and scholarly individuals were living examples of clowning and comedy for me; they planted the seeds that became the inspiration for my ongoing desire to work as an entertainer and somehow to include the arts among my serious pursuits in life. It was advanced childhood play, but it was also how we learned, how we came to understand the new ideas we encountered. Play helped us to release academic and life stress; through play we learned to be creative as a group. It was probably one of the best times in my life, even though my emotions were so fragile then, and my insecurities high. How would we, we worried, become successful members of society? Would we make it or fail? Would our delicate dreams stand a chance out there in the cacophonous world that awaited beyond our sheltered classrooms and dorms?

My talent show offering during my junior year turned out to be a classic Dave Mampel accidental clown, although I didn't plan it that way. I played my great-grandfather's electric Gibson, a 1930 hollow-body guitar with Charlie Christian pickups, the first electric guitar ever commercially produced, and I sang a song I wrote for a girl I had a crush on. As that performance progressed, it turned into a folky-jazzy groove when a friend unexpectedly came out onto the stage to join me and blew an awesome solo on his saxophone.

As I was playing, I began to sense a wild commotion in the audience. I looked out into the crowd--about a thousand people--and saw the girls in the front row screaming like crazy. My old childhood dream had come true. Girls were screaming while I played and sang my music! I was so excited; I was certain in that moment that that performance would lead to my one day being a rock star. However, when my friend and I left the stage after the song, he started laughing and pointed to my crotch. My zipper was wide open and my undies were clearly visible. I peered out into the audience again and saw all those girls in the front row rolling with laughter and pointing at me. Once again, my comic relationship with underwear had made an unexpected appearance. Every time I think I'm hip, slick, and cool, something embarrassing happens to show me who I really am: a clown. This still happens to me: All. The. Time. In fact, Daffy Dave is patterned on this "act cool and end up looking ridiculous" comedic formula, which is, of course, how Daffy Duck's character provokes laughter, too. Obviously, Daffy Dave's character is loosely based on that great duck's.

~.~

One of my best memories from my years at Augie happened during the time I was taking all independent studies and writing poetry during the last quarter of my senior year. I approached the secretary of the Religion Department one afternoon and asked for the key to go up into the dome of Old Main, the college's oldest building, whose tall dome is the campus's chief landmark and a treasured icon. When she questioned me about my purpose, I told her I needed to write some poems for one of my studies. Shrugging, she handed me the key.

Twenty or so of my rowdy, good-natured friends, by prearrangement, joined me there. Together we opened the unmarked door on the third floor and walked into the interior of the dome. Enchanted, we gazed at the old dome's cavernous innards. Someone opened a bottle of wine and we settled in to enjoy the afternoon. One thing led to another and another bottle of wine made the rounds. Before long, jokes and stories and raucous songs had given way to original poetry, which had to be immortalized somehow, don't you know. Magically, a couple of markers made an appearance, and first one poem and then another was scribbled onto the fusty wooden walls and arching beams on the inside of the dome. We weren't the first ones to do so, by a long shot. Our literary efforts joined those of others whose graduation dates preceded ours by decades.

Four of us dared to climb up the old ladder that led to a door at the very tiptop of the dome. When we opened the door and climbed through the opening, nothing but a low balustrade and a few pillars holding up the apex separated us from the spectacular view below. The greenish copper of the roof of the main dome curved away below us, and the majestic Mississippi River wound its way through farmland and low rolling hills to the north. The city of Rock Island looked like a beautiful little fairy city from that height, and we pointed to and named off the landmarks we recognized. It was all breathtakingly beautiful.

I saw President Tredway walking across the campus far down below us and yelled out to him, "Hey Treds! How's it going?"

Tredway looked up and yelled back, "Mampel, is that you?"

"Yeah," I said, laughing.

"Hold on," Tredway shot back, "I want to come up! I've never been up there before." These days, when I get together with Kirk Chilton, John Blommaert, and others who were there that afternoon, we fondly remember President Tredway joining us as another bottle of wine was passed around, there on the top of Old Main's dome and enjoying the breathtaking view.

I was a daredevil in those days, making it a regular practice to run down the hallway on the third floor of Carlsson Dorm and out onto the fire escape, where I would grab the iron railing and flip myself down to the second-floor fire escape. I was a pole vaulter on the track team and felt confident about doing such acrobatics, but it was still a stupid thing to do, especially since I did it more than once.

~.~

On the other hand, when I made the mistake of reading too much Sartre and Camus all at once, I got very somber. Kate reminds me that when I fell into these dark moods I would say things like, "It doesn't matter if you have a relationship; you still dream and die alone." I am so glad I had these fun and interesting friends to shake me out of my seriousness. I still have a tendency to brood, but these days clowning works as a kind of spiritual medicine for my soul. Without clowning, I would likely take myself too seriously, become pessimistic, and sink into despair. Jim Carrey has said that if he weren't a comedian, he would be picking off people with an AK47 from atop a tall building. I understand that.

The parties we invented in college couldn't possibly be replicated, and they were so much fun. We all agree that one of our top five soirees was one we called the "Human Bowling Party." At this party, a person designated as the bowler rolled a cabbage down the floor toward a group of us who had set ourselves up in bowling pin formation. When the cabbage hit the group of humans, we would fall down and wriggle on the floor. We were kind of like the early Dadaists, celebrating the absurd. Another favorite was naked tennis, played at three o'clock in the morning just outside Carlsson Dorm during late spring and early summer, when Rock Island turned hot and muggy. Once, we all got together at Esbjorn House to watch the film *The Sound of Music*. Someone brought along a rubber chicken and a clothesline, and at the point in the movie when the Mother Superior sings "Climb Every Mountain" to Sister Maria, the rubber chicken danced its way across the screen to dangle in front of the good nun's face as she sang.

One evening, Greg Owcarz took a mattress from his dorm room and somehow managed to haul it up to the top of a hundred-foot tower above the train tracks. He and his girlfriend spent the night up there like eagles in a nest. Another evening we dressed like bums, walked down to the Rock Island train depot and hopped into a box car, where we lit candles, drank wine, and smoked pipes, pretending, imagining, discussing, joking, and imitating funny characters. When that grew old, we hopped off the box car and walked the tracks toward Jimmy Sullivan's, a local café famous for its biscuits and gravy served at two in the morning. Empty Sky plunged his head smack down on the napkin holder so that the napkins splayed out in a fan shape. Then he carried the dispenser around the eatery and

in a smartass New York accent invited the other patrons, pros-
titutes and bums for the most part, to take a napkin. We were
all pretty drunk by then and thought we were hilarious, but the
bums and prostitutes--except for one guy known as Vince the
Heathen--recoiled from our antics. When the situation got too
dicey, it was our laughter in the end that saved us, and even
Vince backed down in the face of all that laughter.

One summer, a whole bunch of us stayed in Rock Island
and worked in the college cafeteria or at other menial jobs.
Classes were out for the most part and most of the other students had all gone home, which left us eccentrics to enjoy a
free-spirited summer. I read, improved my cooking skills,
played music with Kirk and others, and wrote poems. However, after a few weeks, we got tired of going to Sam's or Hill-
top Tavern for a beer, fed up with the Sloppy Joes at the Maid
Rite, weary of Jimmy Sullivan's and Lee's Tavern, and just
plain bored. Kirk, John Blommaert, and a few others of us were
commiserating about this state of affairs over stale beer. "Rock
Island is fun when Augie's in session," said John, "but summers
in Rock Island are the most boring summers in the world." We
all nodded in laconic agreement. John sang in the Augustana
Choir with Kirk, was a DJ of classical music at the college radio
station WVIK, and was well known for his witticisms and his
rubber-faced imitations of people we knew. A play he wrote
called "All My Fallopian Tubes" was much admired. John
looked up over his beer mug with a glint in his eye, stuck his
index finger in the air, and said, "I know!" Alert, we waited for
more. "Since Rock Island is so boring in the summer, let's have
a Boring Party!"

After a moment of utter silence, someone laughed and
said, "Yeah! We could serve lukewarm water and lightly singed
white toast."

"We could play elevator music in the background," someone else chimed in.

"We could have an auction playing on TV," said Kirk,
"but turn down the sound so all you would hear is the elevator
music."

"We could have boring presentations," I offered. "We could read from the 1981 and 1982 income tax rules."

"I could read a page from this book I found in the stacks at Augie Library called *A Century of Lutherans in Ohio*," John said.

We called all our friends and invited everyone we knew to the Boring Party. It turned out to be the best thing going on in Rock Island that summer. As promised, John read from *A Century of Lutherans in Ohio*, and as he was reading, he came upon a sentence that was broken by three dots. He stopped reading and said, "Wait. Who knows what the grammatical term for three periods in a row is?"

Without missing a beat, one of our friends, a geeky English major said, "Ellipsis."

"You are boring!" said John, and everyone laughed.

My presentation was a C chord on a guitar strummed for five minutes straight without changing chords. More laughter. We were failing miserably at being bored.

The final boring presentation was a group effort. We sang every verse of "One Hundred Bottles of Beer on the Wall," tape recorded ourselves singing all one hundred verses, played back the tape and listened to ourselves singing all one hundred verses again. Before we knew it, the boring energy of the boring party had shifted to a lively one, and a pretty girl who was visiting from Greece taught us to dance the Greek circle dance.

What happened to us that evening was what my dad likes to call "the law of reversed effort," a concept he borrows from Alan Watts and others. Basically, the law of reversed effort applies to those moments in life when the harder you try to do something, the further away from your goal you get, such as when you try to go to sleep and end up wide awake, staring into the dark for hours. We tried, really tried, to be bored at that party and ended up having a wonderfully lively time, with lots of laughter and some great memories.

The law of reversed effort is the heart and soul of clowning. It's what Daffy Dave is all about. It's what poetry is all about, too. Richard Hugo said, "Poetry is saying the right things with the wrong words." The concepts of negative space and "less is more" come into play here, too. Physicists tell us that all existence emerges from dark energy, and some theologies tell us that God created the world from nothing, *creatio ex nihilo*. Comedy depends on these models, too. The opposite of what's expected is often comical. It's the same with magic. The magician leads you to expect one thing, then surprises you with another, unexpected, action.

~.~

When I was fifteen or so years into my vocation as Daffy Dave, I learned about the Native American concept of Heyoka. The Heyokas were clown shamans who did everything the opposite of what was expected. They would walk backward everywhere they went, mock the arrogance of the bravest warriors, and basically upset the status quo of the tribe. They were contrarians, mirrors for the culture. The Heyokas compelled the people in the tribe to look at their everyday behaviors and laugh at themselves. April Fools' Day is a remnant of a period in medieval church history wherein jesters would take over the Mass to make fun and light of sin, a ritual soon suppressed, sadly. In China, some people, mostly the elderly these days, walk backwards in a circle for about twenty minutes as a way to reverse karma and cleanse the mind. Today, in my own way, I see myself as a kind of Heyoka, or mystical shaman clown. I have the coyote spirit, the "trickster" in me. The law of reversed effort became my favorite philosophy of life somewhere along the way and I still live by it today. It permeates all of my clowning around, my sometimes dark and strange sense of humor, my word play and joking with friends, my songs and my stories, and it guides me in coping with stress and dealing with my own shadow. Thanks to the law of reversed effort, I bob and weave through tough spots brought on by other people's darkness or by life on life's terms. I've learned to simply laugh it off as I journey through this very brief life.

Before my final quarter of college, I had been making plans to attend seminary in the autumn after I graduated. My plan was to obtain a Master's of Divinity degree and become an ordained minister, a career path I had settled on in high school, but the wild rebel kicked in again just before my college graduation. Suddenly and impetuously, I abandoned those plans in favor of my passion for poetry. I took a summer job with family friends on their horse farm in Minnesota. Country life would be the ideal setting for writing poetry, I thought. The Summer of Poetry would naturally lead, I imagined, to an autumn in Minneapolis where I would be a published poet and a folk singer in the café scene near the University of Minnesota, following in the footsteps of Bob Dylan and other folk singers I admired. I look at this time as if, in my own ordinary way, I had the spirit of a young Van Gogh. He, too, floundered in early adulthood. He became a minister for a short time but left his ministry to become a full-fledged painter. My version of creative glory was to become ordained, pastor a small church for four years, and then leave the ministry to become a clown.

Chapter Nine:
Mystical Interludes

I am at heart a mystic. Having grown up in the church as a preacher's kid, I rebelled against organized religion. I felt such pressure to be perfect, to be nice as a child. Maybe that's why mysticism and esoteric spirituality so deeply appealed to me. I felt in my heart that God is everywhere, that there is a greater intelligence and a higher love woven into the fabric life. When I was a teenager, these intimations became stronger, and powerful visions of this mysterious force gave me a deep inner sense that I was meant to cultivate spiritual awareness and somehow share it with others.

I cautiously write about my experiences here because I do not want to trivialize them in any way. These things that have happened to me are certainly not something I dwell upon or seek out, and I include them here only to illustrate what they meant to me and how they shaped my world view. To some, what I am about to write here may remind them of a sensationalized occult documentary on History Channel 2, but I have learned that I am not the only one to experience such things. Others have had similar experiences, as I've learned from sharing these stories with select people open to such experiences.

Throughout my life, at various moments, I have experienced out-of-body episodes that at first frightened me, then left me at peace and filled with joy and inspiration. I was frightened because I seemed to have no control over my soul leaving my body, but I was at peace and feeling other-worldly joy because, once I left my body, I was outside of time and space. Each time it happened, I left fear and ego, pain and suffering behind. When it happens, my ears start to ring and my body vibrates intensely but not uncomfortably. I feel myself lifting and leaving my body, then I am conjoined with or led by a source of brilliant yet calm light.

I had my first such episode when I was about fifteen years old; my family was living on the island of Kauai at the time. I had been reading books about religion and philosophy, and spiritual insights came to me rapidly at this time in my life as I contemplated Christianity and other religions, the Bible, and all the new ideas I had been reading about.

It was a calm Sunday afternoon, and I was alone at home. I was lying on my bed, thinking about these things, when my ears started to ring and my body started to vibrate. I felt my body rise and float above my bed. I rose into a swirl of clouds and lightning, and thunder rolled around me. "Are you God?" I asked.

A voice answered, "Yes." The voice was not a human voice, but a visceral communication that went directly into my mind. Afterward, I lay on my bed in shock, frozen with fear and awe, for what must have been about an hour. These visions recurred every three or four years after that. I don't know why I had them, but I grew to welcome them, as they made me aware of a larger story behind our ordinary lives. They inspired me with the notion that life was grand and mysterious, and that there was much, much more for me to learn.

My second out-of-body experience occurred when I was seventeen years old and in my freshman year at Augustana College. I was visiting my Uncle Ed on Chicago's South Side over Thanksgiving break. Most of the other kids I knew had driven or flown home to be with their parents for the holiday, but I was strapped for cash and couldn't afford a plane ticket; my folks lived in Seattle by this time. I called up my Uncle Ed and asked if I could stay with him and his girlfriend over the long weekend. "Okay," he agreed, "but I've gotta work."

"That's okay," I said. "I'll help." Uncle Ed delivered pizzas in his beat-up Volkswagen bus. I didn't have anything better to do.

I boarded a Greyhound bus in Rock Island, Illinois, lugging a big suitcase I had gotten as a high school graduation present from my mom and dad the previous spring. I arrived on a gloomy November evening, having only the foggiest notion of how to find my uncle's place.

As I walked along Chicago's dark streets that night carrying that heavy suitcase, I couldn't help but remember I had also been given a blanket at the same time. My mom and dad and sisters all watched as I opened up my presents. Sitting on the floor with ribbons and wrapping tossed aside around me, I looked at the suitcase and the blanket, then looked around at my sisters and my mom and dad, shrugged and said, "Ok, I get the hint."

They all laughed and protested, "No, no, no. We're not trying to tell you to leave or anything." Remembering that laughter with my family helped me on that dark and gloomy evening. I walked about nine or ten blocks, and I wasn't in the safest of neighborhoods. I had my uncle's address, but the street signs and house numbers were hard to see in the dark. I approached a guy who didn't look too dangerous and he confirmed I was going the right direction, at least. I was pretty worried that I might get mugged.

Ed is a free spirit with a wide-ranging blend of eclectic views that include a wild array of notions about life, including conservative ones. He's a good writer, and his book *Hot Plate Hotel* is an amusing collection of stories about life in Chicago's worst neighborhoods. My pops jokes that Ed can quote Shakespeare and John Wayne in the same breath.

Ed is very funny, and he and I love to joke around with language. When he was a kid, he and his friends started a group they called "Corny Cracks Incorporated," and they put on a funny skit for their Boy Scout troop. They sang "Home on the Range," but at the end of each phrase, they stopped singing to make a corny crack. "Oh, give me a home," they sang, then suddenly stopped. One of them said, "Wait a minute! Who would just give you a home? Don't you have to buy it?"

After the phrase, "where the buffalo roam," another of them piped up with, "What? With buffalos all around it?" They went on like that, stopping after each phrase to crack jokes, until the stern scout master, a former Naval commander, left the room because he was laughing so hard. My dad, Ed's older brother, tried and failed to keep from laughing, too, thinking that as a patrol leader he should set an example for the young scouts. Clowns and humor run in my family.

When I call Ed or get together with him today, he still cracks me up. One morning I phoned him where he lives now in Kingsland, Texas, from my home in California. When I realized I had probably called too early, I apologized and said, "Oh, sorry, Uncle Ed. I didn't mean to wake you up."

Without missing a beat, he said, "That's okay, Dave. I had to get up to answer the phone anyway."

When he visited our family in Seattle a few years ago, we were driving to Pike Place Market. On the way, we drove under the now-demolished Alaskan Viaduct where railroad tracks crisscross, ran alongside, and were even laid right down the middle of some of the streets. I noticed we were driving down a street with tracks under us and I said to Ed, "I get the feeling we're heading down the wrong track."

To which he responded, "Oh, Dave, you have such a one-track mind." A fountain of puns spewed forth.

"Ed, I think you were born on the wrong side of the tracks."

"I wouldn't know, Dave. I can't keep track of my life."

I finally found his house that night, a shabby little rental in a scruffy, worn-out neighborhood. I was feeling anxious and a little homesick when I walked up his stoop to knock on the door, but when I saw his face, I immediately felt better. I was so relieved just to see a familiar face, if nothing else, and Ed is one of my favorite people.

His girlfriend at the time seemed to me to be a bit manic, maybe even a little crazy, but she was nice enough. A tall woman, she reminded me of a character out of a Mary Shelley novel. Ed and his girlfriend were sipping beers and smoking cigarettes. I was uncomfortable and wished I had some pot to help me relax. I hated beer, but I think I drank a little that night. When it was time for Ed to start his wee-hours shift delivering pizzas, his girlfriend and I went with him. (I'll call her Julie, not her real name, to protect her privacy.)

I hung out with Ed and Julie at the pizza joint to wait for a call to deliver. While we waited, we had some pizza, and when a call came in, Julie, Ed and I hopped into Ed's faded white Volkswagen bus. Ed drove. He knew Chicago; he knew where to go. Some of the addresses we went to that night were creepy and scary--apartments in dilapidated buildings and old houses that looked like they might be haunted.

On one call, I carried a pizza into a creaky old elevator. Without thinking, I had placed the delivery wallet stuffed with cash on top of the pizza box instead of jamming it down into my jeans pocket. When three really stoned, drunk dudes got in with me, I quickly grabbed the wallet and tried to hide it. Too late. The scary guys had noticed and were staring at the bulge it made in my jeans. Ed and Julie were in the bus, waiting while I took the delivery up. Heart thumping, I prayed silently and earnestly for safety as the elevator groaned and screeched its way to the floor where I was supposed to deliver. Those dudes stared a hole through me, but they didn't mug me and I got off the elevator unharmed.

I found the right apartment and knocked on the door. A greasy-looking guy opened the door, and two fat women sitting on a couch inside the apartment turned to check me out. A pornographic movie was playing on an old-fashioned tripod movie screen at the other end of the room. I handed over the pizza and took the guy's payment for it, surreptitiously checking for the tip. One of the two women gave me a lusty look. "Why don't you stick around, son? Come on in!"

"No, thanks," I said. "I've got to get back to work." And I high-tailed it out of there.

Later, as he drove, Ed suddenly slammed his hand to his chest, grimacing. "I can't breathe," he groaned. His voice sounded tight, constricted, as if he were forcing the words out. At first, we didn't take him seriously, Julie and I, but it got so bad he pulled over. "Dave, you drive," he said. Scared, I got out, walked around the old VW bus, climbed into the driver's seat, and took the wheel.

I didn't know where I was going. Ed was hunched over

on the passenger seat beside me, face contorted with pain, but still he gave me directions, looking up to point the way now and then. "Left here," he croaked, or, "Right, just ahead." By the grace of God, we made it to Cook County Hospital and checked Ed in.

Julie and I waited and waited while he was checked in and examined, then we went to see him in his room as soon as the hospital staff said it was okay. It must have been nearly dawn or even after. He looked drawn but not so scared, and he seemed a little more relaxed. I relaxed a little, too. Julie walked over to Ed's bedside and to my utter astonishment, offered Ed a cigarette. "Do you want a smoke, hon?" she asked.

"Julie!" I admonished angrily. "He just had a heart attack! He can't smoke now!" She gave me a look that indicated she thought I was the one who was nuts, but she put the pack of cigarettes away.

Ed was released from the hospital later that same morning, and I think I must have driven us all back to Ed and Julie's place. Gratefully, I flopped down on the bed in their spare bedroom. I was so bone-tired, I thought I would go to sleep right away, but I lay there for a while, thinking, praying, and thanking God for getting us through all that danger.

Suddenly, my ears started ringing. My body started to vibrate and I felt myself floating in the air. I was really scared; I thought I was going to float right through the ceiling. I cried out to God for help. That's when a glowing silver and white dove appeared. It flapped its wings, and I felt a rush of air on my face. I floated back down to my bed. Afterward, I lay there in a state of shock wondering what had happened. I knew I had had some kind of mystical vision, and I felt that God was letting me know I was being taken care of and that there was a Providence beyond my understanding in life.

I had another of these mystical experiences after our family moved to Seattle. Again, I was lying on my bed in a basement bedroom. This time, too, my ears started ringing and my body began to vibrate. The next thing I knew, a golden light came out of my head and pulled me out of my body and off the bed. I floated above the floor, circled back to the bed, and came back into my body. I lay on the bed for about an hour afterward, once again in shock from the experience.

The next time it happened was when I was a sophomore at Augustana College. I was about nineteen. I had been in pain from severe acne on my chest, back, neck, face, and shoulders and hadn't been able to sleep for days because of it. I was feeling suicidal and stressed, ashamed about my appearance, and was critically sleep-deprived. I had started to believe that I would never attract a girlfriend, and I hated how my body felt and looked. I had begun questioning my beliefs about Christianity at about this time and had decided I could no longer accept the rigid beliefs I had once held. In this state of mind, I was walking on campus when suddenly my ears started ringing and my body began to vibrate. Hovering about fifty feet above my physical body, I looked down and saw myself walking. This time, I wasn't scared but felt peaceful and energized all at once. I had the thought that this vision was a gift that would help me get through this difficult time in my life. It was a powerful spiritual event that, together with my broadening views, moved me away from a literal view of Christian faith and toward agnosticism, even a brief period of atheism, as well as a general skepticism of all organized religion.

I had another of these mystical experiences toward the end of my time as a pastor in Idaho Falls, an experience I write about later in this book.

For a while, I thought of myself as a "detached observer" and tried to think like an atheist so that I could know what that felt like. I had grown up with a very strong sense of pantheism, a belief that God is everywhere, but this was not that. I quickly moved through my atheism phase toward a strong attraction to Zen Buddhism by way of D. T. Suzuki's works and Asian art. I still have a kind of abstract sense of a Power greater than myself, yet this Power is personable, too. It is a life force, a mysterious luring toward evolution and enlightenment, loving and approachable, but not "God" in any conventional sense. On the other hand, it's ineffable and as intimate as breath. My brief phase as an atheist helped me to cultivate a deeper understanding of this Power in a significant way.

My dad considers these mystical events to be "confirmations," and I agree. Each experience confirmed for me that life is worth living and gave me hope and strength to live. Each one seemed to occur when I was going through a period of trauma or a significant transformation in my consciousness. They also confirmed for me that there is a Divine presence in life, and that, as Shakespeare says, "There are more things in heaven and earth, Horatio, than are dreamt of in your philosophy."

Later on, when I was in seminary, I shared these visions with a fellow seminarian from a Native American tribe. My friend told me that in her tribe, when someone has visions like the ones I described, the purpose of those visions is to open the person up and help them be more empathic with the suffering of the world. She told me to pray for the strength to keep going in the vision next time. She said I was supposed to fly around the world by means of astral projection and see and feel people's suffering. That was too much for me to handle. I wondered where the humor was, because I was certain it had to be there, somewhere. Maybe the funny part is how crazy it all sounds. Maybe next time it happens, I'll yawn and casually say, "Oh, brother. Not another mystical out-of-body experience! Really? Like, c'mon! I'm right in the middle of the season finale of *Breaking Bad*." I had no interest in flying around the world feeling others' suffering. I felt overwhelmed by the implied responsibility. Whatever the reason, I have not had visions as intense as those I had in my youth since that conversation.

I stopped thinking about most of these visions soon after they happened. Occasionally, they would come to mind, but I revealed them only to trusted friends or counselors. It wasn't until I started writing this manuscript that it made sense to me to describe them in detail, as they elucidate my soul's story in powerful ways. I have come to believe that it's more important, however, to live mindfully day to day, choosing to live a meaningful life in the here and now. These experiences are simply confirmations, gifts that I needed at those times in order to move through difficult phases in my journey.

Coyote spirits have a reputation for learning things the hard way, but I'd like to put in a request to the Great Spirit to adopt a new policy for us. There's got to be an easier way to transform and become whole! On the bright side, we coyotes are able to become powerfully focused and produce a great deal of positivity once we finally learn what we need to learn. Still, I've had enough of the jackhammer on the skull to last me a lifetime. Next time, I'll just settle for a good bout of the flu or maybe an unexplained fever that passes quickly. Better yet, how about a dream or a thought that just comes to me, allowing me to shift my consciousness painlessly and swiftly? Give me a break, oh, Cosmic Divine Force or whatever your name is!

These visions and out-of-body experiences had the effect of instilling understanding and a deep feeling that, although my consciousness is connected to my body in this life, it is also somehow separate from my body. Over time and because I've had several of these episodes, I have been able let go of what other people think of me and become more carefree. I no longer fear death so much, and these experiences have freed me up to play a vulnerable clown portraying embarrassing human moments in ways that provoke laughter. So in a way, these extraordinary experiences are a gift to people around me, too, as I have a fresh ability to inspire others to laugh, to let go of at least a bit of the ego struggles that come from living in the flesh, the crux of the human condition.

~.~

Mystical interludes expand limited consciousness. The ancient Greeks spoke of kairos, which means a lapse in time or a moment when time has no meaning. Kairos breaks the spell of chronological time, called kronos in Greek. Kronos can hypnotize us into thinking we are only separate egos. When we are trapped in chronological consciousness, we lapse into suffering because of our limited perspective of our own tiny, mundane concerns and dramas. This is why the Buddha said, in effect, that the self and attachment to the self's desires create suffering.

Nowadays, I take "time outs" to tune into the Divine: morning meditations, hikes in the hills near my home, or silent retreats away from city life. A road trip to see the leaves changing in their autumn beauty or time spent gazing into the Milky Way or out beyond Mother Ocean's endless horizon can give me a feeling of wild, spontaneous peace laced with creative passion. Such moments shake up routines that have grown stagnant and inspire me to grow and evolve in my life no matter how much I have mucked it up. They help me to find my smile when I've been brooding too long. Thus the Infinite makes itself known in everyday time and space, keeping life fresh and free-spirited.

Chapter Ten: Portrait of a Young Clown in Seminary

The summer after I graduated from college, I worked on a horse farm in Maple Plain, Minnesota. I cleaned horse stalls, baled hay, and played some gigs at the Blue Heron Café in Minneapolis and at the Landmark Center in Saint Paul, a community and cultural center housed in a historic building. Here's one of the poems I wrote from that time, with a few revisions made recently:

Initiation on a Farm
--Dave Mampel

Fumbling on the rickety hay wagon,
the thirsty farmhand anchors his fingers
under parallel twine
to lift and stack the bales
as if performing a forgotten rite.

Dan chugs the tractor into high gear,
quickening the drip from our brows,
sucking the green earth into eighty-pound struggles
that spit out onto the conveyor as fast
as Tony, Rick and me can grab 'em.

The sultry afternoon burns through our skin
until heat swells and changes muscular growth.
Coke and cool water rinse out
the dusty dryness between each wagon load.
The young farmhand collapses in swaying shade
that makes me wonder about work and hunger.
Could my pain and exhaustion grow into a strength
like his arms?

Shouts from the half-finished field
force the boy-becoming-man
from a quiet revelation.
A simple song beats forth in his head to keep time
to the steady heaving for survival, so that,
by the last hour of Minnesota summer light,
as orange and purple ripen the clouds,
tender legs tighten
silence of breath
Alfalfa and clover
arouse dewy death
he drifts like smells
off sides of naked grass.

~.~

I faced a thorny conundrum and I knew it. How was I going to make a living as a poet and café musician right away? Autumn was fast approaching and the farm work soon would be ending. What would I do after that? I didn't have another job lined up and the student loans would start coming due unless I went to graduate school or seminary. I was desperate, so I talked to my dad. He persuaded me to pursue the ministry and assured me that parish ministry is conducive to creative pursuits. I would be able to use my artistic talents from that position and spend lots of time composing poems and songs. He pointed out that he himself had published poems while he was a minister, and he reminded me that he recited poetry in almost every one of his sermons.

His arguments made sense to me. I felt enormous relief when I made the decision to take his advice, at least for a while. I figured I could buy some time if I continued my education in divinity school, learn whatever I could, and follow my dream of being a poet and a musician. I contacted United Theological Seminary in New Brighton, Minnesota, just barely in time for the deadline for the fall quarter. Thus began my pursuit of a Master of Divinity degree.

~.~

I arrived late for the orientation on my first day at UTS, feeling keenly the loss of my starry-eyed vision of being a coffee house musician and poet. The simple truth of the matter is that I had run out of money and was taking the most practical route my life offered me at the time, a good dose of the medicine of "practical idealism," I supposed. I soon discovered that most of my classmates at seminary were twice my age and married, and I missed my fun, eccentric college friends. Fortunately, one of my good pals from Augustana, John Watkins, moved to Minneapolis to attend the University of Minnesota at about the same time. He and I got together occasionally to hang out in trendy North Minneapolis. Sometimes, we would go to Dinkytown, near the University of Minnesota, and sip sassafras tea at New Riverside Cafe, enjoying the strange and funny musical groups that played there. There was, for instance, a certain trio that included a musician who played an accordion with a fake pink flamingo attached to it; another musician played a Vietnamese stringed instrument. I enjoyed John's quick wit on those leisurely days, and his friendship eased some of the longing I felt for our good old times at Augie.

United Theological Seminary of the Twin Cities is a small, ecumenical seminary just outside of Saint Paul, Minnesota, in the sleepy suburb of New Brighton. It attracts students from a wide range of denominations, including lesbians and gays and nuns who have left the Catholic Church. Couples I know who got ordained together at UTS now serve their churches as married ministers. The school also includes a Native American theological program, which provided me with an opportunity to learn about Native American spiritual practices and a variety of other earth-centered spiritual beliefs and practices. I attended a sweat lodge and met a medicine man; I learned about vision quests, peace pipe prayer ceremonies, and give-away ceremonies. In a give-away ceremony, everyone brings their most prized possession and exchanges it for someone else's favorite thing, as a way of detaching from earthly possessions and remembering more important values such as love and friendship.

At UTS, my studies introduced me to centuries of church history that I had never been exposed to before. I learned about witch and heretic burnings, the Inquisition, Gnosticism, and the books of the Bible that never made it in the sanctioned canon we have today. I read about mystic Christians such as Saint John of the Cross, Juliana of Norwich, and Saint Theresa of Avila. In class we discussed feminist theologies and the rise of feminism in the church. Another of my classes was a "Sexual Attitude Reassessment Seminar," a course I found to be greatly beneficial on many levels.

~.~

Throughout my time in seminary, I did find more time and opportunities to write and perform songs and poetry. At the same time, however, I also started yet another consuming pursuit, which was liberal political activism. My classes and student discussions at seminary woke me up to injustice in the world, both historical and current. I worked as a progressive political organizer for Clergy and Laity Concerned, a nonprofit organization cofounded by Dr. Martin Luther King, Jr. I coordinated church groups to protest against the contra war in Nicaragua and apartheid in South Africa. With other demonstrators I intentionally got arrested for blocking the entrance to the Federal Building in Minneapolis. I helped organize protests against Honeywell's production of cluster bombs and against their toxic wastes on Native American lands, and I participated in several other demonstrations, letter-writing campaigns, conferences, and a clean-up of the Mississippi River around Saint Paul with the folk singer Larry Long and several social activist groups. At one point, there were one hundred social action groups working together on all of these issues in the Twin Cities. It was an amazing effort and brought together people from all walks of life.

I fell deeply in love with a young female artist, a fellow seminarian. I envisioned myself being married, working on progressive political issues, and using my creative energies for these pursuits. The idea of being a parish minister became more appealing, and my dreams of life as an artist slipped onto the back burner again. Seminary life was making me more mature, I felt. I wanted to be married to the woman I loved, and life as a full-time poet seemed incompatible with that dream. I wanted to be married, have a home, and be a responsible adult.

I wrote intensely political poems and songs during this phase, but they lacked the depth and breadth of the poems and songs I wrote at other times in my life, as they were limited to and by progressive causes. Gradually, I became less politically active because I felt angry and bitter when I constantly exposed myself to injustice and fought against "the system." I felt this anger leaking into my relationships with my friends and family and robbing me of a deeper spiritual awareness of life. Furthermore, I was becoming serious about being a pastor toward the end of my seminary education and didn't want my left-leaning politics to alienate members in my parish. Most churches I was familiar with and involved in comprised a variety of people with a wide range of beliefs and views. I sometimes still expressed my progressive views in sermons or by encouraging and supporting liberal causes, but I tried to tone it down, pick and choose my battles, and practice being more tolerant of views that were different from mine. I felt the most important lesson for me at this time was to listen, be compassionate and open-minded to others, and develop trust by focusing on common ground and being of service to individuals and the community.

~.~

Eventually, I made some wonderful friends at UTS, among them Judy Bagley-Bonner, whom I still count among my good friends. She and her whimsical, spiritual husband Brian are from the Cleveland area and are salt-of-the-earth folks, one of the minister couples I referred to earlier. Judy has a deep love of poetry and literature and a quick and intelligent sense of humor, and we hit it off right away. Brian worked as a camera man for a local television station. When Brian's workday was done and Judy's and my classes were over for the day, we'd all three get together in the lounge at the student apartments. It was 1983 and Reagan was in his first term as president. We'd bring our dinners out from our cinderblock rooms to the lounge, watch the news, and discuss the politics of the day. Then we'd watch *MASH* before we headed back to our rooms where Judy and I studied Tillich, Von Rad, and other theological heavy hitters and Brian relaxed for the evening.

I had hardly any furniture in my room, just a mattress on the floor and a rickety kitchen table. When Judy first saw my empty room, she asked, "Mampel, where's all your furniture?" I told her I was a minimalist and didn't need it, and we both laughed. "Well, maybe you could at least build some shelves for your books," she admonished laughing.

"Okay," I agreed, then took the thought a couple of steps further. "Hey! Maybe we could start a shelf-making business, eh, Judums?" We joked about the idea for a while and even came up with a name for our imaginary business, "Shelf Esteem Builders."

Judy and I became good friends, joking around and sharing insights, such good friends that when I said, "Hey, let's get together and have dinner at your place," she just laughed and teased me about my gaffe.

"Are you inviting Brian and me to make dinner for you?"

"Well, yeah, I guess I am," I said, a little embarrassed. I explained that I wanted to talk with her in private about the struggles I was having in my first-year internship at a church in Minneapolis. She agreed with much good humor to "invite" me to dinner.

My internship had started out well enough, especially because the congregation was such a radically political one. The church gave sanctuary to Salvadoran refugees, organized protests against apartheid and racism, and pretty much protested every social and political injustice of the day. Truly, they were Protestants in every sense of the word. Their Sunday services were held on the half-moon stage of a funky old theater, and their minister wore clogs and read from Lao Tzu. Musically, they departed from the Charles Wesley favorites and instead of hymns sang union songs and shape-note Appalachian folk songs, which I really loved. I appreciated the atmosphere of political dharma, but it seemed to me that it was all geared toward disillusioned hippies from the sixties. Meanwhile, I was relegated to delivering church fliers door to door in the cold, slushy snow and leading the Sunday school for three or four little hippy offspring in a small, ugly basement room while the good reverend led the worship service upstairs. When I went to see him to let him know how unhappy I was about this state of affairs, he said, "It sounds like you're trying to collect experiences," a response that left me baffled.

It only made matters worse that I was secretly smoking pot again.

I felt used and confused and lonely for my wonderfully funny and now scattered friends from college. I felt I had abandoned my summer dreams of becoming a professional musician and poet, and I felt out of place at seminary. I was one of the only young white males right out of college who was going to school there, and I felt like an outsider. When I shared this painful feeling of not belonging with Judy, she proceeded to make me laugh. She called the minister "Big Daddy" and that just cracked me up. We proceeded to imitate him and teased that he was like Flip Wilson's character, "Reverend Leroy." Big Daddy would have made a great assistant pastor at Reverend Leroy's "Church of What's Happenin' Now," we joked. Judy and Brian both made me laugh and teased me out of my dark brooding. I left their home that evening feeling a little more hopeful and encouraged.

When the time for finals rolled around, everyone around me acted all stressed out, and all my classmates were cramming for their upcoming tests. I causally walked into the lounge one evening during that time and asked if I could borrow a Bible. People looked up from their books and papers in astonishment. Laughter rippled through the room. Someone said, "Mampel, you're in seminary and you don't have a Bible?"

"No," I replied. "Was I supposed to bring one?"

In our Old Testament class, we learned about the different traditions woven into the writings of the books in the Bible. There was the priestly tradition and the Yahwist and the Eloist traditions, along with other sources that offer differing views about historical events and doctrine. For example, there are two creation stories in Genesis, the first book of the Bible, because of these different traditions. At one point, Judy and I were sitting next to each other in the back row and the professor was talking about how the priestly version of God was concerned with rules and regulations. I was reminded of a scene performed by Monty Python that illustrated this priestly view of God. I leaned over toward Judy and said in my best deep, priestly voice, "Oh, God, you are so big."

Judy laughed and said, "Cut it out, Mampel."

"You are so very, very huge, God," I continued.

Judy struggled to hold back laughter and her face turned red. "Stop it, Mampel," she whispered furiously.

"And, God, we are so itsy bitsy small. Please, God, don't crush us." Judy told me later she just about peed her pants, and some of the other students near us were cracking up, too. Titters and little bursts of laughter spread through the room, and the professor's brow furrowed up, but, bless him, he continued with his lecture and didn't kick me out. I couldn't stop giggling and I knew I should stop, but I turned to Judy one final time. Her eyes watered from trying to hold back laughter, but I just couldn't help myself. "Oh, God," I intoned, "please help me!" Then I excused myself and ran to the restroom.

In another class, the professor asked everyone to share two emotions they were feeling. Students offered up emotions such as fear, sadness, insecurity, and vulnerability; the room took on a somber tone. When it was my turn the professor asked me what two feelings I was feeling. "Cold and itchy," I said. I didn't say it to be funny; it really was what I was feeling at the time, but Judy, who was sitting nearby, surprised me with peals of inappropriate laughter. To my way of thinking, I was simply and sincerely stating my truth.

~.~

Even though the wild antics of my college years were behind me, my drug use continued. I justified it in numerous ways: "It's just how I relax," I would say, or "Jesus drank wine, and wine comes from a plant; God created plants, pot is a plant, so I'm being just like Jesus when I smoke pot!" Little did I know it, but I was headed for a rude awakening.

A master's degree from United Theological Seminary takes most students three years to achieve. Seminarians refer to the first year as "deconstructive theology" and the second year as "constructive theology." In other words, the program is a sort of "break you, then make you" process. By the spring of 1984, I was definitely broken, but it wasn't because of the deconstruction of my theological views. My active addiction had crept back into my everyday life again. I justified my using by telling myself that no one knew about it but me. Besides, I wasn't hurting anyone, or so I thought.

One night after dinner, I went back to my room to smoke a joint. When I came back out to the lounge, I ran into Judy and she stopped me. I was pretty stoned, but even so I could tell that Judy's eyes looked troubled. Maybe she's having trouble in one of her classes, I thought, expecting her to talk about something like that.

However, what she said stunned me. "Dave," she said, "I know you're getting high." I stood there, horrified. I had thought I was the only one who knew my dirty little secret. She took a deep breath and continued, "You're an addict, Dave, and you need help." I wanted to crawl back into my room and hide there forever. She went on, relentless. "I have family members who have problems like yours," she said, "and I know the symptoms." She paused a moment, searching my face. "I think you should start going to recovery meetings and get help." A sudden lump clogged my throat and my guts knotted up. I felt as if something were tearing apart inside me. Then Judy spoke the words that caused a tiny crack to begin forming in the walls of my denial. "It really hurts me to see you high, Dave," she said.

My cover was blown. What was worse, I could no longer

deny that my using drugs and getting high were hurting another person I really cared about. I had failed even in my inauthentic mission of being the caretaker. But deeper than that, my authentic, compassionate self, buried deep down, below the emotional numbing the drugs provided, began to wake up. I was broken. I hurt. My deconstructive year at UTS culminated in this confrontation by my friend, a moment that turned out to be truly more important for me spiritually than all of my studies that year, more important than all the theology, Biblical scholarship, and church history combined.

I admitted to Judy that she was right. "But life is so raw without getting high," I complained. She sympathized, but she encouraged me to seek help and at least try going to meetings. When Judy's husband, Brian walked in on the conversation I opened up to him, too. "How do you relax," I asked him, "without taking drugs?"

"I take hot baths," he said. I laughed a little at that, but I took him seriously, too. As I continue my life without the use of drugs, I follow Brian's example. I love taking hot baths, soaking in hot tubs, and taking regular trips to Wilbur Hot Springs in Northern California, near where I live. I have found that Brian's hot bath habit really works; soaking in hot water relaxes me, and taking a hot bath these days is an integral part of my spiritual recovery.

Judy explained to me about recovery programs and told me a little about how they work. I looked up Twelve Step meetings in the phone book and went to my first recovery meeting the next evening. It was held in a church in a rundown neighborhood in southeast Minneapolis in another one of those ugly basement rooms. The room was so filled with cigarette smoke I could barely see or breathe, and the meeting consisted of a bunch of scary-looking biker dudes sitting in metal folding chairs. It seemed to me that everyone there had tattoos and long scraggly hair and talked about kicking heroin. I felt completely out of place and failed to notice that, just like me, they felt compelled to use their drugs just as I used mine: They used drugs to change the way they felt and to escape reality, just as I did. The drugs they used were different from mine, and I thought that made me better somehow. I wasn't anything like them, I thought.

I wasn't listening for the ways in which I was the same as them; I heard only the differences. I didn't see how I, too, was obsessive with my pot use and felt uncomfortable in my own skin. I failed to see how I, too, was dependent on intoxication to help me feel normal. My intoxicant was different, and I thought that made me different. "These guys are hard-core heroin junkies," I thought. "I'm just a pothead." I was so scared of the tough-looking biker dudes I left before the meeting ended, grateful for the smoke-free air outside of that dingy basement room. These days, no one smokes in recovery meetings, thank goodness.

I went to a few more meetings that spring just because I thought I should, and I stayed clean for about a month. It would be several more years before I would be ready to re-enter the rooms of recovery and allow myself to feel a part of the group. That spring, though, I just wanted to get high again, far away from anyone who might care enough to talk with me about it, so I told my friends I needed an academic break. I had been going to school and sitting in classrooms my entire life, I said. I needed some time to experience the work world if I were ever to be an empathic minister someday. With those justifications firmly in place, UTS granted me a year-long leave of absence from seminary.

While my reasons for that sabbatical were plausible, they were not true. I suppressed the truth, though, lying even to myself. "I'm too young to quit now," I told myself, "I need to take a leave of absence from such heavy responsibilities before I have to work for the rest of my life. I need a time out to have some fun and see if the ministry really is for me." The lies ran on and on, and the rationalizations poured forth.

~.~

By the time spring break rolled around, I had not used drugs or alcohol for a month. I had wanted to get high again, but somehow I stayed clean anyway. All that kept me going was that I knew I was going to leave seminary at the end of the term, and I was looking forward to smoking marijuana again, once I was away from the observant eyes of my dear friends. At about this time, I experienced my first sweat lodge.

Organized by the students and teachers from the Native American Theological Program, the "sweat" was open to anyone who wanted to experience it. A Lakota Sioux medicine man from northern Minnesota visited the campus, and the group set up a wigwam in the field behind the student apartments. The weather on the day of the sweat had a springtime energy, with partly cloudy skies and a light breeze, and buds were emerging on flowers and trees. A handful of us, wearing light clothing and carrying towels, walked over to the wigwam. The first sweat was for men only, and the men stripped naked and crawled inside the sweat lodge. The medicine man called it the "womb of mother earth." The lodge was dark inside, with a small round fire pit in the center of the dirt floor. Once everyone was settled around it, hot rocks were placed in the pit.

An elderly medicine man led the ceremony. It was so dark inside the lodge that I couldn't see him very well, but I had the impression of tanned and weathered skin and long gray braids. Before he began, he told us that the ritual was from the earliest times of his tribe, a time no one could remember. Ancient himself, he was soft-spoken and gentle of spirit, but there was an inner fierceness about him, too. The ceremony, he told us, would cleanse, purify, and strengthen us and all our relations. He explained that the heat would get intense, but encouraged us to let it happen and pray to be strong. Whenever the temperature inside the lodge got too hot for anyone, they could say, "*Ho mitakuye oyasin*," which means "all my relations," and which was a signal for the flap to be opened briefly to allow cool air inside. It would be okay to leave, the medicine man told us, if the heat became too intense. My heart beat fast and I felt a little scared, but I knew I wouldn't want to leave.

The naked men who sat in a ring around the fire pit were an eclectic group. There were students from all over the campus, including one student from Africa who had ritual scarring on his cheeks. Red hot rocks were brought into the lodge and placed in the pit and the flap was then closed. The medicine man sprinkled dried cedar and sweet grass on the rocks then poured water on them to make a pungent, fragrant steam. The heat built up quickly, and as we sat, he directed us to pray for strength for our families and relations and for ourselves. The medicine man chanted and prayed to the Great Spirit and the heat intensified as red sparks from the cedar and sweet grass bounced off the rocks. I was sweating and breathing deeply, and I longed for a single breath of fresh, cool air, but I remembered to allow myself to be in the heat and pray harder as it got hotter. With each breath, each prayer, I felt stronger and lighter at the same time, and I felt the strength of the others, too. I prayed for my family, for myself, and for others; I prayed as hard as I could. Someone uttered, "*Ho mitakuye oyasin,*" and fresh spring air swooshed inside the hot, steamy sweat lodge. Men breathed sighs of relief as the cool air brushed their skin, and then the flap dropped back into place and the ceremony continued.

As the heat intensified I felt a connection to hundreds of generations, and the ceremony, as it proceeded, began to seem familiar and comfortable. Oddly, I felt as if I belonged. The raw and edgy feeling I had experienced during my month of being clean began to subside, and I felt strength seeping into my very being. I felt connected to life, to the earth, to the other men in the sweat lodge, to the generations who had passed this ceremony on to us, and to the Great Spirit who was continuously summoned during the ceremony. Although I didn't realize it at the time, that feeling of belonging was exactly what I most needed. The feeling of being connected to all of life, to my own authentic self, and to a Power greater than myself gave me an eventual reason to stay away from drugs, or in Twelve Step parlance, to stay clean. That spring, though, I was still not ready.

As the ceremony went on and on, my resistance melted and I relaxed into the heat. The sweat lodge became the entire world, and I lost track of the passage of time. Suddenly the chanting stopped. It was over.

I stepped outside into the darkening twilight, feeling as if I were floating. I felt cleansed and renewed, strong and confident and inspired. Each of us in turn gave thanks to the medicine man and made an offering, then we dressed, hugged each other, and talked softly about our experience before we parted ways. I walked back to my apartment and wrote a poem that night called "Sweat Lodge." The experience was a powerful one for me, and I wanted to mark the moment so that I would never forget it.

Sweat Lodge
--Dave Mampel

Naked
nine of us enter the sweat lodge
of bent sticks and green canvas

Kind and strong the medicine man
dips the pan in water
gives it to the sacred stones
dashing against our faces a new level of purity
from the hot spray of this friendly ritual
Faster the chants
salt and sage my mind the images flow
Breath short and precious like God
we sing to God pray chant and grunt
to the Great Spirit
"God
clean me go around the world
and strengthen me with the poor!"
I'm not sure of my prayer
I'm only sure of my body.
It melts into earth
leaps out through the sky
and I am back
"All my relatives" is spoken
the flap is open

Jim says we all look different
We do
Medicine Man speaks
gives good words
I am full and empty ready
to burst with nothing
The peace pipe comes forward
when breathing balances like twilight
or a flame in stillness
We smoke
pass it around
I blow my final puff upward
then give it to
my closer brother
The water calls forth
we drink of it
we splash down
our hot and slippery skins
we pass the cup
and pray gently
until we pause
in unexpected thanksgiving

Leaving behind
a silent memory of Mother Earth
we change in the early spring wind
outside the Sweat Lodge
Our bodies dry and tickle to the touch
We fly to freedom or walk within it.

~.~

Dr. Gabor Mate' writes in his book, *In the Realm of Hungry Ghosts: Close Encounters with Addiction*, that the epidemic of modern-day addiction springs from the rise of industrial capitalism and the subsequent alienation and isolation people feel. A cold-hearted attitude by those in power which values profits over the well-being of people leads to a break in belonging on a societal level. When cultures were more in harmony with nature, the Great Spirit led everyday life, and a system of elder wisdom gave a deep sense of the vertical, a sense of a transcendent dimension in life, along with a connection to ancestors. Meaningful vocational roles were available for everyone and addiction did not exist in the epidemic proportions we experience today. While ritualistic drug use or even the occasional drunken episode might have been acceptable, there was not widespread chronic addiction in all corners of the world.

Recovering addicts like me find Twelve Step recovery programs and fellowships to be a healing balm, a way to feel connected with other human beings. When I finally did surrender to my addiction--in other words, when I fully accepted that my addiction was real--I allowed myself to return to Twelve Step meetings. That time, when I stepped through the door and sat down, I felt as if I had come home. Over time, I have come to experience care and love, spirituality, meaningful growth, and purpose in the rooms of recovery.

~.~

When I left my first year of seminary behind I bought my first car, a light blue Dodge Demon, which I thought was a car that was perfectly named for a lapsed seminarian. I bought it from another student for five hundred dollars, and I got what I paid for. If you substitute the letter L for the letter D in Demon, you'll have its more accurate name: Lemon. That car had already been through several winters in Minneapolis, where the roads are salted after every snowfall, so the frame was rusted nearly to the core. I know God looks down on all of us, but He has to employ angels overtime to watch over clowns. Somehow I made it back home to Seattle without a major mishap, despite the fact that I had to cross over two major mountain ranges on my way. For good measure, my sister Jeanie and her boyfriend Craig Swanson, who is now her husband, made the trip with me in their car. I was hoping to find some kind of work in Seattle, and Craig and I were planning to live together as roommates in my Great Aunt Vangie's home in West Seattle. Aunt Vangie had recently died, and her home had not yet been put on the market and sold. When we arrived at my folks' place, the parsonage for Beacon Avenue United Church of Christ on Beacon Hill, I stopped in to unpack, visit, and discuss plans for our living situation at Aunt Vangie's.

I hadn't been home for more than a couple of hours when I decided to hop in the Demon to drive north on Interstate Five to see if I could buy some pot from a drug dealer I knew. As I pulled out of the driveway, I waved to my dad, who was watching me from where he sat at the dining room table. I backed onto the road, and I heard a loud crack. The steering wheel swooped up over my head, and the seat I was sitting on suddenly dropped. The car refused to budge. Bewildered, I looked up and saw Dad at the dining room window, laughing at my predicament.

Since it was my first car, and a cheap used one at that, I had expected to have to take it in for repairs, even a lot of repairs. I expected maybe to have had to fix the brakes, change the alternator, or buy a fuel pump. But my first car broke right in two! The rusted-out frame had cracked all the way through.

Feeling a little shaken, I reflected that I had been about to drive on the freeway in that car. I might have seriously hurt myself or someone else. Dad ran out of the house and helped me to climb out of the car. By the time I was on terra firma again, we were both laughing. "Son," he said, "your angels were watching out for you!" I nodded in agreement, a little too numb to speak. I called for a tow truck; the driver offered me fifty bucks and said they would use it for scrap. That sounded like a pretty good deal to me.

I got to use Great Aunt Vangie's car that summer, so things turned out pretty well for me on that front. All the same, though, I was facing another dark chapter of my life, although I didn't realize it at the time. I spent the next two years consumed by active addiction, with confusion and uncertainty the dominant themes.

Chapter Eleven: Waking up from Seattle

I floundered in Seattle. I worked as a cashier at the cafeteria at Seattle Pacific University and served as a part-time youth minister for Prospect Congregational Church. Craig and I played our guitars together, and when we did I almost felt as if I were living back in the dorms at Augustana College again. Craig was my friend before he met Jeanie, and we had played our guitars together during my freshman year at Augie. I also tried to write a musical because I was so inspired by the film *Amadeus*, but I was so stoned it never got past the early stages. I even tried to take the entrance exam for the English graduate program at the University of Washington, but was so high I walked out during the exam. My addiction really went out of control when I used cocaine for about three months. I soon realized coke was not for me; when I was high on cocaine, I felt like my heart was about to explode. I knew I had a problem with drugs, but I still wasn't ready to quit. I wasn't yet ready to give the rooms of Twelve Step recovery another try.

However, I did have a talk with my dad. While I didn't come clean with him about my use of drugs, I did tell him how lost I felt. "I'm just not sure where to go next in my life when my leave of absence is up," I told him. His answer helped me then, and it has helped me many other times since then.

"Davey," he said, "When you don't know what to do, just do the things you do know how to do, and do them well." I must have looked confused because he paused a moment and continued. "Everything will get clear later on." I got it then, and the idea struck me to the core. The way out of my confusion was to do whatever was in front of me, something I did know to do. Maybe it would be washing the dishes or doing a load of laundry; maybe it would be applying for a new job or starting a college course or calling someone I had lost touch with. I started getting a glimmer of an idea of the way out of my troubles. I would do the next right thing and do that well, and things would become clear with time. "I've learned that you have to create possibilities in life before the opportunities can come," Dad said. "If you don't know what job to work, volunteer somewhere. If you want to get published, start submitting your poems to magazines."

~.~

After my conversation with Dad about creating possibilities, I decided to volunteer for an organization in my community, I figuring I'd create possibilities by volunteering there until I could see more clearly. I started by helping the director with whatever she needed. I answered phones, interviewed unemployed people and worked to place them in part-time jobs. I helped elderly ladies supplement their Social Security income by finding them piecework contracts such as sewing for local linen companies and dry cleaners. Best of all, for me anyway, was that volunteering there got me out and about and circulating. Giving back to the community in this way boosted my energy and confidence. It stimulated my mind and connected me with others in my field of interest. It was just a matter of time before the opportunities came.

When I had been on my leave of absence from UTS for nearly a year, the school contacted me to ask if I planned to return. I was still unsure of my path in life, and I asked if I could extend my leave. The only way to do that, I was told, was to find a mentor and an internship in Seattle. Perfect! I told them. I would do just that. I already had my volunteer position, and that became my internship. It wasn't too long afterward that the director at that organization stepped down and the board of directors asked me if I would like the job. Thrilled and excited, I accepted. John Cannon, a retired colonel and a long-time member of Dad's church, consented to be my mentor.

My dad's wisdom about creating possibilities got me started, and John Cannon's pragmatic leadership built my self-esteem and confidence. I started learning how to use a daily planner, and I have used one ever since. I learned that if I need to remember something, I need to write it down in a place I refer to regularly where I can find it later. If it's in my planner, I don't have to try to remember it. I can write it and forget it until I need it again.

During my internship, I learned to make cold calls to possible job sites for our clients, and I began to catch onto the idea of creating possibilities for grants by writing one or two letters to possible grant funders each day. Once I was installed as director, a big part of my job became soliciting grants, along with all the other stuff I had already been doing as an intern. It was such a thrill when the grants started coming in and I was able to fund my position for the year. I learned how to be more organized, how to lead board meetings, secure contracts, create financial reports and budgets, work with clients and volunteers, write grant applications, and manage all the other day-in-day-out details of running a nonprofit organization. I used those skills when I returned to UTS the following year and took an internship with Clergy and Laity Concerned. They came in handy again and again, helping me to be a more organized and confident pastor and eventually enabling me to establish my own entertainment business as a professional clown and run it well. I am forever indebted to everyone who helped me learn the ropes back then. I am extremely grateful for their guidance and support.

I was so busy that year that the time passed quickly, and when the year was up, I knew I had to make a decision about whether or not to return to seminary. My drug use was an obstacle, and I knew it. However, I was starting to feel a sense of purpose with social ministries such as the one I was working with, and that inspired me to return to seminary. I wanted to specialize as a minister for social programs rather than being a pastor, a notion that fit my emerging political views. Then, too, I didn't want to merely imitate my dad; I wanted to find my own voice, my own identity as an individual. None of that could happen, though, as long as I was stuck in active addiction. I had to clean up my act and change my ways before I could go back to seminary and become an ordained minister. Thus motivated, I went back to Twelve Step meetings, accepted that I was an addict and needed help, and stayed clean for the next four years. The year was 1986. I was clean and felt ready to return for my final two years of seminary.

~.~

I drove back to Illinois from Seattle in my new car, that is, in my late Great Aunt Vangie's Malibu Classic. I felt more grown up and I was free from the slavery to drugs. I didn't feel so out of place at UTS when I got back, and I even fell in love. I worked two half-time jobs that served as internships for my course work, and I carried a full load of courses. I was extremely focused and the floundering was over.

That was when the nightmares about my dad's accident began. As I mentioned in an earlier chapter, I woke up to the suppressed trauma of hurt, fear of abandonment, and feelings of resentment, anger, and grief. Psychotherapy helped me to access these feelings and start to express them. For about two months, I was not able to speak to either of my parents at all. As I reflect on this time in my life now, I believe I had reached a point of maturity so that I was ready to handle those deeply buried feelings. The drugs had made their way out of my system and my ego was a bit more mature. I believe now that this is why the nightmares came to me at this time in my life. It was because I was finally ready to release the pain and allow the healing process to begin.

I ran into our old family friend Professor Henry Gustafson one evening in the hallway of the student apartments. I was struck by how much like my Uncle Ed he looked. Professor Gustafson had been my dad's New Testament professor and now he was my New Testament professor, too. After we exchanged greetings and pleasantries, I found myself telling him about my therapy. I told him it centered around my dad because I was so angry with Dad and was having a hard time forgiving him for his accident and the way it traumatized me. Henry had such compassion, and he said exactly the right words that helped me start to forgive. "Well, Dave," he said, "just remember your father is not perfect and he didn't mean for any of this to happen." We talked a little while longer, but his words stayed with me.

As soon as I got back to my room I immediately sat down to write a letter to Dad. In it, I tried to tell him the truth about what I had been thinking and feeling. He wrote me back almost at once and his response touched me deeply. He had no idea, he wrote, that I had reacted to his accident all those years ago. He was so sorry. He told me his own dad had abandoned him at about the same age as I had been then, when his father and my grandma had split up during the Depression. He had promised himself, he wrote, that he would never abandon his own son. But with my letter to him, he learned that unwittingly he had done just that.

When I read his letter to me, I felt so sad for him. I had never known these things about my dad, but now I knew that he and I were the same. I felt his pain, his compassion, and his grief, and forgiveness began to melt my heart. I have since learned that forgiveness is not a single event; it is a process. I still had more work do, but for the moment it was enough.

~.~

During my final year at UTS, I was heavily involved with organizing against the Contra War and apartheid through my half-time position at Clergy and Laity Concerned. I began to notice how much anger all that work was creating in me; I was becoming quite the radical. I was concerned that it was too much for me and making me miserable in spirit. I went to hear Abbie Hoffman speak at Macalester College in Saint Paul and afterward I went up to him while he was sipping on a bizarre infusion of herbs. He and I got into a big argument about organizing strategy, both of us adamant about our positions.

At another time, I found myself playing peacemaker in the middle of a crowd of angry protestors who were trying to shut down the Minneapolis Federal Building as riot police approached with billy clubs. I noticed the poet Robert Bly standing nearby on the sidewalk watching the spectacle, and, since I wasn't having much success at my peacemaking role anyway, I slipped out of the crowd and went over to talk with him. I told him how much I loved his poetry, especially his fairytale translations and his work with Coleman Barks, one of the best translators for Rumi. Despite the fact that I was on the fringes of the protest discussing poetry with an erudite poet while chaos swirled nearby, the next day a photo of me accompanied a story about the demonstration on the front page of the *Minneapolis Tribune*.

Another time, a group of us succeeded in blocking the federal building until we were dragged away in handcuffs. The handcuffs were actually plastic cables fastened very tightly around our wrists, and they really hurt. We were thrown into a paddy wagon and taken downtown to be booked. As we sat together in the paddy wagon, I started reciting Yeats' poetry to help me cope with the pain in my hands from the tight bands. Then I remembered I had a nail clipper in my back pocket and I twisted and squirmed until I could grab it. I clipped off my cuffs then helped everyone else get out of theirs, too. When we walked out of the wagon to be booked, the cops didn't seem to notice that our cuffs were off, and we thought that was pretty cool.

When we went in front of the judge a few months later, I pleaded innocent and quoted from Thoreau's essay on civil disobedience. I stated that the government of the United States was breaking international law with the Contra War and our actions were essentially an attempt to stop that illegal war. I pointed out that we were following a higher law, a defense that is often used in court for protests involving civil disobedience. We were all acquitted and set free. Our victory was exhilarating, but I decided then and there I had done my fair share and my protesting days were over.

~.~

All this time, another influence was quietly working during these last two years of seminary, more subtle than social activism or the pastor I was becoming. This influence is personified for me by the late Bruce Carlson, a dear friend of my dad's and then director of the Schubert Club in Saint Paul, Minnesota. He and Tom Tredway arranged and published Dad's poetry books, among many other kind deeds.

While Bruce was in many ways a major player in the arts and music scene of his day, he operated under the radar. Garrison Keillor recognized this about him and wrote a short story based on his life that was featured in one of Keillor's books. Bruce had a sharp wit and was extremely well read. He could even be said to have been shrewd, and yet he was kind and supportive, and he helped me get one of my first paid music gigs at the Landmark Center in Saint Paul. He founded a museum that featured unusual and fascinating musical instruments, and in his office were photographs of Leontyne Price, Itzhak Perlman, Yo-Yo Ma, and other big names in classical music. He had worked with them all.

Bruce introduced me to classical music when I was a kid when he played a recording of *Peter and the Wolf* for me, helping me to hear how each instrument was made to sound like the different animals and characters in the story. He exposed me to literature as a boy when he read to me from Maurice Sendak's children's stories. Later in my life, he gave me tickets for classical concerts to use for raising money for Clergy and Laity Concerned. He got me a "sermon gig" at a Swedenborgian church, where the congregation consisted of a few eccentric old ladies. The beautiful design and architecture of that church intimated a lonely mysticism, and my preaching experience there reawakened my love for esoterica and poetry on a deeper level, somehow making the social activism I was engaged in at the time seem a little less significant.

Emmanuel Swedenborg was a contemporary of William Blake's, a theologian who was considered a threat by the established church in London during the late eighteenth century because of his mystical philosophy. William Blake sought him out; it is rumored that Swedenborg's church was the only one Blake attended. Swedenborg believed that church leaders obscured spirituality and kept it obscured to protect their privileges in society. In his book *Divine Love and Divine Wisdom*, published in 1788, which Blake owned and annotated, Swedenborg elucidated at length about how the Divine in the natural universe had been concealed by churches. He complained that "all the Things of Religion, which are called Spiritual, have been removed out of the Sight of Man," by "Councils and certain Leaders in the Church" who have misled Christians to "blindly" believe that, being born to a "natural" world, they cannot perceive anything "separate from what is natural." To preserve their worldly privileges, he argued, the religious tyrants at the head of the church have conned their subjects into believing that the "spiritual" world "transcend[s] the Understanding." They deceived churchgoers by describing "the spiritual Principle to be like a Bird which flieth above the Air in the Aether where the Eye-sight doth not reach." Swedenborg contended that the spiritual principle of the world is visible to those who break the mental constraints imposed by churches. "By the Sight of the Eye is meant the Sight of the Understanding," he wrote. The spiritual world is "like a Bird of Paradise, which flieth near the Eye, and toucheth its Pupil with its beautiful Wings, and wisheth to be seen."

However, it was when Bruce took me to meet the author Brenda Ueland that he gave me the gift I most cherish. On a brisk, beautifully orange-lit October day, Bruce and I walked together into the author's home in Minneapolis. I immediately felt her presence flowing down from her upstairs room like a warm and brilliant light. A silver pyramid hung in the middle of her living room, a noble talisman that reminded me of my early mystical experiences with pyramid power as a teenager on Kauai. Together Bruce and I walked up the stairs and stepped into her room. She lay on her bed, an elderly woman in her nineties, skinny and wrinkled, but with eyes that shone like stars. She quickly looked me over, darted her eyes toward Bruce, and exclaimed, "Oh my, and he's a handsome one, too!" I blushed and Bruce introduced us. I told her I felt humbled and honored to be in her presence and that I had given up running so that I could walk like she did so as not to miss a thing in nature. I told her how much I loved her book, *If You Want to Write*, which I had just read. She encouraged me and told me to keep writing and signed my copy of her book, with this notation: "The great William Blake said, 'if the sun and moon were to doubt, they'd immediately go out.'"

Bruce had discovered and republished her book, my dad had read it and strongly recommended it to me, and once I started reading it I couldn't put it down; it reawakened the poet and mystic within me. In it, she wrote, "I learned... that inspiration does not come like a bolt, nor is it kinetic, energetic striving, but it comes into us slowly and quietly and all the time, though we must regularly and every day give it a little chance to start flowing, prime it with a little solitude and idleness."

She had mystical visions and wrote that she heard William Blake in the thunder. Of Blake, she wrote, "And yet this creative power in Blake did not come from ambition.... He burned most of his own work. Because he said, 'I should be sorry if I had any earthly fame, for whatever natural glory a man has is so much detracted from his spiritual glory. I wish to do nothing for profit. I wish to live for art. I want nothing whatever. I am quite happy.'" And this,"...He did not mind death in the least. He said that to him it was just like going into another room. On the day of his death he composed songs to his Maker and sang them for his wife to hear. Just before he died his countenance became fair, his eyes brightened and he burst into singing of the things he saw in heaven."

I felt a surge of power and a deep sense of mystery and quiet joy after visiting with Brenda Ueland. A connection to a deeper dimension, one that I had sensed before, opened up in me again. My spirit, sorely in need of soulful nourishment after all my social activism and the anger that had engendered in me, felt nurtured once more. My encounter with Brenda Ueland saved my artistic soul and helped bring it back to life just as I was embarking on my career as a pastor.

Chapter Twelve: Leap of Faith and Earthly Angels

"We must not cease from exploration and the end of all
our exploring will be to arrive where we began and to
know the place for the first time."
--T.S. Eliot

Parish ministry, I slowly came to realize, was my dad's calling, but it was not truly my own. I began to see that the role of pastor, at least for me at that time, came from my continuing to try to be the caretaker in my family system. My choices in that regard were made by the still-wounded eight-year-old boy within me who was desperately trying to save his family. I was playing out the role in the family that I unconsciously and emotionally believed was mine. This was my own unresolved trauma manifesting in my life, but I was starting to wake up and see the lie that it was. I began to see that I was trying to help others, my family in particular, at the expense of my own needs and my soul's truth and destiny. These burgeoning insights and emotions came together inside me and became so painful that, after four years of being abstinent from drugs and alcohol, I relapsed into active drug addiction, and thus plunged toward the worst and lowest point in my life.

When I finally left the ministry, I first told members of my parish, then I told my friends, and they were difficult conversations, all of them. But the most difficult conversation of all was with my dad and mom. At first, Dad thought I was just planning to find another parish. "I did the same thing, son," he said. "It was such a relief to leave that church in Brainerd and go to the United Church of Christ in Minneapolis."

"No, Dad," I said. "That's not what I mean. I'm not leaving Idaho Falls to find another church. I'm leaving parish ministry for good."

Both Mom and Dad were shocked and dismayed. "What are you going to do? How will you survive?" Dad asked.

"Have you lost your faith?" asked Mom.

I explained as well as I could. I did not want Mom and Dad to know the exact circumstances surrounding my resignation from my parish, but I also needed to let them know that I was not going to return to the ministry, not now, not ever. I told them how unhappy I had been, how I had come to the realization that Dad's calling was not my calling. "Mom, Dad," I said, "being a minister just isn't for me." I reminded them that I was still young and single. "I need this chance to follow my own dreams or I'll regret it for the rest of my life." I reassured them (and myself) that I could always go back to the ministry if it didn't work out after a time. "My friend Kate offered me a place to stay until I can get on my feet," I told them.

"Kate?" said Dad. "Your friend in San Francisco?"

"Well, the Bay Area, yes."

"In California?" The way Mom wailed it, you would have thought I was going to the moon.

"Yeah, Mom. I'm going to be a musician." Then I hurried to say, "Don't worry. I'll find other work as I need to until I find my way." She wasn't convinced. Neither was Dad, or maybe I just felt they weren't because they both sounded so worried and concerned. "Listen, you two have always encouraged me to be myself and have faith. Well, I'm doing just that."

They were very worried. I could tell they were trying to be supportive, but I could hear the fear and disappointment in their voices. I didn't want them to be worried for me, but going back was no longer an option for me. I was scared when I heard their fear, but that door was closed to me. I knew I had to do move forward on my newly chosen path or I would fail myself, lose my way on my soul's journey.

I didn't want to feel the conflicting feelings these changes in my life stirred up, so, as I had done so many times before, I numbed those feelings by returning to active addiction. What did it matter? I rationalized. I was back home in Idaho wrapping things up, but I was on my way out of the parish, I reasoned, and I didn't need to be all that "responsible" any longer. I convinced myself that I could use drugs again, because I didn't have to be a spiritual role model anymore.

My wild side morphed into the rebel, and while I tried to hide it from members of my church, I was not as successful at hiding my drug use as I imagined myself to be back then. One of the members of my church pulled me aside at my going-away potluck party. "You know, Dave," she said, "you won't be able to be a successful musician if you continue getting high." I knew she was right, and even though I tried to forget what she said, her words haunted me. They were good seeds planted in my subconscious mind that, with other events to come, would help me to get back into recovery six years later.

~.~

My final year of parish ministry was 1992. In the summer of that year, I packed up all my belongings, turned my mobile home over to a property manager to rent it out for me until I could sell it, and said my goodbyes. Eventually, I sold my mobile home for a loss, but another loss was harder to bear. I gave my four-year-old golden retriever, Woody, to a nice family who welcomed all one hundred ten pounds of him into their home. It was a very difficult decision, but I couldn't bring Woody to California. There was no room for him at my friend Kate Ague's modest home in Menlo Park. Besides, I was dragging along about thirty thousand dollars in debt, and I couldn't very well bring along a one-hundred-ten-pound dog as well. Besides, I had no job prospects and no idea where I would live after my temporary living situation at Kate's.

Woody and I had been together since he was only six months old, and he had been with me almost the whole time I was a pastor. He was so loving, even though he could be a bit clumsy at times. I think he never quite adjusted to how big his dog body was. He would wag his big tail excitedly and knock down toddlers while he was looking the other way. Wanting to play with the neighborhood kids while they rode by on their bikes, he'd jump up to try and lick them as they rode quickly past, in the process knocking them over sideways onto the ground. Luckily he never hurt anyone.

I named him Woody after Woody Guthrie, one of my heroes, but his name took on a whole new meaning when I came home from the church office one day and found him in the backyard pulling logs off my newly stocked wood pile. As he dragged the last log to the middle of the yard, he suddenly saw me and stopped. "Woody! What are you doing?" I yelled. Roughly two hundred logs, maybe more, were scattered around the entire yard. He was so proud of his accomplishment, excitedly bounding up to me, that I had laugh. I laboriously put all the wood back into a neat pile, but the next day I returned to find the same mess! He really was in love with wood, and his name made even more sense to me. From then on, I took him with me in my car everywhere. Assuming he had been bored before, I took him out for runs on the back roads between the Idaho potato fields, and the wood scattering became a thing of the past.

My favorite story about Woody, though, is about the time when I was soaking in my new hot tub on a winter night. Woody came over to the tub and looked at me wistfully. "Woody, do you want to come in?" I asked. He seemed to answer in the affirmative, so I stood up in the chill winter air, and dripping wet, pulled him into the tub with me. As he submerged into the heated water, he moaned with pleasure and I burst out laughing. Woody was my pal and I will forever treasure him in my heart. He lived a happy life with his new family after I moved away, and they let me know when he died of cancer a few years later. I still think of my wonderful friend from time to time and miss him and his ever-faithful love.

As I write this book twenty-one years later, I am preparing my home for a new doggy love. I have built a patio and a fenced-in area, and I am making plans for having another dog this year. It's taken me a very long time to be in a position to have another dog and be able to give it a good home. Maybe I'll get a smaller dog and call it Daffy Doodles, train him or her to do tricks in my show while wearing a little clown hat and clown collar. However, Doodles will have to be the last act in my show. I can't have Daffy Dave being upstaged by the clown dog!

When I got together with my music friends in Idaho Falls for my final going-away party, I was filled with energy and happiness. I felt so relieved to be leaving the ministry behind, and I was excited to begin pursuing my dreams of being an entertainer. But right there, right in the middle of the party, while I was outside playing with the kids, it struck me. I was going to miss my musician and soul friends in Idaho. A wave of melancholy laced with fear washed over me. I turned to my friends. "What am I going to do?" I asked. "How am I going to make money? I don't even have a job or a gig lined up in California."

"Why don't you do something with kids, Dave?" someone said. "You're always playing with them and making them laugh. They love you."

"Yeah," another chimed in, "Why don't you dress up like a clown, call yourself 'Crazy Dave' and charge those California yuppies $150 bucks for a birthday party?" Everyone laughed, including me.

"Yeah!" I said. "That's a great idea!" Everyone laughed again and the jokes started flying back and forth. I assumed they had been half-joking, but I noticed with surprise that even though I imagined most people might have been insulted or uninspired by such a suggestion, I felt complimented and excited! And not only that, but I felt relieved, too. I started to relax a little and began to feel happy again. Of course I could do that. Of course I could! I would do the silly clowning thing on the side until I was able to put a hip, slick, cool band together. Crazy Dave would pay the bills for Rocker Dave. Right after that party, I got some business cards made up for "Crazy Dave." I already knew a few magic tricks and kids' songs, for starters. I would buy a clown costume and learn more tricks and balloon art when I got to California, I figured.

~.~

I loaded up the camper shell on my red Ford Ranger with all my essentials and left Idaho for California in July of 1992. I was on my way! I drove all day and all night. I felt so free and alive. Driving into Northern California on Interstate 80 wearing an African tie-dyed shirt, I sang and shouted at the top of my lungs out the windows of my truck, hopped up on marijuana and the thrill of changing my life. San Francisco Bay. The Golden Gate Bridge. Redwood trees. The Pacific Ocean. Fragrant orange blossoms, lemon trees and magnolias, colorful flowering bushes and palm trees assaulted my senses. It was almost as if my life on Kauai had come over to join me on the mainland. I shed the tight suit of Reverend Dave like a snake-skin. I was doing it! I was taking the first steps of living out my dreams of being an entertainer. I had heard someone say, "If you take the first step, the universe will take a thousand more for you." I really believed that, and I sensed the life of my dreams rushing toward me.

I rolled into the driveway at Kate Ague's house in Menlo Park at about one o'clock in the morning. Kate, my sweet, eccentric friend from college days, was my godsend, my angel. When I arrived, we hugged and chatted a bit, and then Kate made sure I was comfortable in her guest bedroom. The next morning, I woke with life surging through my veins, happy and thrilled to be alive. The world awaited, ready for me to pluck it, like the ripe fruit I could see in practically every yard I passed in Northern California. Already, the universe was taking a step for me by providing me a place to live by way of my friend Kate.

Now that I had taken that most difficult of steps, the first one, the universe was coming to my aid. Invisible as well as visible hands helped me. So many people reached out to assist me during that time; opportunities fell into my lap almost unbidden; ideas flooded my mind, and resources were mine for the asking. I began to understand the saying, "Heaven helps those who help themselves." I was on a roll. New songs poured out of me, and a few gigs came my way. Through Kate, I met another musician and recording engineer, Steele Harris, who helped me come up with a demo tape that I used to find more gigs. Kate's wonderful harmonies inspired us both to create a duo we called Lunar Disguise, and she and I sang at some local cafés. When Joan Baez walked in on one of our local performances, I was thrilled. Even though I didn't get to talk to her, I felt her presence there was an encouraging nudge from life to continue pursuing my dreams. Kate said our little duo lifted her spirits, too. Her poetic musician's soul had been longing for some freedom, and she had been feeling stuck at her job in the city. She got so much joy, she said, from singing with me.

One of the songs I wrote at this time was "Goes Around, Comes Around." It's a jazzy folk rock tune that's filled with the energy and inspiration I felt at this time.

Goes Around, Comes Around
--Dave Mampel

Get me downtown! I'm tired of uptown.
Meet the people, try to find another sound.
Strum your guitar, sing a new song,
Watch the children make a playground.

All your stories, all your motion,
All your dreams and all your notions,
All your wishes, all your feelings,
All the hope that's worth your screaming.

No use denyin', there's people cryin'. No use for tryin', all the lyin'.
So, keep it open, make it happen, throw away dissatisfaction.

Goes around, comes around, goes around, comes around.

~.~

I met so many interesting musicians and entertainers, artists, and poets during those first few months. The Bay Area was riding the wave of Silicon Valley's expanding computer industry boom times, despite an economic recession taking place in the rest of the country and the last throes of a years-long California drought. I didn't worry about such things; I seemed to live outside of such mundane matters. I felt happy and free. Positive vibes were everywhere.

~.~

All the same, I struggled to make enough money to survive. When things got tough, I remembered the advice Dad had given me before when I was struggling in Seattle: When you don't know what to do, do the things you know to do--and do them well--and everything will get clear later on. I remembered what Dad had said about the importance of creating possibilities, too. I remembered that my volunteering had led to my being in the right spot at the right time so that I could become the director of a nonprofit organization in Seattle. Now in California, I once again needed to create possibilities in my new pursuit of being an entertainer. It was time again to follow leads, to network, pitch ideas, and volunteer. I had learned from my own experience that just doing anything at all would be enough to get the juices flowing until the "right" connection happened. Once I had jumpstarted my life, I knew, I would hear of a better opportunity. Get out there, then, I told myself. Make yourself available, useful, and exposed. I knew that if I didn't take strong, effective action, possibilities wouldn't have a chance to show up.

I tried doing all the things I knew I could do, and I did them as well as I could. I took part-time jobs of all kinds, any odd job I could find that could help me pay the bills. I played music for tips at Lytton Plaza in downtown Palo Alto; I gave guitar lessons; I worked as a host cashier at a restaurant, baby-sat for a local therapist, officiated at some weddings. Despite my best efforts, I struggled financially. My odd jobs were only occasional at best. I only lasted three weeks at the restaurant, for instance. Payments on my student loans, modest rent at Kate's place, credit card debt from my days as a minister in Idaho, gas, food, insurance, and other expenses all added up to a good deal more than the tiny streams of revenue I managed to bring in.

Finally, I landed a job performing at a birthday party as

Crazy Dave. They paid me eighty bucks.

I shared my job struggles with a local café owner, and he told me about his early days of washing windows for a living. "It's a low-overhead business, plus it's flexible, and it's lucrative. It helped me get through college." It sounded like a practical and feasible idea to me, so I started a window-washing business and called it "Dave Does Windows." I put an ad in the local paper, and next to all my other fliers for guitar lessons, weddings, birthday parties, and babysitting, I tacked up new fliers for my window-washing business. Almost at once, I started getting window-washing jobs that helped me generate a little more revenue.

But it still wasn't enough. I still was not making ends meet, and I felt anxious and depressed about it. When rain fell day after day in late fall, as it sometimes does in the Bay Area, I got even more depressed. No one called for window-washing jobs, or much of anything else for that matter. I started to question my decision to follow my dreams, and despair crept into my thoughts.

I prayed that I could learn to trust in a friendly, abundant universe, and while I was praying I had a thought about how to practice faith: I was down to my last fifty dollars, and I decided to spend it all on celebrating my new life with as many of my new California friends as I could. I went to a specialty grocery store and bought the ingredients for a five-course East Indian meal, then I went home and cooked up a storm. Kate and I called our new musician and artist friends and invited them over to Kate's house for a musical dinner party. People came, the food was delicious, the music was beautiful, and everyone had a fun time. I could hardly believe how calm and happy I felt. I was broke, but I had an inexplicable feeling things were going be okay, that things already were okay.

What happened next was nothing short of a miracle. I truly believe that when I spent my last dollar on that dinner party, I was performing a powerful act of trust. It demonstrated to life that I believed in abundance, that I believed assistance from the universe would come my way and that Divine Providence would come to my aid. I have no way of proving this belief actually led to what happened next, but I have experienced this kind of help so many times in my life that I simply see the pattern. My energy and enthusiasm for life, combined with faith in an abundant universe, magnetically attracts to me positive solutions, ideas, assistance, and prosperity. Not only that, but my mind is clearer when I operate in this fashion, and my positive attitude enables me to solve my problems more effectively. My attitudes, my thoughts, reflect back to me precisely what I have sent out, as if they were a mirror.

~.~

If you have heard about or experienced the Law of Attraction before, you know about these things: You are what you think. Perceptions create reality. Thoughts become things. I am a walking, talking demonstration that the Law of Attraction really does work. I don't know how it works or if it always works. I don't seem to be able to manipulate it strictly to achieve my own selfish ends, for instance. But I have learned from experience that when I am aligned in love with my own highest aspirations for myself and others and I love and cherish life and am grateful for what I do have, this powerful Law truly works in my life. Gratitude for what I have attracts ever more abundance into my life.

I believe that if I had allowed my negative beliefs and creeping despair to gain the upper hand, if I had acted on the belief that the universe is limited and that resources in the infinite cosmos are scarce, my fear and despair from that perspective would have closed me off from what was lined up to come to me. I would have given up on creating possibilities and pushed away or missed opportunities for wealth and success to begin reaching me.

Nonetheless, being fully human, I awoke the morning after that wonderful musical dinner party feeling anxious and scared. I was totally broke, and I felt the lack of money like a disease. Immediately, I started to pray. I prayed to God, to the universe, to any angels who might have been listening. My prayers were sincere and passionate, and they were answered almost at once.

As soon as I said, "Amen," the phone rang.

"Hello," I answered.

"Is this Dave of Dave Does Windows?" I pictured a perky little old lady by the sound of her voice.

"Yes, ma'am," I said. "This is Dave."

"My name is Mary," she said. "Can you come over this morning to clean my windows?"

I felt a quick surge of relief and grinned into the phone. I looked up and mouthed a quick "Thank you!" toward the ceiling. "Yes, ma'am!" I said to Mary. "I'll be right there."

I got her address, hopped into my truck, and drove the few miles to Mary's townhouse in Palo Alto. The last shreds of despair fled out the windows of my truck into the sunshine. "Thanks, God," I prayed as I drove. "Your timing is perfect, as usual. As You know, I sure could use a little cash!"

Mary showed me around her townhouse, giggling. I counted windows as we walked through her home. She grinned often and appeared to be suppressing a hearty laugh. She was chirpy and energetic, and I guessed she was in her early eighties.

"Okay," I said when we had circled back to her front hallway. "I can wash your windows for thirty-five dollars."

"What?" she protested.

I was afraid I was going to lose this job, and I really needed the dough. "All right, then," I said. "How about thirty-three fifty?"

"You can't do that!" she exclaimed. My heart sank in my chest. "Thirty-five dollars is not nearly enough for all of these windows."

"Huh?" I said.

"I am going to pay you more than thirty-five dollars for doing my windows," she said firmly.

I cleared my throat and tried to recover my dignity. "Well," I hesitated, then seeing the determined look on her face, hurried to say, "I only expect you to pay me thirty-five dollars. If you want to tip me, that's fine, Mary." I grinned and she returned my grin. "Thanks!" I said and got right to work.

Before I knew it, Mary was helping me wash her windows. "Hey, Mary!" I protested. "What are you doing? No, no. Let me do this." I tried to stop her, but she just laughed and continued washing windows with me. As we worked together, side by side, she asked me about myself. I told Mary my story of leaving the ministry behind to follow my dreams of being an entertainer. I told her about my odd jobs and all the things I was doing to get on my feet.

"There!" I said, when we had finished, and I started packing up my equipment.

But Mary wasn't done with me yet. She made lunch and insisted I eat it, which wasn't too hard since I had rushed out of Kate's house that morning without breakfast. After lunch, I finished packing up my supplies while Mary wrote me a check. When she handed it to me, the first things I saw were a five and a zero in the space for the payment amount. Wow! I thought. Mary paid me fifty dollars for this job! I was happy. But then I looked again. There was a second zero I had not noticed before. I gasped and looked at Mary in disbelief. "You can't pay me this much, Mary! Not five hundred dollars!" Mary just giggled. I wanted to hug her. "Are you a saint?" I asked her. She giggled. "An angel?" I swear I saw her face light up like the sun. She just giggled again. I tried to hand the check back to her, but she would have none of it.

"Don't tell me what to do with my money!" she said, laughing. "I can pay you whatever I want." I could tell I was losing this battle. "And besides," she continued, "I want you to come back in a few weeks and help me out some more."

"Wow! Are you sure?" I said.

"Yes," she answered.

I carefully placed her check in my wallet. "I'll come back and do whatever work you can find for me to do. I owe you now."

She shook her head, still grinning, then, "Wait just one minute," she said, and disappeared into a bedroom. She came back out with a plastic bag full of loose change and handed it to me. "Here, take this, too." The bag was heavy, and when I counted the loose change later, it ended up being about a hundred and fifty dollars. But she still wasn't done. She opened the front hallway closet and pointed to a microwave oven sitting on the floor there. "Take that thing, too," she said, pointing.

Humbled and amazed, I stammered, "Wow, really? Thank you, Mary! You *are* an angel." I could hardly believe my good fortune, or as my dad says, my blessing. I thanked Mary profusely and told her to call me if she needed anything at all.

I got back in my truck flabbergasted and happy. I could hardly wait to tell Kate. I drove to where she worked and ran to meet her when I saw her on the sidewalk, waving the check and jumping up and down. We danced and hugged right there on the sidewalk. "Davey, you're so magical!" Kate said. "Everything you do turns to gold. You don't know how much power you have."

Well, I didn't know about that. I still don't know if the power that came through me that day flowed from some higher aspect of my own being, as Kate said, or Divine grace. Still, I appreciated Kate's confidence in me; I have always loved her for that. Later, when I did the math, I realized that Mary's check would cover the payments that were due on my two big student loans that month and I'd still have money left over for food and gas. I gave the weighty bag of change to Kate for partial payment toward rent.

My faith grew as a result of what I came to think of as the "miracle of Mary." My trust that I was being taken care of, even when I wasn't aware of it, was stronger. I was more convinced than ever that a loving, mysterious Divine presence cared about me, that I lived in an abundant universe, and that following my bliss produced magic within and around me, despite imperfection, evil, pain, and lots of times when things had not turned out the way I hoped. My personal confidence expanded. Life itself was encouraging me to live out my dreams.

Finances continued to be something of a struggle as I built the foundation for my new life. On some days my faith was strong, and on other days doubts crept in. I began to notice that faith and success seemed to be somehow connected for me. I was still using drugs, for one thing, and getting high continued to fog my thinking, interfere with my faith, and cloud my life. My addiction kept me eddying at the edges of the river. All the same, as I slogged my way through the days and nights during this period, help was always just a prayer away. As I look back on this time in my life, I see now that I was watched over and protected even when I rebelled and acted stupidly. Grace, unearned and Divine, carried me through life more often than my foolish pride wanted to admit.

The money Mary paid me for washing her windows was soon used up, and I continued working all my other part-time jobs to make ends meet. I hoped Mary would call me back soon, but I didn't sit around and wait for her call. I spent any money I made that didn't immediately get used up on living expenses to pay for the demo tape Kate and I were making for our duo, Lunar Disguise. My so-called leisure time went into learning balloon art and simple magic tricks. I bought my first cheap clown costume, complete with rainbow wig and messy face paint, for twenty dollars at a novelty shop. I spent the next year or so learning basic skills for being a birthday party clown. I made up some new Crazy Dave fliers and posted them everywhere I could think of. I went to the local library and volunteered to make balloon shapes at their upcoming book sale. I had learned by then how to make a dog, a sword, a mouse, and a bunny rabbit. I started asking around about other children's performers in the area and joined the Golden Gate Clown Association. I answered an ad I found at the Stanford Student Center and became a kids' "fun fitness instructor" for Barry Ruttenberg's Fit Kids classes.

~.~

Barry ran his Fit Kids business at several Bay Area schools and recreation centers. He introduced me to the world of preschool in 1992, and he helped me learn how to entertain four-year-olds. He showed me how to work with groups of kids by teaching them exercise, games, and teamwork in fun, silly ways. He taught me how to lead kids in parachute games and field hockey; eventually he paid me to step in for him and do his fun fitness routines at private birthday parties.

Barry is a natural clown. I loved it when he and I improvised slapstick routines that made kids laugh. There's nothing like hearing kids belly laugh. It's so cute and pure. It brings me joy every time I hear it, and it makes me happy just to hear that sound.

Barry's classes and parties helped me to cultivate the physical comedy I now use in all of my shows; he encouraged and inspired me as I developed my fledgling clown show. He even booked "Crazy Dave's Magical Musical Show" at some of his parties. When I told him about the miraculous help I received from Mary, he said that I had lots of good karma built up from helping people when I was a minister and that's why I had the "money miracles" from Mary.

Whether or not that was true was not nearly as important as the fact that he said it to me. I respected Barry, and when he recognized that my positive actions had positive consequences it corroborated something I already felt and was beginning to truly believe, that the universe is organically responsive to us. Human beings, microcosms of the universe, interact with the macrocosmic universe and it co-creates life with us. We reap what we sow. Barry's comments reaffirmed my belief in a friendly, abundant, interactive, and moral universe. Our actions play a part in the ongoing creation of the universe. For every cause, there's an effect. What goes around comes around.

Every time the bills loomed large and it looked as if I wouldn't have enough money to pay my bills, I would pray about it. I know this sounds made up, but it's true: Every time I was down to my last dollar or less and prayed about it, Mary called. She even asked me to drive her to her bank in Oakland and paid me a thousand dollars, in cash, for the service! I could never force it, and if, in my fears about the future, I tried to pray for her to call me before I truly needed the money, it never worked. Her calls always and only came when I truly needed money. My friends used to tease me that Mary wanted me to be her gigolo, but she never asked me for anything other than rides to her bank in Oakland or help with washing windows or moving furniture.

And here's the eerie thing: As soon as my clown business took off, she never called me again. I called her from time to time, because I cared about her and I wanted to know if she was okay. Several years later, I got a call from a state agency asking if I knew Mary. She had died and my thank you cards and notes had been found in her home; they thought I was a relative. I'll always be grateful for my "earth angel" Mary for helping me to get a good start with my new life as an entertainer. She showed me generosity not only with money but with love and time, too. In many ways, Mary's generosity inspired me to be a more generous person myself.

All in all, Mary called me eight times. Most of the money she gave me went into launching my birthday party business. I spent five hundred dollars for a professional clown costume from Priscilla Mooseburger Originals, took out a quarter-page ad in the *Peninsula Parent Magazine*, purchased some ads in the yellow pages, hired a photographer for head shots and slick business cards, and bought some better magic tricks, juggling props, and other necessary tools of the clown trade. If it hadn't been for Mary, I might not have been able to purchase these materials and kick off my clown business within that first year, surely not as quickly as I did.

As my dreams began to take on more reality, and the clown and the rock star I wanted to be began to materialize, life became a lot more fun for me. I was having the time of my life. I remember driving down El Camino Real one day in Menlo Park thinking, "Here I am in sunny California." I had to pinch myself to make sure I wasn't dreaming. I had spent the morning shopping for magic tricks at the House of Humor in Redwood City and was excited to get home and practice. I was giggling as I drove, because ideas of how I was going to tailor the tricks to fit my first-ever clown show filled my mind. Then it struck me. I felt like a kid again. I was reliving a part of my childhood,

I reflected, the part that had become suppressed at the time of my dad's accident. Crazy Dave and the budding rock star with Kate in Lunar Disguise signified a journey back to my childhood dreams; I was returning to the person I was meant to be. I was picking up where I had left off when I made my sisters and friends laugh as the Sunday school class clown. I was even getting to be like Paul McCartney, too, not just by "playing" a broom, but by actually playing, with some skill, a real, adult-sized guitar. I felt happy, innocent, and free, but now I was also an adult and I was beginning to experience some prosperity, kind of like Richie Rich, I thought with a grin. I was even able to buy some of the things I had wanted to buy as a kid. The kid and the adult were consolidating inside of me, and I was having a blast. I was arriving at the place I had started from, but knowing it for a second time. The momentum of my life continued on an upward swing, and the miracles kept coming. I was a sponge, and I soaked up new ideas and influences around me.

Those first few years of doing Crazy Dave shows would never have continued without Barry's fun fitness classes and parties. When Barry obtained a purple dinosaur costume, I had an opportunity to make a lot more money by playing Barney the Dinosaur. Although I cringe now to admit it, I portrayed Barney quite well. In some ways, Barney was the low point in my quest to become a well established, full-time performing clown, but it paid the bills at that time and gave me lots of party entertainment business. For about a year, I played Barney, sometimes for as many as eight parties per weekend. Looking back, I think I really paid my dues.

At the end of that phase, three back-to-back parties where I played Barney turned out really awful. The first was yet another birthday party, after which the honoree's dad took me into his garage to pay me. I was still dressed as Barney, and let me tell you, that costume could get really uncomfortable, especially on a warmish day, as that one was. After he handed me cash, the dad pointed over to the washing machine where lines of cocaine were laid out for Barney to snort. "You can't give Barney lines of blow!" I protested. "That is just wrong!" I pictured Barney with white powder all over his purple snout, sniffing, wiping his nose, and talking too fast. The kids I had just connected with would be bewildered and confused if they saw that, I thought. "No, thanks," I said, and left, more than a little shaken.

The next event was a picnic for postal workers held in the Santa Cruz Mountains. Again, I showed up in my big Barney costume. The drive from San Mateo should have given me time to calm down, but something about the day felt wrong to me, and I was still feeling out of sorts from my encounter with the birthday party dad with the cocaine. The picnic, set among the redwood trees, was no picnic for Barney. The day was more than a little warm, and I was hot and sweaty in my big purple costume. The show must go on, I reflected, and approached a group of kids to get started. Suddenly, out of nowhere, one of the adults at the party, drunk and trying to impress the other picnickers, kicked off the show by giving Barney a left hook.

I had had enough. I tore off my Barney head in a rage, and little kids screamed and ran away frightened. "Barney took his head off!" a child screamed in dismay. I reprimanded the drunk as calmly as I could and walked away disgusted. I didn't even care that kids were running away from me, completely freaked out. I slammed the door of my truck and drove to the next party.

When I got to the next party, I put the Barney costume on again and walked into the back yard. I didn't see any kids at all, but only several scantily clad and very sexy women. It was a hot day, after all, and there I was, sweating away inside my Barney costume. And then I saw him--one little three-year-old kid. "Uh, hi, boys and, uh, girls," I stammered. "It's Barney the Dinosaur!" I exclaimed with forced glee. To the mom who hired me, I whispered, "Where are all the kids?"

"Oh," she said, "this is just for my three-year-old. He loves Barney."

"Ah," I said. "Okay. Well, then c'mon, everybody!" I did my best to generate a little enthusiasm, but I was wilting inside that stuffy costume. I motioned for the sexy moms to circle up, because you couldn't expect one little three-year-old to do the hokey pokey all by himself with Barney, right? "Okay, boys and girls," I encouraged, "let's do the hokey pokey." Everything was going pretty well for a little while, and we circled up and sang and danced the hokey pokey. Then, suddenly, the little boy darted off and ran toward the house.

"Where are you going?" his mom yelled after him.

"I have to go to the bathroom," he said and disappeared into the house. There I was, standing in a circle of women wearing tight shorts and tank tops. My range of vision with Barney's head plopped over my own was limited, to say the least, but even so I managed to get an eyeful of this lovely gathering of the female form. In a flash, though, the moms dropped below my line of vision and I couldn't see them anymore. It was as if they had all disappeared. I could hear them laughing, and I was tempted to take Barney's head off again, but I remembered what had happened when I did that at the postal picnic. Instead, I moved Barney's head to the side just a bit and peeked out from under it. The women were rolling around on the grass, laughing hysterically. Just then, I felt something warm and wet on Barney's right leg and propped open Barney's head at the neck a bit more to look down. That adorable little three-year-old boy had his pants down to his ankles and was peeing on my leg!

I handed my pee-soaked costume to Barry later that day and said, "I quit." I never did that stupid gig again. Thus began Daffy Dave, full time.

~.~

After a while, once my birthday party business was well established, I visited my parents in Seattle. By then, I had a store of memorably moving experiences with kids, and I shared a touching story with them from my clowning experiences. Mom and Dad laughed at my story, then sighed, nodding. They had similar stories about their grandkids, my nieces and nephews. "You know," Dad said, "I truly believe that our job as adults is to give kids good memories. That way, when dark times show up, they can draw on those positive, happy memories and gain hope, strength, and faith that life is worth living."

"You're right, Dad," I said. "I remember lots of happy experiences from my childhood, and truly, when I think of them, they do reinforce in me that life is basically good and worth living."

I believe that people are basically good. Many of the good memories I have of growing up came from adults who, probably without thinking about it, gave me good memories to draw upon later. I remember one of my dad's friends juggling oranges in our kitchen in Minneapolis in the late 1960's. I remember another of Dad's friends, Phil Johnson, playing basketball with me when I was five. I remember another of Dad's friends taking Kevin Bauer and me for a thrilling ride to the corner store in his shiny new red Corvette Stingray. I remember my dad taking me to watch the Minnesota Twins; I remember these and a thousand more good, positive, happy experiences, many of which I described earlier in this book, that adults gave to me when I was a kid. They gave me good memories that continue to uplift me in direct and indirect ways, confirming in me a deep faith in the goodness of life and trust in the universe and other people. Now, as an adult, I am privileged to give good memories to kids as Daffy Dave whenever I make them laugh and encourage them to sing, dance, and marvel at the magic of life. Life circles back to where it started and expands to a kind of second innocence that blesses the world if we seek to follow our bliss back to it and let it flow through us.

Chapter Thirteen: Springtime for Daffy Dave and Comedy

"A thousand clowns I'll bring you
Just to make you laugh
A blue baboon and a red raccoon
A lavender giraffe...."
--from the song "A Thousand Clowns"
by Judy Holliday

In those early days of performing as Crazy Dave and doing all those odd jobs, during 1992 and 1993, there were sometimes long spells between gigs or the miracles of thousand-dollar errands for Mary. The work of building my business was real work. It took time and effort to learn magic, juggling, balloon art, basic comedy and performing skills, not to mention the marketing and salesmanship techniques that I needed to acquire and perfect, along with all the other nuts and bolts of running a business. Every now and then, I'd learn a new trick or skill, make up a well received funny bit in a show, or book a last-minute gig that would pay another bill, and I would feel hopeful again. But depression skulked in the wings, and I often felt discouraged. Was I just a hack? I wondered if I could really make it as an entertainer. I felt intimidated when I watched established performers with advanced skills, and I doubted I would ever measure up. I once told one of them that I felt that way, and his response was, "We're equals, Dave." It was a generous response, and it was just what I needed to hear; I was encouraged to go on.

By the spring of 1993, Crazy Dave had become Daffy Dave, and I entered what I think of now as my honeymoon phase with being an entertainer. I had good days and bad days during this time. On the good days, I bounded out of bed in the mornings, excited by the creativity that filled my life and thrilled about new friends, exhilarating work opportunities, and fresh ideas. On the bad days, I struggled with addiction, financial difficulties, and performer burn-out. My self-image took some serious blows with some failed romantic relationships, and I found myself wondering what kind of woman would want to date a clown anyway. The hard work of building my business seemed tedious and difficult, and I thought more than once of returning to my old life as a pastor. I missed the security of a steady income, and my old quiet life looked tempting to me.

Finances were an ever-present struggle. I constantly felt stress to make ends meet financially, and every month was a new challenge just to survive. I was burdened by debt, so much so that I dreaded answering the phone for fear it was another call from a collection agency. I was using drugs again, especially marijuana and alcohol, and my addiction was draining my energy, scattering my focus, and leaving me feeling depressed, guilty, ashamed, anxious, apathetic, and downright miserable. When I look back on my journal entries from that period, I can see that, over and over again, I tried to quit using drugs, but I simply could not do it on my own. It is very painful to me now to reread those entries as I write this book. Those old feelings, the secret remorse and misery I carried during those days, come back to haunt me. It was a heavy burden. Today, the memory of that pain serves to remind me how much I appreciate being free from active addiction and compels me to work my recovery program daily so that I don't return to that personal hell.

One of the main reasons I wanted to quit using drugs was that I was seriously considering a return to parish ministry. I knew without a doubt that I would have to leave drugs behind once and for all if I were to go back to my old profession; I couldn't go back to being a pastor if I were still an active addict. Returning to parish ministry as a drug user was simply not an option, but I was getting desperate about my short-term survival. My entertainment business appeared to be in danger of utter collapse, and I was beginning to get a sense that my drug use might be the root of the problem. On the other hand, I was afraid that if I weren't using drugs, I would no longer be funny. Life would be boring, I thought, and so would I.

~.~

On Christmas Eve 1992 I made this entry in my journal: "...I feel the confusion of my lost place in the world without a career, compared to my siblings.... I mean, even though I do have work with clowning, [washing] windows, etc., and my band is gradually developing, I still feel like I'm just in a period of blind experimentation and that my new creative career is tenuous and possibly really not for me. Sometimes I wish I could just die or check into a mental ward, but I'm so disillusioned with modern mental wards that dying seems a better option or maybe running away into the wilderness...."

I kept going, though, and by the summer of 1994, some of that hopelessness had fallen away. I was two years into developing my dream to be an entertainer, and I was growing more confident in my performing skills and my ability to run my entertainment business. Here's a journal entry from July 1, 1994: "I've lived in California for almost two years now. I'm living on the edge, but hey, I'm still paying the bills, even if it's one at a time and the slightest unpredictable auto, home, or health expense could possibly ruin me. Yet, I've never been so close to 'trust' before. I have to trust! The edge I'm on almost demands this of me. [It] would simply drain my energy if I took the half-empty-glass approach to life."

In another journal entry later that same month, I wrote: "Who knows what all this new level of performing activity is doing to me? It feels like I'm definitely entering a serious point of no return with music and clowning, etc. [It's] as if I'm reaping [the fruits of my efforts and persistence in] the lifestyle I set out to live [two] years ago, like I got what I wished for and now I [need to] deal with it, manage it, not let it overwhelm me and consume my soul. Surely it is a vibrant and 'Dave Mampel-friendly' vehicle to express myself [in], and I thank my higher self for guiding me into this mode...."

Later in the same entry, I wrote: "I'm getting back to balance and economy of motion again, but, oh God, I could use a vacation away from all my contacts and scenes here...." As I see it now, I was beginning to become aware of my introvert's need not to let the extroverted activities burn me out. This was the beginning of my awareness of how vacations and travel were ways to save myself from becoming devoured by creativity and performing.

~.~

As my fledgling clown business started to grow, I knew I wanted my clown character to be colorful, funny, magical, musical, clumsy yet acrobatic, and silly. I did not want him to be scary, or at least, not too scary. I knew for sure my rudimentary clown character needed to change. The "Crazy Dave" moniker was too crude and not very marketable. I searched for a kinder, gentler clown name. I wanted it to sound cute and have alliteration; I got that inspiration from a local kid's magician who was successfully performing and running his entertainment business. I brainstormed about a number of possible new names, wrote them down, and mulled them over. That very day, two people, one of my guitar students and a client of Dave Does Windows, both suggested "Daffy Dave." Ding! It was perfect! I loved it and so did everyone else. One of my friends, who also entertains as a clown, nailed it when she said, "Daffy Dave is a big kid who loves kids."

While I felt a little disappointed that I had not come up with my new clown name or basic character description on my own, as I look back on it now, it was as if life itself knighted me with this new name, this new character, through the people in my life. Like a Native American brave, I had received my new spirit name from the tribe. This new character, Daffy Dave, conferred upon me by my community, reflected the transformation my consciousness was making from pastor to clown, from false persona to real self, from wounded child to a big kid who loves kids. It represented psychological integration, actualization, healing, wholeness, and personal truth. I once was lost, but now I was found. I didn't understand these things at the time, and maybe I'm waxing a little too philosophical about it now, but this is how I understand it today. Daffy Dave felt at home in my skin. It was as if Daffy Dave had been hiding inside of me since my own eight-year-old self went underground after my dad's fall. Daffy Dave was already who I had been for most of my life; Daffy Dave came out to play in college, in seminary, and even when I was a minister, but especially, Daffy Dave was who I was as a young child before dad's accident. Once again, other people knew who I was before I did.

~.~

I stopped wearing white face paint when I noticed that some kids were scared of clown make-up. An all-white face suggests death, so it's no wonder that kids and even some adults are freaked out by clowns. I was trying to build my business, so in a very practical sense, I wanted kids and parents to like my show. Any decent parent would probably not want to hire a clown with a reputation for traumatizing children. Besides, I didn't want to walk into a roomful of kids just to hear them scream and cry. It's hard to be funny when your audience is terrified. Clowns already have a reputation for being crazy and scary. Remember Stephen King's horrific clown, Pennywise, in the movie *It*? That movie ruined things for a lot of party clowns who were trying to pay the bills.

However, I soon learned that just a little fear helps to keep the aggressive kids at bay, among other things. Personally, I loved being a little scared as a kid, and I think it's good to scare kids sometimes, but not too much. Studies have shown that some fear-inducing situations actually expand the brain's synapse patterns and help us to learn problem-solving skills. I know that when I'm a little nervous or afraid, but not overly so, especially before a big show, the adrenalin starts flowing and I think more quickly on my feet. I become more lucid and articulate with my lines, my gestures, my timing, and my humor.

The Pueblo Indians used the Kachina doll ceremony to scare children intentionally. They wanted children to learn to run to the elders in the community for protection, comfort, and guidance when they were frightened. The ceremony taught the children of the community that real life had scary moments in it. If they could be taught these things before terrible things happened to and around them, they wouldn't be so traumatized by life's sad and frightening events, and they would be more likely to develop courage and wisdom. The Kachina doll ceremony created a bond between the generations and helped to strengthen the entire Pueblo culture. Fairy tales teach kids these same basic lessons. Bowdlerizing fairy tales and scary stories for kids not only makes these stories less readable and enjoyable, it does children a disservice by diminishing the effect of the story and making it less potent. It deceives children and robs them of opportunities to face their own very real fears and grow beyond them--always with the help of caring elders nearby, of course. We need to be there to comfort kids when they hear these scary stories and interact with them to strengthen their faith, courage, and problem-solving skills.

Daffy Dave took flight like the Wright Brothers at Kitty Hawk, and as he did, I found it harder and harder to find time and creative energy for my evolving folk/pop/rock band, The Shift. I loved The Shift. It allowed me to experience my dream of being a cool rock star for a while. Kate sang back-up vocals and played tambourine, and she sang solo on one of our cover tunes, "Fever." She was developing a great onstage presence. David Wilson, a long-time Bay Area magician and entertainer, helped fine-tune our endeavor, played bass, and sang both backup and lead vocals. We had a super lead guitarist and a drummer, too. I delighted in being up on stage and looking out over the crowd to see folks dancing to my original songs. I loved to feel the ecstasy of singing harmonies with a full band; the way the various instruments and voices amplified the music was thrilling to me.

After a successful gig for about a hundred people in a Kundalini Yoga class at the Masonic Hall in Menlo Park, we decided to start recording rough tracks for an album, and we joked about possible titles. I suggested "When The Shift Hits the Fan." Dave said our second album should be called "Bull

Shift," and our lead guitarist said our final album could be called "No Shift, Dude." Our rehearsals took more and more time, our equipment got heavier, and my marijuana-altered mind stumbled a lot. Sometimes, I forgot the words to songs right in the middle of performing. I wondered if I had what it took to be a rocker. I was losing momentum, not to mention poise. My former parishioner's words came back to haunt me: I wouldn't make it with my music if I continued to get high.

My mental hard drive was maxed out with Daffy Dave shows, too. I would play all night with the band and then be too worn out to optimally practice, prepare, and perform my clown shows for kids during the day. Daffy Dave was paying the bills, and I knew I had to make a choice. I knew I couldn't continue living both lives. I needed to cut back on the time and energy I spent on the band to protect my "day job" as a clown. Other interpersonal issues popped up among the band members, too, and played a part in my decision. I did some painful soul-searching and reluctantly decided to quit the band. Telling the others was hard. Dave understood since he made his living from family entertainment, too. It was tougher for the rest of the band. Most of all, I hated to disappoint Kate; I felt I was really letting her down. I could see how happy and confident our music had made her feel.

I took Kate to lunch and tried to explain myself. I simply couldn't handle both endeavors anymore, I told her, and she tried to understand, but it was hard for her to accept. A few years later, I was happy to hear that Kate had joined other bands. After that, she found her own niche in family entertainment, leading kids' classes and parties in a kids' music program called "Music Together." She later thanked me for inspiring her to pursue her own dreams. How gratifying it was to me to know that in pursuing my dreams I also inspired Kate to follow hers.

~.~

After the band broke up, I felt a huge sense of relief. I was able to focus all my energies on developing my Daffy Dave character, honing my comic entertainment skills, becoming more

189

proficient with juggling and magic, and running my business. I continued working some of Mr. Barry's Fit Kids parties to fill the gaps in my earnings as Daffy Dave, but I was able to drop my odd jobs because I was making enough money as a clown to pay the bills, if only barely. My clowning business continued to grow, and I gradually raised the prices I charged per show. In the beginning, I would perform for a birthday party for only eighty dollars, but eventually I was able to charge one hundred seventy-five dollars for the same package.

However, in the late winter of 1995, I hit a wall and found myself once again struggling to pay the bills. Dave Wilson and his wife Colleen invited me to their home for dinner on a regular basis because they knew I could hardly afford to buy food. I got really depressed about my situation and decided to see if my family in Seattle would put me up if I moved back home. I'll never forget that call. Mom and my sisters loved the idea. "Oh, come home, Dave," Mom said, "as soon as you can!" But when Dad came on the line, it was a different story.

"So, what do you think, Dad?" I asked. "Would it be okay with you if I came home?" There was a long silent pause. "Oh," I said. "You're right, Dad!" I felt pretty embarrassed. I read my dad's silence to mean that I should man up and deal with life, not go running home just because things were tough for me.

After a moment, "It's not that you can't come home, son," he said. "Of course you're always welcome here." He paused again. "It's just that...."

I interrupted. "Oh no, Dad, you're right. I'm glad you were silent. Your silence says it all."

"Dave," he said, "I just think you've got to give it another try."

Swallowing both my pride and my fear, I said, "You're absolutely right, Dad. Thank you. I will." I hung up the phone feeling chagrined, but also feeling a measure of confidence I hadn't felt before. Dad believed in me and my new life as Daffy Dave! He didn't want me to take the easy way out, to give up. I felt chastened but also reassured. Somehow, Dad's fatherly response to me had increased my stature, as well as his, in my eyes. He became a stronger father to me again in that call, and I felt he was wise not to acquiesce. That moment led to healing as time went on. I began to let go, bit by bit, of trying to be the father of the family myself, and, inside myself, I gradually allowed the family authority to flow back toward my dad. The spell cast by the scared little eight-year-old inside of me began to crack when my dad kept his silence for those few seconds on the phone. I grew up a little, and my relationship with my dad took a turn for the better. Sometime during all of this, I had a heartfelt exchange with my pops and he said, "You're smarter than me, Dave." Without missing a beat, I shot back, "Yeah but, Dad, you're wiser than me." Pops quickly retorted, "You see, son, your saying that I'm wiser than you proves that you're smarter than me." We both laughed, and we still joke about that exchange.

That very night, right after my sobering phone conversation with Dad, I met my good friend Steve Koehler and his girlfriend at the time, Shawna, for tea at Printer's Inc. Café in Palo Alto. I told them how hard life had been for me lately and how depressed I had gotten about trying to make ends meet as Daffy Dave. I shared with them about the phone conversation I had just had with my dad. I looked up to see Steve and Shawna smiling at each other. Shawna turned to me and smiled. "You're not going to believe this, Dave," she said, "but they want you to work full time at C.A.R." C.A.R., now called Abilities United, is a not-for-profit organization that provides services for developmentally delayed individuals. Shawna and Steve both worked there and had invited me to perform for their adult clients. I had performed a free Daffy Dave show there just a few days earlier.

"What?" I said. "Are you kidding me?" A real job? With benefits? And just in the nick of time, too. I had been having knee pain, and I knew I needed surgery. I could hardly believe my good fortune.

This was not the first time in my life that I had volunteered somewhere and then a job opened up, as I mentioned in previous chapters. Here it was again! This was yet another living example of creating possibilities out of just doing the next right thing. This is how it works. This is what you do. I know that when I do things for the wrong reasons, life generally doesn't work out so well; but when my heart is in the right place, when I genuinely come from love and service, sometimes life falls into place in the most remarkable ways. The universe will meet you halfway if you're making yourself available by getting out there, volunteering, trying new ventures, ideas, experiments, making phone calls, whatever it is you know how to do. This way of living continues to work for me over and over again.

Beginning in March 1995, I worked seven days a week for a full year. My weekdays were spent working with developmentally delayed adults at C.A.R., and I performed as Daffy Dave on the weekends. I even worked as Daffy Dave some weekday evenings, too. I was determined to take advantage of this opportunity to finally pay off all my debts and get those creditors off my back. My new medical benefits allowed me to get my knee taken care of, too, for which I was very grateful.

My new job at C.A.R. left me humbled and grateful in other ways. I worked with severely disabled human beings who surprised me with their humanity and their humor. Gratitude for my own abilities and my life in general grew within me, and I learned compassion for folks with Down syndrome, autism, cerebral palsy, and other conditions that lead to developmental delays in human beings. My heart opened and I became more accepting and patient of others. My own humanity evolved, and I became a more tolerant person as a result of my time at C.A.R.

Even my sense of humor and physical comedy underwent a subtle change. I would clown around with the clients, pretending to trip or "accidentally" bang into a door, in efforts to get them to laugh. They loved my jokes and slapstick routines, but even better, they made me laugh, too. Some of my guys were very funny. There was this one guy who, I remember, would hold a phone to his ear and pretend to have a serious conversation; or someone would pretend to be an animal. Sometimes I still miss my dear C.A.R. clients and their antics.

~.~

One year later, in March 1996, I resigned from my job at C.A.R. and marched into March as Daffy Dave, full time and debt free. During the preceding year, I had paid off thirty-four thousand dollars of debt and grown as a person. I had gotten surgery on my knee, and my wisdom teeth had been extracted. I had spent almost two thousand dollars on new promotional packs and tricks for my business. I had reduced my drug use significantly, for the most part because I simply did not have the time to spare, and therefore had about half as much "toxic fog," as I called it in my journal. "It's been a fruitful year," I wrote in my journal on March 18, 1996, "though very draining and lots of times [I was] sick or burned out and [was] barely able to enjoy myself, my shows, my friends." With my resignation from C.A.R., springtime for Daffy Dave was upon me.

That year was a watershed for my confidence as an entrepreneur and as an entertainer. In June 1996, I broke my previous revenue records when I had my first four-thousand-dollar month in gross sales as Daffy Dave. I fell in love, too, this time with another clown, a woman with whom I was so smitten that I actually quit using drugs during the six short months we were together. When she and I broke up, my heart broke, too. I was a mess for quite a while afterward, and I fell right back into active addiction. All the same, I blossomed during that time, and in many ways I started to hit my stride as Daffy Dave. I surged with new energy and confidence. I remember thinking to myself that I had done so many clown shows during the previous four years that my brain was permanently altered. I found myself "thinking in clown." How, I wondered, laughing, could I ever re-enter society as a serious, normal person? I doubted that I could go back to another job even if I wanted to, and I certainly didn't want to! The fruits of Daffy Dave were ripening in 1996. I was now inspired and curious to see how many harvests I could garner from this wonderful new tree in the orchard of my new clown life.

Chapter Fourteen:
Dark Night of the Clown

"Comedy is a man in trouble."
--Jerry Lewis

Addiction continued to keep me in its grip, and its darkness was distracting and draining. By December of 1997, things had gotten really bad. Pot didn't get me high anymore; it just made me feel depressed. My thoughts were garbled, and my conversations were dull. I could hardly read books anymore. All I wanted to do was stay in my room and get high. In my efforts to change my ways, I started attending church whenever I didn't have birthday shows on a Sunday, and I found a spiritual director to whom I could turn. I went to an acupuncturist and herbalist, Joan Kobara, for some stomach pains I had been having for about a year, and her work with me made those pains go away. But I was still unhappy. I knew by then that my drug use was at the root of my problems, but I couldn't stop using marijuana, even though I truly wanted to stop. I needed help to deal with my addiction and I knew it. I was desperate, and that's a horrible feeling. It wasn't until I returned to Twelve Step recovery in early 1998 that I would learn that my desperation was a gift, a gift that led me to stop my destructive behaviors.

The medieval Christian mystic Saint John of the Cross wrote about the dark night of the soul. As I understand this concept, it is a common human experience that we often think of as depression, but it is more of a spiritual cleansing. What happens to us in a dark night of the soul is that we lose interest in everything that usually engages and excites us. We don't like the food we eat, we lose interest in our favorite hobbies, our lovers bore us, our vocations become meaningless, nature doesn't inspire us with its beauty, music doesn't lift our spirits, and so on. These days, this experience can be mislabeled as clinical depression but, depending on the individual, such may not be the case. These experiences of apathy can instead be necessary for personal renewal.

It's important to honor and accept the dark night of the soul as a natural process of growth in our lives. If we can let the darkness be and allow it to pass naturally, it will cleanse us of obsessive or meaningless attachments to interests and activities that no longer serve us. Such a process can reveal to us what we need to change to make our lives happier and more meaningful. This cleansing of our attachments will renew our appreciation for what interests and engages us in our lives. It's like letting a field lie fallow for a season or two so that nutrients can rebuild in the soil and new growth can begin. It's like the phases of the moon. Sometimes we wax and sometimes we wane. Sometimes we're bright and full of light and sometimes we become dark and hidden in the sky. I have learned--and had to relearn--how to recognize these cycles, and then how to accept them and let them teach me what I needed to learn. I've learned that, after the darkness, the new moon appears and new growth takes place. When the moon grows full, we savor and celebrate that growth, and then the cycle repeats itself. The waning moon grows dark again and offers us a time to empty and reflect.

~.~

"In the middle of the journey of our life I found myself within a dark woods where the straight way was lost."
--Dante Alighieri, Inferno

My understanding of the medieval mystical concept *via negativa* is that a person can learn what God is by discerning what God is not. However, I have found it even more useful to apply *via negativa* to self-discovery; I can learn who I am by being who I am not in a process of elimination. I've practiced *via negativa* this way my whole life and will probably continue to do so until I die, maybe even beyond. In my lifetime so far, I've tried many ideas, pursued various vocations, worked at a variety of jobs, and experimented with my values, spiritual practices, religions, hobbies, clothes, dating partners, relationships, residences, towns, sports, books, films, music, and on and on. Some of these ideas or pursuits have changed because of personal growth, or I've become curious about an opposite idea, or my interest has faded over time; but some have remained because they've continued to delight and fascinate me and advance my self-actualization. Those pursuits that remain fit my personality and align with my essential, overall life values; they continue to interest and engage me. *Via negativa* assists me in this process of self-discovery.

I tried to be a minister and discovered its tight suit was too restrictive for me. This was a process of *via negativa*. I learned more about who I was by being who I was not. I left behind my dreams of being a rock star in order to allow Daffy Dave to grow and flourish. This, too, was a process of elimination. Again, I discovered who I was by being who I was not. This process helps me to accept my need to have lots of quiet time to restore my introvert energies. When I spend too much time in extroverted activities, I become over-stimulated, which leads to my feeling grumpy and distressed, even sick.

My family likes to remind me of the time I was in one of those states when I had just come off a long run of shows in December a few winters ago. Our family had rented a big cabin on Mount Baker in the Cascade Mountains for our annual get-together. When everyone poured out of their cars and into the rental house, the cabin exploded with loud and chaotic activity. I responded by getting really upset and yelled out, "Whose idea was it to bring all these kids and dogs anyway?" Dad and my sisters laughed and shooed me upstairs to take a hot bath.

Still feeling grumpy, I wanted to add oil to the bath to soften my dry skin, but all I could find was olive oil. When my brother in-law Troy Olsen went up to use the tub later, he noticed a ring of olive oil in the tub. He came downstairs and asked, "Hey, who cooked spaghetti in the bathtub?" Everyone looked at me and laughed. By then, I was feeling better, so I joined in the laughter, too. When my family gathers and the stories start flying, this old chestnut always makes an appearance.

I played the diversion of getting high on drugs through to the bitter end, and I very painfully learned who I was not. Concerning my addiction, however, I was confronted by a paradox. I learned both who I was and who I was not. When I finally accepted that I was an active addict, I broke through the chains of denial that held that addiction in place. I now fully accept that I am an addict and will always be an addict. Today, by God's grace, by the power of the universe, through life's own beautiful mercy, I am an addict in recovery. Every day, I must choose newly to be an addict in recovery. Today, I want only what works for me and aligns with my deepest values and most cherished passions, desires, and interests. I choose to live in ways that resonate with my own highest truth.

Via negativa is an ongoing process. It teaches me about my love of gardening, travel, films, and music. Through its unfolding I find meditation styles that fulfill my needs, and I gravitate toward friendships and relationships that best fit me. Reflective endeavors such as writing that help me to observe, create, and be myself are an important part of this process. Writing, conversation, contemplation, meditation, and prayer reinforce the insights of self-discovery that come to me by way of *via negativa*, and they help me to let go of the elements that fall away from me in this process of elimination. In introspective moments and reflective activities, I become more focused. Discernment of what I like and dislike, what I value and what I do not want, what I need and what I can discard, who I am and who I am not, become clarified and affirmed.

I went through a period of performing adult shows at big corporations, and that was yet another *via negativa* phase. During that time, not only did I learn a lot about who I was not as a performer, I gained a lot of practical show business experience, too. My poise improved, and my chutzpah swelled. I developed new comedy routines, and my comedy writing got better. My confidence increased, and I felt a renewed appreciation for my background and my values, my skills and my talents. Best of all, that experience taught me that I was better suited for family entertainment; I have an incredible connection to kids. Once more, I learned who I was by being who I was not.

From 1996 to 1998, four to six years after I left the ministry to become an entertainer, I was engaged in a struggle to accept wholeheartedly who I was in the world, first as a comic performer and then, as a non-intoxicated "clean clown." I was growing as a person and a performer. My confidence in my skills and stage presence increased. I was making more money than ever before as a clown and was learning the art of being funny. I had finally decided the rock star wasn't really me, although I still love to play music and jam with other musicians. These days, playing music happens either in amateur settings or as a clown persona when I am the front man for the Daffy Dave Band. Working as a serious professional musician, especially performing in a band, is too over-stimulating, too intense, too focused for me. I find I'm just not able to remain present on stage with live band music, but I am able to be fully present while I'm performing solo clown routines. At least for now, that's how it is for me.

An entry from my journal on November 4, 1996, illustrates the energy I felt during that time in my life:

"Phew! Tired from eleven shows this weekend [I'm sure this included Friday night], but feeling an "alchemical" shift from being steeped in clowning, performing, and around other performers--so much validation from them, too--even an attractive, stronger older woman too! "[You] have great energy" she says! "Charming," she says, attracted to me. "Marry me," she says. You must be drunk! I think. She asked for my card to hire me for combo gigs with her "Rainbow Friends" group in schools, etc., plus for an adult show at her CD release party. Cool! Lots of other great feedback, too. It was like this huge shot in the arm, huge self-confidence boost, albeit externally based, that really helped put that big "clown grin" all over my body the next day (Monday). Geez, almost sweeter, maybe 'tis sweeter than sex with a true love!" I was so happy from all this validation, I blew off getting high that day.

During this time when my confidence as a comic performer and entrepreneur was growing, I was simultaneously struggling with several issues that delayed and distracted my growth in my new vocation. I was hurting inside from a break-up with a female comic entertainer; I was experiencing "performer burn-out" and trying to invent different characters and shows; my body was suffering from intestinal pains, knee strain, and other health issues; I was questioning whether or not I should go back to the parish ministry or even consider another career altogether; money was sometimes tight. Although I had almost all my debt paid off, I hadn't started a savings/investment strategy yet. By far the biggest drain was my continued use of drugs.

As I mentioned earlier, I had relapsed into active addiction after a romantic breakup. My drug use, in combination with the breakup itself, caused my self-esteem to sink to new lows. I had doubts that I would ever be able to have a committed relationship with a woman if I continued to perform as a clown. My anxieties reached new heights when I considered the fact that it had been a female clown who had broken up with me! But I also had to wonder if any woman at all would ever want to be in a committed relationship with me. I thought and even spoke aloud, "Yeah, like any woman is going to want to marry a clown. I mean, can you imagine her writing home and saying, 'Dear Mom and Dad, I just met this great clown....'"

My anxious logic followed this depressing path: If a woman clown doesn't feel comfortable being with a man clown, how would some non-clown woman be able to handle me? I found that some women were attracted to me at first, loved my sensitivity and humor, but then found they just couldn't commit to me because my life as a clown wasn't secure or stable enough for them, or it was too weird and unconventional for them. I wasn't good "nesting" material, particularly here in the

San Francisco Bay Area (or should I say, Pay Area?) where it costs about a billion dollars a year just to live in a storage unit. At least, this is the way I felt at the time, and this is how I perceived my romantic issues then. I wrote a song after this clown romance break-up called "Those Darn Clown Blues" and later recorded it on one of my Daffy Dave albums. When I recorded that song, I left out this verse:

"Now I had a lover, but she broke up with me.
How could I be her husband and a clown naturally?
She thought I was perfect in every way,
but when she saw my shoes she said, "No way!"
'Cause I'm a clown who can sing, but I'm also a ding-a-ling.
Yeah, it's true. I fall down for a living. I've got those darn clown blues."

Nevertheless, my overall growth as a comic entertainer and entrepreneur miraculously continued, despite my romantic troubles. I experimented with adult stand-up comedy in the spring of 1996 by going to a few open mic events at a comedy club in Sunnyvale called Rooster T. Feathers. I experienced a few moments of success in this arena, and then had the idea to create an adult corporate comedy show. I got the idea from a scene in the movie Larger than Life in which Bill Murray plays the role of a huckster motivational speaker. I wanted to create a character similar to his and perform comedy motivational seminars for corporations. I wanted to make more money as an entertainer, and I thought a fatter wallet might also help me attract a woman into my life. I figured if I made more money and worked in the corporate world, I would look more stable to a woman with nesting concerns, even if those concerns were unconscious to her. I also felt inspired by this new direction, and lots of ideas came to me, and I thought some of my pastor's training would help me come off as a professional.

~.~

I bought a suit, an easel, and a pointer, and I started writing material. I ended up performing for Chevron, Flextronics, Kent Electronics, and Stanford University, among others. Interestingly enough, my first corporate show fell into my lap while I was still enthusiastically putting together my props and material. I was working on my show at the house I called home at that time. It was one of a series of such houses, as I moved around a lot during that period. The phone rang and I answered. Someone's executive assistant at a big multi-national company asked for Daffy Dave. I hadn't advertised or marketed anything about my idea at that point, but she had found Daffy Dave in the phonebook and asked if I could put on a spoof motivational show. I was stunned. Yet again, the universe had reflected back to me what my heart and soul was putting out there, this time in the form of a phone call to invite me to perform a show I had just started developing. My journal entry from that day, November 8, 1996, captured my excitement:

"Okay, so YES I got that 'motivational guy' gig! Tuesday, November 19 at 12:30pm. YES! Okay, I got some great, great material already started! My character's suit envisioned, an easel board purchased, an outline for the show. Wow! A next level suddenly lifts me up outa nowhere, it appears, and it all converges. My education, experience, ministry, life background, clowning."

I worked on my material extensively after that call and prepared myself as well as I could. I felt I was expanding as a performer and felt renewed hope that my new vocation as Daffy Dave could be diversified into adult shows that would stimulate my creativity, growth, and prosperity. Here's my journal entry from the day of my first adult corporate comedy gig:

"Wow! I'm still flying from that corporate 'motivational guy' gig today! It couldn't have gone better. It really exceeded all my best expectations ('cause, believe me, I had some fearfully stupid-bad thoughts, too!). It represents a milestone in my comedy career. It was marked by utmost concern for those people as human beings, good people who needed from me, in my zany moments, 'ministry' of joy, love, innocence, faith, aspiration, values of love via comedy and fun!"

~.~

I have to chuckle when I think of the gall I had back then to pretend to be a motivational speaker, especially for a successful multinational corporation. Of course, that's what the CEO hired me to do, so that helped. He wanted to play a practical joke on a gathering of about two hundred salespeople, vice presidents, and managers.

I started out by welcoming everyone and summarizing my thoughts about the importance of team-building in any organization, spouting what sounded to me like ridiculous platitudes. Then I pulled out my easel and a large marker and spelled out the acronym I had made up for the occasion: E.A.R. "What do you think the E stands for?" I asked the crowd. "The A?" I paused for effect. "The R?" I got some good responses from the audience and had a fun field day of low-key comedy improvisation at that point.

After a few minutes, I defined the terms, telling them in my best life-coachy voice as I pointed to each letter on the easel in turn, "We can only achieve Excellence when we Remember to Appreciate each other." I paused briefly, "And the only way to do that is by listening, or E.A.R.," I said, spelling out the word "ear." These were the three big qualities, I passionately preached, that would help them grow and prosper. Then, while everyone was still politely pondering whatever it was they thought I was trying to say, I said, "Here, let me sing a song about these important concepts to help you understand what I'm getting at," and I pulled out my electric ukulele.

Then I wrapped a belt around my middle that was constructed to hold four mini amplifiers and made me look like a suicide bomber. "Okay, now," I told the crowd. "I want you to hold your hands up in the air, you know, like you're at a concert, and sway your arms back and forth in time to the music." A few people were starting to get the joke at this point, and the CEO was cracking up in the shadows and trying to hide it. "Lighters up! Help me out here! Show some enthusiasm!" I sang the E.A.R. song, a song I had made up that had a completely silly refrain. I tried to rally everyone to sing along on the chorus like a campy corporate version of "Kumbayah."

Some people in the audience were still politely listening to my pitch as if it were serious. I pulled out my colorful stage juggling balls and started spouting a bunch of hooey about the importance of juggling your career with home life, hobbies, coffee breaks, etc. I juggled the balls in column patterns and talked about the importance of money management. I talked about the value of tracking finances in "columns" and then did a juggling trick that looked like the three columns were still going up and down, but one hand was holding a ball and creating the illusion that a third column was going up and down by itself. I told them my accountant called that trick "fake columns," and that got a big laugh and a few more people started getting it. I did some magic tricks then, and more people caught on.

I asked the CEO to come up on stage along with two of his vice presidents who were in on the joke. "It's much easier," I explained, "to 'undo the knots' of our common problems in the workplace if we all pull together." At that point, the two veeps pulled scarves out of the CEO's shirt. At the end of a long sequence of scarves, out popped a black lacey bra, and of course I pretended to be completely flabbergasted as if that weren't supposed to happen. "Well, I guess there are all kinds of ways to deal with problems at work," I joked. What was remarkable to me as I reflected on my performance later was that I really and truly felt sincere, innocent, and caring during the whole performance, and I'm sure my pastoral presence came through, because folks warmed up to me.

I did a series of adult corporate comedy shows during the two-year span between 1996 and 1998, but the first one I did was the best of all of them. I spent hours and hours and hundreds of dollars on marketing and upgrading these shows, and I even went down to Los Angeles to network with other potential clients for their team-building seminars and health fairs. However, I became disillusioned with this venture when my adult motivational show bombed at a drunken after-hours corporate party in Palo Alto. What followed was a fairly icy reception at another corporate event in San Ramon.

However, there were enough successful moments in these shows that I gained more poise in performing for adults as well as for kids. I also discovered a lot about the importance of being vulnerable when performing comedy. I learned how much better comedy is when it is based on real, human, awkward, truthful experiences. I think back on the innocence I felt when I performed at my first spoof motivational gig. Maybe that's what made that particular show go over so well. What's so funny about perfection? The more I made mistakes, the more I discovered humor in the mistakes, the foibles, the imperfections, the pain, and the troubles a person can get into.

~.~

Jerry Lewis was right when he said, "Comedy is a man in trouble." Of course, it's not funny when I'm in the middle of the pain, or when I feel hurt, but when I can laugh at my troubles or the absurdities of life, I know I have transcended the Maya, the illusion of opposites, the transitory field of time and space. I believe this is the truth of alchemy. Laughter signals the transmutation of opposites without doing away with either position. Laughter is life energy exploding like atoms clashing. Laughter captures what Hegel meant in his discussions of the dialectical process toward wholeness. We take all our opposites into the whole and grow larger in our actualization. We realize our boundless selves then get back to doing laundry and washing the dishes.

I learned that I could take more risks with performing if I was willing to be myself, to be vulnerable, to speak my heartfelt truth and to do so fearlessly. The Yiddish word chutzpah revealed this secret to me. I still had fears, of course, but I learned to perform these adult shows despite my fears. Having fears about something and doing it anyway is not fearlessness; it's courage. Courage is doing something despite having fear.

What was it that allowed me to be willing to be vulnerable and look stupid on stage? It was the notion that nothing is perfect, that we're always growing and changing, that life evolves. From that notion came courage.

Courage also comes from faith that a greater divine and caring grace guides and strengthens me and anyone else who seeks its presence in life. My experience has shown me that the more I've turned to this divine source for help and then observed how I've been helped along the way by it, the more my faith has grown and empowered me even further in my life. Being grateful for this ongoing divine help moment to moment has also reinforced its presence in my life, too. This is the "chutzpah" I started to discover more and more as I tried and failed several new ventures in my life, including developing and diversifying my Daffy Dave entertainment enterprise.

The German general, Rommel, was known to have said, "There's nothing worse than the American soldier, at first. But no one learns quicker from their mistakes than the Americans. And, once they learn from their mistakes, they never do it again." The point is that making mistakes is the best way to learn, and the courageous and faithful ability to learn and grow is what leads to success. Knowing this, I have been willing to look stupid on the way to learning what works, what's funny, and what's my truth. I perceive that life is about growing, is seldom perfect and never static. It's a process that includes self-discovery, *via negativa*, and failure as I learn what works and become the person I'm meant to be.

~.~

I never fail to be astonished about and grateful for the responsive, abundant universe that we live in, a universe that mysteriously helps whoever is open to its help. When I got that call for my first motivational gig at the exact moment I was excitedly working on doing a show like that, it further increased my trust in the "law of attraction," the idea that our thoughts and feelings attract to us the things we feel and think about. Then, too, my corporate comedy gigs helped me to reconnect with the positive aspects of being a pastor that I had forgotten about in my quest to be an entertainer and a clown. Some of my pastoral presence came back to me during that first corporate show, and it reminded me how much I missed spiritual community in my life. I realized I wanted to have that positive communal influence in my life again, and I felt renewed in perceiving and expressing spiritual values in my comedy performances. I began to see my comic entertaining in terms of my ministry to the world, or at least, my little corner of it. Maybe that was the whole synchronous gift of this show for me. It wasn't about turning my enterprise into some lucrative corporate comedy business, but rather, it provided for me an awakening of spirit and an epiphany of who I was and what I love. Finally, my corporate comedy act inspired me to put music back into my performing life again. This time, though, instead of trying to be a serious rock star, I allowed music to filter through my affable Daffy Dave personality, and my songs became funny, silly, and humorous.

While my adult comedy period was yet another one of those *via negativa* phases that taught me more about who I am by showing me who I am not, I also gained many practical show business benefits from doing those shows. Along with improved poise and chutzpah on stage, I developed new comedy writing and routines, developed more confidence, and experienced a renewed appreciation for my background, values, and skills. Along the way, I gradually learned that I was better suited for family entertainment because of my profound connection with kids. I still haven't completely shut the door on adult shows, but for now, I've accepted that my niche and passion with entertainment is with kids and families.

~.~

Toward the end of 1997, I became anxious with the intensity of corporate comedy. On the other hand, I was also bored with doing too many kids' shows. I needed to grow. To complicate things further, I felt a longing for some kind of spiritual community and I felt a tug to return to the church, but my active addiction blocked that possibility, along with draining me in everything I did.

However, I was also experiencing a renewal with clowning because I had started teaching clowning to kids. A journal entry from October 29, 1997, captured some of this buildup:

"...[T]hough this has been the hardest year in my life, to my knowledge, especially the hurt from the breakup, the depression, the confusion with career path, suicidal thoughts, fantasies to 'unplug' and live in the wild, back pains, stomach [pains], addiction.... At the same time, it has been a 'rebirth.' I feel a long-lost excitement for clowning and creative humor (and love!). Best of all: teaching kids clowning with ease and passion (praise and love)--class today at 1pm."

~.~

By mid-December of 1997, I was deeply submerged in a dark night of the soul. I lost interest in everything, and I do mean everything. It really scared me when I realized marijuana wasn't getting me high anymore. Pot was my primary way to feel better and cope with all my feelings, my ups and downs, my boredom, my successes, and my failures. I lost interest and passion for food, friends, hobbies, music, nature's beauties, and even clowning. The happiness I had found as an entertainer deserted me, and my dream profession lost its meaning. I was in the "dark night of the clown," but I didn't know it. All I knew was that I was depressed, and I felt isolated and lost. One gray afternoon during that difficult month, I was alone in my room and I just started sobbing. I didn't know what to do.

Later that month, I took my usual two-week Christmas break and went north to visit my family in Seattle. While I was there, I went to church with my family. When I met the joyful church members at my dad's parish in Seattle, it became clear to me that I had lost touch with my core values of faith, love, and service. I recognized that my active addiction had progressively extinguished my spirit and my connection to God, despite the fact that I had experienced so many miracles when I left the ministry and started becoming Daffy Dave. All of my success up to that point, all of the wonderful breakthroughs that had inspired me, counted for nothing. I was an emotional mess, spiritually bankrupt and morally lost. I knew I had to change. I didn't want to lose whatever meaning and positive momentum I might still have going for me as Daffy Dave. It became clearer to me than ever before that my active addiction had cut me off from the true source of my good fortune and blessing, my relationship with the Divine. My relationship with a Divine power was there in theory, but not in practice. I had no conscious, authentic contact with the Divine. I was emotionally numb, and my spirit was locked inside a prison deep within me. A true conscious contact with God was no longer mine, and I felt the loss deeply. It was like death to me. I felt like a ghost floundering in the world, barely able to look people in the eyes anymore. I felt miserable and ashamed. I was a hollow shell of a human being.

This experience was truly the most important experience in my life. In Twelve Step programs, members call this "bottoming out" or "hitting bottom." Basically, this is a psychological state of wanting to stop using drugs or at least stop the misery of addiction. For many of us, our drugs have stopped working. They no longer soothe our emotional pain. Such a bottoming out process seems to be a necessary experience for many addicts so that they can come to terms with their addiction and begin taking the necessary actions to treat it. If I had never had this awful breakdown, these feelings of loss and desperation, I would never have been motivated to change, to seek help and get into recovery. Why would I have wanted to change if I had been feeling happy? Why then would I want to live differently? I was miserable and was sick and tired of feeling that way. This phase in my life was similar to the time when I finally took the leap of faith to leave the ministry and follow my dreams. The disgust and misery I felt became greater than my fear of change, my fear of the unknown.

I tried to talk with Dad about what was going on with me. He told me that if I would return to the church I would probably feel better again, and I tried to believe that for a while.

Whether it was to save my career as an entertainer or to return to the church as a prodigal pastor, I was finally motivated to seek help for my addiction. My tolerance for misery was at its end.

I knew even then, though, that the church was not sufficient to help me with my addiction. I knew that I needed to go back to the only way that had ever worked for me whenever I wanted to quit using drugs, a Twelve Step fellowship. I had tried it before, but I had never stuck with it. I knew I had never really given it a chance to work before, but I also knew it was there waiting for me. I am still dumbfounded when I look back and realize that although I could see what marijuana was doing to me, even though I truly wanted to stop, I could not stop using that drug. I knew that my thinking was broken and that the Twelve Steps could help mend those broken thoughts, beliefs, attitudes, and behaviors. I knew that if I kept thinking the same thoughts, particularly the thought that marijuana would make me feel okay--especially since it was actually making me depressed--I would continue to feel the same feelings of guilt, shame, regret, and despair. If I kept feeling the same feelings, I'd do the same things again. If I kept doing the same things, I'd keep getting the same results--those feelings of despair and alienation. Unless I made some fundamental changes, I would continue to use drugs in an effort to make myself feel better and end up behaving in ways that made me feel worse and worse about myself. Worse yet, I knew that I would lose my ability to be Daffy Dave and my dreams would melt away into thin air.

I returned to California from visiting my family in the new year with these insights still fresh in my mind. The year was 1998. One evening in early January I attended a meeting of a group I had been involved with during the previous year or so, a small, informal circle in which we discussed our dreams and tried to interpret them. I had begun to realize that many of my dreams were pointing out how addiction was ruining my life and my clowning. I surprised myself by standing up in the group that evening and announcing that I had a problem with drugs and couldn't quit on my own. I told the group I needed help to get clean. I felt like someone else was saying those words, not me, but as soon as I spoke them, I felt a huge and powerful release. An enormous weight fell off my shoulders, and a glimmer of hope and freedom signaled the dawning of a new day and the end of dark night of the clown. I promised myself right then and there that I would find a nearby Twelve Step meeting and start attending regularly again. This time, I vowed, I would follow all the suggestions and stick with the program. Deep in my soul, beginning that moment, I fully accepted that I was an addict, and I accepted that the solution for me was the Twelve Steps. I stepped out into the night after the meeting and noticed a new moon on the rise, and I knew my life was going to get better.

The funny thing about it was that when I stopped using drugs entirely, when I "got clean," as we recovering addicts say, life gradually did get better and better. What's more, once I got clean, I began to recognize for myself that I was good at my new vocation. I had even more fun clean than I had ever had when I was loaded, and so did my audiences. Things got even better when, after about eight months of staying clean, my obsession to use drugs was completely lifted, and I no longer even had the physical and emotional urge to use drugs. That's when I knew in my bones I was good at performing. I began to love my new profession more than ever. I felt guided by God or the Universe or some Power greater than myself to continue performing as a professional clown.

~.~

I've been called a "child whisperer" by some parents who have hired me over and over again. I laugh when I hear this, but there is some truth to it. I have a strong affinity with kids and know intuitively how to deal with them and make them laugh. After years of performing, observing and reflecting on this, I think a big reason is that I empower kids because I don't try to hide the fact that as an adult I continue to make mistakes just like they do. In my act, they get to correct me when I make a "mistake" on stage, and from that they learn they can laugh when they make mistakes themselves. But there's also something in my soul that remains childlike, no matter how old I get. I believe it's part of the coyote spirit I was born with, the blueprint for my soul that I have rediscovered and cultivated over time. It's a huge part of who I am. I really am a big kid who loves kids.

As Daffy Dave gained ascendancy, my last lingering regrets about leaving the ministry faded into oblivion, and I left behind any thoughts of returning to the parish ministry and its perceived security. By this time, I had paid most of my debts in full and was in good standing with a small amount of remaining debt; I had upgraded my props, my magic routines, and my office equipment; I had purchased a used van and had it decorated with colorful business signage. I was growing as a person and as a performer. My stage presence improved as my confidence in my skills increased. No longer was active addiction draining my energies and numbing my mind and soul, and the dark night of the clown turned into a beautiful new sunrise of promise. There wasn't anything funny about being lost in my addiction, but over the years, I have been able to laugh at all the stupid things I did as a result of my troubles with drugs.

Chapter Fifteen: Clean Clown

"If goodness lead him not,
Yet weariness may toss him to my breast."
--from "The Pulley" by George Herbert

No matter how many funny slapstick routines, cool magic and juggling tricks, and silly songs I do in my Daffy Dave show, the big take-away for most kids is the "bad clothes day" routine that starts off my show. My hat pops off my head, my hands get tangled in my suspenders, my socks come off my feet and when I try to pull them on again, they magically stretch out until they're twelve feet long. When my big baggy clown pants fall down to expose over-sized polka dot clown boxers, a collective belly laugh erupts from the audience and gets the show off to a rollicking start. This is my signature comedy-is-a-man-in-trouble routine. It introduces the misfit clown character of Daffy Dave right off the bat and draws the audience in with hearty laughter.

This part of my act also sets up the ultimate misdirection for hiding the secrets of my magic tricks during the rest of the show. Aside from using sleight of hand, palming, and other magical techniques, my foolishness gets them distracted with laughter so that when a wand appears out of a burning piece of paper, they are completely blown away. "Hey, Mom! He can do magic, too!" a kid will blurt out. They aren't expecting a clueless, bumbling Daffy Dave to actually do magic tricks--or anything else, for that matter, which requires skill. I make slapstick "mistakes" throughout the show, and when I finally succeed in performing a trick, the audience is delighted for me and cheers me on. When I juggle balls and clubs while spinning a plate on a stick in my mouth the audience is enchanted.

I think they are happy for my success because they identify and bond with me when they see me make mistakes. Many times, kids will come up to me after the show to give me a hug and sometimes even tell me they love me. This is so precious and truly inspires me. Parents, too, praise me for my shows, give me sizable tips afterward, and ask me to perform again and again. I think it's because I love people and this love manifests in everything I do. I'm still that little "love bug" who gave everyone a hug when I was a toddler at my dad's first church in Brainerd, Minnesota, sealing the deal on my dad's first pastoral gig.

My philosophy of clowning has evolved over the years. Today, it's about portraying our common humanity by means of the bumbling slapstick of vulnerable Daffy Dave. I become a mirror for others to laugh at themselves by laughing at me. They laugh at Daffy Dave's very human mistakes and reactions and thereby laugh at their own mistakes, ego, judgments, shame, negativity, anger, and power trips. Their laughter allows them to release their fears of life. It frees them from whatever keeps them from feeling free and happy, even if only for forty-five minutes.

I nearly always see a transformation in the people in my audiences after a show. Folks will come into the party, whether it's held in an auditorium, a park, a library, a school, a country club, a corporate headquarters, or whatever, exhibiting shyness, bad moods, aloofness, and anxiety, but after the show, after much laughter, their whole being shifts. They walk in bound by something weighty and negative, but during the show they break into smiles and their cheeks turn rosy. Conversation grows animated; their laughter has released them from whatever was binding them. People engage more after the show than they do beforehand, with each other and with me, and both kids and adults joke around and imitate me afterward. People hug each other, and there is more freedom in their faces. The valves of their imaginations open up, and creativity is released. It's a kind of alchemy, a transformation of baser moods into the golden glow of love. I am not exaggerating, either. Of course, it doesn't happen after every single show, and a very few of my audience members appear to be immune, but I've seen it over and over again. For this reason, I now consider clowning to be a ministry of laughter. This is the true magic of being a "magician clown."

To date, my baggy clown pants have "accidentally" fallen down in front of other human beings more than six thousand times over the course of twenty-one years. It leaves kids shrieking with laughter and adults dropping their jaws, some shocked and embarrassed but some laughing, too, rolling their eyes and not quite sure what to make of it. I figure I've made about a million dollars, all told, by dropping my pants for a living. It's not a bad way to go through life. It took me years to develop the art of having a bad clothes day, and I use this routine to introduce my character at almost every clown show I perform. However, I usually don't do the pants drop at schools and churches. And in today's overly sensitive, "politically correct" society, which is fear- and shame-based in my opinion, I've even lost a little business because some folks are too uncomfortable with my "edgy" underwear jokes and pants drops. But most clients love it and even request these bits in my show and are disappointed if I don't do them. When kids see me after the show or out and about in public with their parents, they love to remind me of my antics, usually cackling and giggling. "Daffy Dave," they'll say, "remember when your pants fell down? That was so funny!" Of course, there's nothing new about a clown dropping his pants for a laugh. Bill Irwin as Mr. Noodles did it on Sesame Street. When his pants fell down, he pretended to hide sheepishly behind a skinny hat stand, which, of course, is too thin to hide behind, making his act even funnier.

Initially, my routine started simply enough, with only baggy pants dropping to the floor. I'd come out in front of the audience, warm them up with a few silly questions, get them to clap for me and loudly say, "Welcome to the Daffy Dave Show!" Then, I'd quickly slip my arms out from under my suspenders so that my very loose-fitting rainbow-checkered pants fell to the floor. My large and colorful polka-dot boxers and bare legs would be exposed and hilarity would explode throughout the room. Kids have laughed so hard at this bit that they've fallen down on the floor with tears in their eyes, their faces red and veins popping out on their little necks. A few times, kids laughed so hard they peed in their pants, and frantically embarrassed moms had to whisk them off for a quick clothes change. I'm always tempted to put yellow caution tape around the little puddles they leave behind, but so far I haven't done that.

~.~

As my routine has evolved over the years, I've added a long pause after the pants drop, pretending to be oblivious. Let me tell you, it takes a lot of moxie to pull this off, pun absolutely intended. Most kids go nuts with hilarity; a few little girly girls will cover their eyes. Some moms will drop their jaws if they don't smile or laugh, or they will laugh after a moment of quiet shock. Some dads will giggle, chuckle, snort, chortle, or loudly guffaw. I pretend to wonder innocently why everyone seems to be shocked, which just cracks them up all the more. I stand there and look around the room, pretending not to notice that my pants have fallen down.

I'll ask a couple of kids what they're trying to tell me, pretending not to get it, shiver, and ask if someone just turned on the air conditioner. I look all around, behind me, to the sides, but not down to where my pants are heaped around my feet. The kids in the audience delightedly or helpfully point out that my big pants have fallen down. When I finally look down and see why everybody is yelling and pointing at me, laughing hysterically, I shriek with mock embarrassment. Again, they laugh even harder. Quickly, I pretend to try and cover myself, thanks to a suggestion by one of my later directors, the famous pantomime artist Leonard Pitt, by bending down to pick up my pants. As I pull my pants up, my hat falls to the floor. Loudly complaining, "Great! Now my hat fell down," I bend down again to get my hat, only to have my pants fall down a second time. Again the audience hoots with delight. I repeat this cycle a third time, finally getting my pants and hat both back in place at the same time. Feigning innocent embarrassment, I apologize and say emphatically, "That was soooo inappropriate!" As I try to secure my suspenders, my hands become hopelessly entangled with them. Then I notice my socks have fallen, too, so I pull them up. That's when my yellow-and-white horizontally striped stockings "magically" stretch up through my pants, becoming twelve feet long. There's more, but it's best to see a live show to get the full effect.

~.~

I describe the essence of my clowning to point out that this is what I didn't want to lose when I finally decided to get clean on February 1, 1998. After my third and longest relapse, I was finally done digging that massive pit in my life and ready to put the shovel down. I had been digging a hole with active addiction, on and off, for nineteen years, and I knew I was digging an early grave. Each time I got stoned, I pounded another nail into my coffin, committing slow suicide. My world had shrunk. I spent more and more time alone in my room getting high. My thoughts were confused and my emotions numb, and I felt split off from my real self. I was cut off from the Source of my spirit. I had fallen in love with being Daffy Dave and all the laughter and love he brought me, but I could feel that wonderful bliss dissipating and slipping away. I didn't want to lose it; that was the main reason I finally made the choice, deep in my heart and soul, to get clean and stay clean. I wanted to grow spiritually again. I didn't want to die stoned. I wanted to die authentically, in peace and with true release, when it was my time to go.

As I struggled to stay clean in 1998, the hardest part was feeling the continuous physical and emotional urge to use, but choosing not to use drugs anyway. Everybody I met in the program encouraged me to just stay clean; the obsession to use would eventually be removed, they assured me. I grieved the loss of all my old using friends, especially the musicians and entertainers I once hung around with, but I knew I had to remove myself from their company or I would be tempted to use again. Some of them didn't understand even when I explained my reasons, but many of them did and supported my recovery, and I am still grateful for that support. I was willing to do whatever I had to do to get and stay clean. It takes time and history to make new friends anywhere in life, including the rooms of recovery, and I was in between my old life and my new life for quite some time. These initial weeks and months of transitioning to a new way of living are the most difficult time for any recovering addict. During this time, those of us in recovery have to remain vigilant every single day, sometimes every single moment, and celebrate each day we stay clean.

I finally realized that addiction is a spiritual sickness, not a shameful moral issue. While I do feel shame and regret when I think about the moral wreckage in my past that resulted from the compulsive behaviors I engaged in while I was in the throes of active addiction, working the Twelve Steps has enabled me to clean up that wreckage as well as I possibly can so that in the present I can live fully and joyfully, as God intended for me all along. In recovery fellowships, we say that in this way we are restored to sanity.

At first, I was ashamed of the knowledge that I was an addict. Today, I am grateful for my addiction, because it led me into a more spiritual way of life. Addiction is a powerful affliction, and it compels me and many others like me to seek spiritual solutions to everyday problems on a continual basis. We have to, in order to stay clean and live life on life's terms. This is true for us every day, not only when life is a struggle, but also--sometimes especially--when life is going well. We addicts are inclined to use drugs about anything and everything. We want to console ourselves with drugs when things aren't going well, and we want to celebrate with drugs when life is good.

As I've matured in my recovery, I've become acutely aware of how grateful I am for what the seventeenth-century poet George Herbert called "repining restlessness." The spiritual disease of addiction is a warning system for my soul. When I have flare-ups of obsessive-compulsive thinking and behavior, I am reminded me that there is still much work for me to do on myself. I am prompted to return to values I consciously choose for myself, values such as love and peace. It's a strange razor's edge because success, mastery, material abundance, beauty, new inner growth, creative intoxication--all the good things in life--can easily seduce me into forgetting my limits, my needs as a physical being, my transitory nature. I love abundance, but abundance is not the source of what is good and true in my life. Good times can be the sirens that lure me, as they did Odysseus, away from the journey home. In recovery, we try to practice honesty, open-mindedness, willingness, faith, love, and other spiritual principles we find in the Twelve Steps, in order to stay clean. We discover along the way that not only do the Steps keep us from relapsing into drug use, they also make us happier, more loving, and freer people in every area of our lives. When we look beyond our own small world and find ways to support other suffering addicts in their efforts to stay clean and recover, we make up for some of the harm we caused in our active addiction; we make amends for the damage we created to those around us in society, and we "keep what we have," our recovery, "by giving it away."

~.~

Statistics show that many of us don't make it, but those who diligently stick with the program have a much better chance at recovery from active addiction than those who don't. The first year of being clean can be the most difficult. It's so important for someone new to the program to build a sturdy foundation during that first year. Such a foundation will make things easier later on, especially during those inevitable times when life gets hard. Difficult times happen for everyone, not just addicts, but addicts are vulnerable to relapse during such times.

It has been more than fifteen years since I last used drugs and decided to make my recovery from active addiction a priority in my life, and I still go to meetings regularly, stay in touch with my sponsor, and continue to work the Twelve Steps. That is my foundation. These days, when I work the Steps again with my sponsor, I work on issues such as my vocation, my family, or romantic relationships. In addition, I sponsor other men into the recovery program of which I am a member, and I give back to the community of recovering addicts in my area by being in service to the local organization, and I practice prayer and meditation on a daily basis.

I feel it's very important to let newcomers know about the grieving process that can happen in early recovery. Someone trying to get clean and stay clean needs to understand that it takes time to adjust and accept this new way of life without drugs. I felt so lonely during my first three months of living clean. One afternoon in my small, rented room in Palo Alto I felt so lonely that I started to sob. I fell to my knees and asked my Higher Power to help me. I needed strength to deal with the loss of my old friends and my old drug-using lifestyle. I fervently prayed that I would begin to feel comfortable with my new way of life in recovery. As I was praying, a deep, calm, warm, and overwhelming feeling of love washed through me. I looked up and saw a misty light on the ceiling and palpably felt Love's divine presence in my room, reminding me of the feelings I had felt during some of my out-of-body experiences. My painful tears melted into peaceful tears of joy and love, and I knew my Higher Power was giving me a gift of encouragement to keep me going in my recovery. I went outside for a walk immediately afterward and everything looked so beautiful. I felt an enormous sense of love, and I must have emanated that feeling because a couple of the neighborhood cats came up and rubbed against my legs as I walked.

I continued to work the Steps. By the time I had eight months clean, I was working on my Ninth Step, which is the one where we addicts begin to make amends to others for the harm we have done. Dad and I took a road trip together, just the two of us, in northern Canada. The time we spent together on that trip gave me ample opportunity not only to apologize for my hurtful behaviors but also to learn from him what he needed from me in order to make things right between us. I experienced forgiveness from him, and I began to forgive myself. I felt a new sense of freedom from shame and guilt.

When I attended my first world convention of a Twelve Step fellowship, I was privileged to hear a very famous rock star playing on stage to twenty thousand of us recovering addicts in that auditorium. There were no drugs anywhere in that room; not a single whiff of pot smoke could be detected. After the sixth song, this rock hero of mine announced that he, too, was a recovering addict. He was one of us. Deafening cheers ascended to the rafters with his announcement and threatened to blow the massive roof off. I burst into tears of joy and wept during the remainder of that concert, with a feeling that I had finally come home. My heart opened and I allowed my new friends in. Fun and soulful joy commingled in my heart, and I allowed my heart to unite with the hearts of members my adopted spiritual family. As we rejoiced together in our fellowship of recovery from active addition, my grief for my old ways of living fled and has not since returned. I accepted without reservation my new way of life, chose freely this new spiritual path, this solution to my affliction of addiction, and warmly welcomed my new, empathic friends in recovery.

The next day, I woke up and noticed that I no longer felt the urge to use drugs. As my new friends in recovery had assured me would happen, my obsession had been lifted. Just stay clean and continue to work your program, they told me, and the miracle will happen for you, too. I was overjoyed to discover that they were right.

From that point onward in my recovery program, I focused on changing the negative attitudes and destructive behaviors that had contributed to my active addiction in the first place. Self-centeredness and fear, I learned, were the source of my addiction. My drug use was a symptom of the underlying spiritual malady, self-centered fear. I wholeheartedly embraced the solution of recovery by way of the Twelve Steps as my primary spiritual path toward wholeness, and I began to truly enjoy my new way of living. I was flabbergasted to realize that I had never before experienced anything as spiritual as my recovery program, not growing up in the church, not attending seminary, and not even while I was being a pastor. The spirituality

I found in my Twelve Step program was a practical, nuts-and-bolts, everyday spirituality. All of my intellectual and religious training paled in comparison to the spiritual examination I conducted with the help of my sponsor and the love and support I found in Twelve Step fellowships. I felt humbled. I knew my education and training had been an arrogant defense, a shield that kept me distant from this way of life until I was ready to surrender to it, until I was so desperate, so weary of the misery of active addiction that I was open to new ideas and willing to try what had already worked for so many others.

As I continued to stay clean and became more involved with all aspects of my recovery on a daily basis, every other area of my life improved, too. I cleaned up my diet and started to exercise more. My intellectual and vocational pursuits took on a new life, and my hobbies and friendships became more nurturing. My finances improved, as did my health. Romance graced my life and long-lost dreams to travel the world began to come true. So many things that I had either stopped doing because of my drug use, or had not had the courage or means to do while I was using, now became manifest in my life. In every area, my life progressively got better. Sometimes I still struggled, and painful and difficult situations and feelings continued to come my way at times. But as long as I stayed clean through these times by using the tools of my Twelve Step program and relying on the loving support of the fellowship, I grew even stronger. I have learned to stay clean through the hard times and painful emotions that inevitably come to everyone by turning to a Higher Power for help and by allowing myself to experience the loving support of my close friends in recovery. I make it through the beginning, middle, and ending of painful emotions without the use of drugs, and I have learned that all emotions, both painful ones and joyous ones, do pass. I have learned that when I used drugs to numb the pain I stunted my own growth. Today, I try to move with dignity and grace through life's challenges.

Eventually, I learned that I could stay clean even when death took people I loved. I stayed clean through romantic break-ups, financial loss, surgery, boredom, depression, and a heart attack. I stayed clean when I moved to a new area because I immediately found a Twelve Step fellowship there. Most importantly, I have learned that I can stay clean and deal with any and every emotion that washes through me, despite the fact that dealing with emotions can be very difficult for us recovering addicts. During our years of actively using drugs we intentionally numbed ourselves; we wanted to escape our emotions; we didn't want to live in reality. Learning to feel our emotions as they occur, to name them, be with them, and simply to get through them is a new experience for many of us.

Over the next few years in recovery, I saved up money for travel and went to Europe four different times. I also traveled to Costa Rica, Hawaii, and various locations throughout North America. By learning to save money for travel and taking trips to visit with people I love, I became more actively involved with my family and friends, reunited with long-lost childhood friends, and experienced more success as Daffy Dave.

Sometimes I made these trips so that I could make amends to people I had harmed in my active addiction. Today, I vigilantly work on my relationships in order to "keep my side of the street clean." Today I can say that I am a man of integrity. I have learned to love and respect myself enough to honor my limits. I maintain healthy boundaries to the best of my ability and to the extent that I am willing--and I work at being more willing. My relationships with others are healthier and more respectful, and when I do hurt others or myself, I do what is necessary to make things right again as soon as I am able. Freedom from active addiction has allowed me to blossom into the person God intended me to be and given me a life beyond my wildest dreams. Today I continue to follow my bliss. I am a clean clown, one day at a time, thanks to recovery in a wonderful Twelve Step fellowship.

~.~

I am struck by the irony in the fact that long before I got clean, my entire Daffy Dave show was about "how to clean your room using magic" and included a song I had written about cleaning your room. The tag line in that song is, "My name is Daffy Dave; I'm a real clean clown." I can't help but think now that my unconscious was bubbling up with that act and that song, creating imagery about cleaning up during the time when I was still using drugs, while I was "dirty." I think now that my soul and my Higher Power were conspiring to encourage me with a foreshadowing of the clean life that awaited me, once I was willing to learn to live clean.

I have learned to pay attention to these impulses, these nudges from my soul and from my Higher Power, which come to me in the form of dreams, notions, images, and otherworldly coincidences. Where once I might have failed to notice them, I am getting better at recognizing them when they show themselves. And when I do, I am reassured that I am walking in the right direction. When I watch, remain teachable and humble, open and willing, I am better able to feel my way through the darkness that life sometimes is. "We think by feeling," writes the poet. "What is there to know? I learn by going where I have to go."

Chapter Sixteen:
Way Leads on to Way

"Yet knowing how way leads on to way,
I doubted if I should ever come back.
I shall be telling this with a sigh
Somewhere ages and ages hence:
Two roads diverged in a wood, and I--
I took the one less traveled by,
And that has made all the difference."
--from "The Road Not Taken" by Robert Frost

One of my biggest fears about not using drugs when I got clean in 1998 was that I would become bored and boring, and that I would lose my ability to be funny as a clown. I told myself that if recovery did this to me, I would go back to using drugs. In Twelve Step language, this is called "having a reservation" in your program. Early on, though, I shared these fears with others in the fellowship. Their laughter, support, compassion, and wisdom dissipated my fears and gave me hope that I could continue to stay clean no matter what I was going through, just as they were doing. Someone told me that I would become even funnier and better as a clown by staying clean, and that really gave me hope. I still hear wonderful, helpful words such as these in meetings today.

Time and experience helped. When I performed after my clean date, I saw smiling faces and heard laughter from the audience, just as I had before I put drugs aside. I was happy to discover that I was still funny. It took me a while to adjust within myself, though. I wasn't quite sure of my sense of humor when I first got clean, because I was still coming out of a toxic fog. I was grieving the loss of my using friends, scared about living daily life without being intoxicated, and not yet comfortable with my new friends in the recovery community. My brain was pretty impaired for quite a while. It can take eight months or more to restore the natural abilities of the pleasure receptors in a person's brain after a long period of artificial stimulation with illicit drugs. My sisters confided to my dad that I seemed "too serious" and they missed my old self when I first got clean. My dad had to reassure them that it was only a phase and I would find my way back to my jolly self. Pops and my recovery friends were right. I did recover my lost sense of humor, and I became even better at being a clown as I continued with my recovery.

~.~

During that first year of my being clean, I worked my way through each one of the Twelve Steps. I took on service commitments in my recovery fellowship and through them made new friends in the program. I began to feel that I belonged, that my life had direction and purpose, and that I was a part of something larger than myself, something larger than my addiction. In the fellowship, we say that our addiction is larger than we are, which makes us powerless over our compulsions and our obsession to use drugs. Therefore, we addicts need something larger than our addiction to help us to stay clean and recover, and we call that larger something our Higher Power. This Higher Power is uniquely understood by each recovering addict, and the program does not tell us what to believe in any way. However, I've noticed a number of common beliefs about our Higher Power that are shared by every recovering addict I've ever yet met, and that is that this Higher Power, however we experience it, is whatever Force is lovingly helping us to stay clean. It loves us and helps us and is greater than we are.

At the end of my using, when the drugs no longer got me high but I couldn't stop using them, when I had received the "gift of desperation" and hit my bottom, I finally surrendered to this Higher Power and asked for help. At that moment, I was, in effect, admitting I was powerless over my addiction. I was keenly aware that my addiction had become a destructive higher power. As soon as I admitted I couldn't quit on my own and needed help, in that instant, way led onto way, and suddenly people and events started unfolding in my life, and that made all the difference. In that instant, I experienced Step One of the Twelve Steps. I admitted I had a problem and accepted without reservation that addiction was more powerful than I was and that it had made my life a mess, or to quote the Steps, that my life had "become unmanageable."

Right after I first admitted my powerlessness over my addiction to myself and others in my dream group in December of 1997, I went to my seamstress's home to pick up my new Daffy Dave magic prop box cover she had sewn for me. When I walked into her sewing room, I saw a Twelve Step symbol on her desk. I gasped and said to her, "Wow! Are you in recovery?"

With excitement in her eyes she looked at me and said, "Oh! Are you an addict, too? Hey, there's a noon meeting today, do you want to come with me?"

"Oh no," I stammered. "I was just curious."

"Okay," she answered, shrugging and turning back toward her sewing machine. She seemed a little embarrassed.

"Well, actually, this is too weird," I said, reconsidering my hasty response. "I've been thinking I need to go back to the rooms because I've been struggling with my addiction."

"Great!" she said. "Let's go." Before I could figure out what was happening to me, I was plopped down into a chair in a meeting beside her. Thus began my recovery in earnest. As soon as I sat down in that room, a warm feeling came to rest deep in me. I found I could honestly identify with other recovering addicts sitting near me. I saw similarities between me and others wherever I looked. I saw our common feelings, or common obsessions and compulsions, our common issues. This time, I wasn't looking for the differences between me and other addicts. While it's true we used different drugs, we dressed differently from each other, and we came from a wide array of socioeconomic and educational backgrounds, those differences no longer existed as excuses for me to keep myself away from Twelve Step fellowships. I could no longer afford to believe that these fellowships could not possibly work for me. I was out of options.

As I sat in that meeting room with my seamstress that afternoon, something that had been tight within my chest relaxed, and I felt a glimmer of hope. Maybe, I thought, just maybe, I too, could stay clean and recover. This was the beginning of Step Two for me. I had admitted and accepted my problem (Step One) and now I was having some hope that a Power greater than I was could help me stay clean. At this point in my recovery, my Higher Power was the group itself, other recovering addicts who were staying clean by working the program and participating in the fellowship they found in the rooms of recovery. I heard this admonition over and over again: "Let us love you until you can love yourself."

After a few days, I asked another member to sponsor me. A sponsor in a Twelve Step program is a member of the program who has already worked through all of the Twelve Steps and guides you through working the Twelve Steps for your own life. Working the Steps is an amazing process, and it offers the miracle of self-awareness. You get the opportunity to shed those things about yourself which are harmful to yourself and others. You get a chance to repair broken relationships and clean up the wreckage in your past. And you come to experience forgiveness and freedom from shame and guilt. You learn to maintain spiritual growth with ongoing daily awareness and the practice of living by spiritual principles such as honesty, open-mindedness, and willingness.

For most of us, regular, ongoing meeting attendance is essential to maintaining our recovery and staying clean, as is regularly improving our conscious contact with our own Higher Power. We learn to ask for strength and guidance, and "we keep what we have by giving it away" to others, particularly the still-suffering addict. We do this by sharing our experience and hope with still-using addicts who are open to hearing our message, and we help other addicts who have found their way into the program to work their Steps by becoming a sponsor ourselves when we are asked, once we have worked all of the Twelve Steps, too.

Since 1998, living the recovery way of life has gradually deconstructed my personality from the weakened, tortured state in which active addiction left it. I have learned to live clean day by day, risk by risk, event by event, living life on life's terms. No longer do I try to escape my feelings and reality with the use of drugs, and progressively I have transformed into a happier person and a more successful clown. Because I got clean, I was able to continue following my bliss as Daffy Dave and become more truly myself. My shows have improved exponentially. I have learned how to be creative without having to use drugs to "inspire" me. I let go of my fear that I would be bored and not funny once I got clean.

It took me a while to relearn how to be creative without using drugs, but that reservation eventually vanished, too. As a matter of fact, that whole first year of getting clean took a lot of focus and energy, and I didn't create much new comedy material at all during that time. For the most part, that lack of creativity came from my being afraid that I would want to use drugs if I started to work on a new magic trick or slapstick or juggling routines. Songs and poems, or anything else creative, were out of the question that year, too. I had such strong associations between getting high and being creative that it took some intense Twelve Step work to release those associations. I shared about my concerns with other recovering addicts, and I prayed for guidance. With time, healing came to me in that area, too, as it has in all the other areas of my life. Gradually, I began to return to creative activities, beginning with playing music. Slowly, as I learned to trust myself again, as I learned to trust the process of recovery, I regained the courage to try other creative activities without the use of drugs.

~.~

Toward the end of my using, I read three books that planted seeds for my recovery from active addiction. They were *The Care of the Soul* by Thomas Moore, *The Artist's Way* by Julia Cameron, and *The Creative Fire* by Clarissa Pinkola Estes.

Thomas Moore's book didn't address addiction per se, but it touched upon it in terms of feelings, depression, and neurotic illnesses that are symptoms of the soul seeking expression. I still have the copy of Moore's book that I read during that time, and there are several notes I scribbled in the margins: "toxic escapes hold off this process!" and "drugs disallow us to 'sustain' these teaching, shaping moods and experience." In the margins of a section about self-love, I wrote, "I seem to still have some of this with my masochistic drug abuse?" The main effect Moore's book had on leading me toward recovery was that I started to sense that by numbing out my feelings with drugs I was blocking my soul's development and splitting myself off from my authentic connection to the Divine.

Clarissa Pinkola Estes's book, *The Creative Fire*, revealed to me the ability that creativity has to burn and destroy artists if they become consumed by the intoxication of the creative process. I saw how many artists in history had allowed this to happen to themselves and how they had destroyed themselves by going too far and ending their lives with overdoses of drugs, by alcoholism, or by suicide, and I started to see myself in that way. I saw the patterns of using marijuana and other drugs in order to maintain the creative fire or to try to calm myself down after a session of intense creativity. As I looked back on my own experience of creativity, I saw that numerous conflicting feelings surfaced when I created poems, songs, and comedy. I saw that many of my creative endeavors came out of painful and troubling experiences and triggered deep feelings of grief, anger, and pain. When I experienced those feelings, I used pot to self-medicate.

Julia Cameron's book, *The Artist's Way*, was the strongest wake-up call of the three. The author shared her own experience with using intoxication to become inspired. She noticed, she wrote, that inspiration in those instances would be brief and would quickly fade into confusion and apathy. Pow! Right between the eyes! I saw that very pattern in myself. Remorse crept into my heart; I feared that many of my creations were immature or incomplete. Worse, I clearly saw that I was becoming less and less able to work on creative projects because I was becoming more and more dependent on just getting high. My creative fire and my soul were bogged down by intoxication. These thoughts made me feel increasingly depressed and desperate. I was in danger, I feared, of being consumed by my own energy and caving in upon myself.

A few years later, after I had been clean a while and was finding my way back to my soul and my genuine feelings and reconnecting with a creative, loving Higher Power, I found I needed time, practice, and reflection in order to learn how to create again. I wanted to find a way to be creative while practicing self-love and maintaining balance in my life. Most of all, I wanted to be creative while staying clean. I ventured out a little at a time, writing a poem here, adding a new routine to my Daffy Dave show there, until I could feel and see that I could create without getting high to prime the pump beforehand or calm me down afterward. Slowly, I learned to build new neural pathways and forge new associations with people, places, and things. I learned to be inspired naturally from the kids in my shows. I found that I could be inspired by other clowns, by movies and books. Ideas of my own began to come to me. I even learned that I could be inspired by the mistakes I made.

I learned how to calm and center myself with meditation, prayer, and journaling. I shared with other addicts and my "normal" friends. I relaxed with massages and hot tub soaks. I took breaks, and I exercised and ate a healthy diet. Over time, I built "clean memories," reference points for a new way of being creative. Today, I continue to build these clean memories, and I draw upon them as I continue. The creative process is so important to me, but I must learn to practice it while being clean and in recovery. Gradually, I built a new foundation on solid, clean, spiritual ground.

~.~

When I was two years into my recovery, my first children's album, *Daffy Dave's Git Down and Funny!* was released. Drawing on my clean, creative foundation, I recorded the main tracks for twenty-six songs in one afternoon with Scotty Smith (alias Dusty Buckles), who was my new producer at the time. It was a major creative effort. Later I merged the songs on this album with my second album, *Get Down with the Clown*, and a couple of years after that I repackaged all of it as *Silly Party Songs*, my most popular album so far, with more than fifteen thousand units sold and countless online downloads and internet radio airplays.

"Soccer Rock 'n' Roll," one of the songs from that album, received airplay on the *NBC Today Show*. "Choo Choo Train," another song from the same album, has gone viral on YouTube. Raoul Pop used this one for his video, "The Toy Train," which has had more than eighteen million views so far. I've profited thousands of dollars from this album and its songs, but I am absolutely certain my good fortune comes as a result of my getting clean and recovering from my addiction to drugs in a Twelve Step program. My foundation in recovery is built upon earlier foundations--positive, loving experiences from my childhood, supportive mentors, friends, events, and Divine assistance that gave me hope in dark times, hope that allowed me to go forward through difficulties. These past foundations set the precedent for goodness to continue from my past and into the present and beyond. Way has truly led onto way and continues to make all the difference.

Chapter Seventeen:
Get Down with the Clown

"You know why I love Daffy Dave?
He makes me pee my pants!"
--Connor, age 5

There's nothing quite as delightful, naturally delicious and wholesome as homegrown tomatoes from my garden during the summer. Tender, tangy, and sweet, they are warm and bursting with flavor, not hard and tasteless like store-bought tomatoes. I pop the first cherry tomato of the season into my mouth, and it explodes like fireworks on my palate. I moan with pleasure and swoon with gratitude.

As I grew more comfortable with my new life in recovery and started to regain lost values of faith, compassion, honesty, and other fruits of the spirit, my clowning ripened on the vine, bursting with natural flavor. In the year 2000, I still stumbled in this area, learning how to stand up for my true nature and my humanity as a clean clown in recovery. Joseph Campbell's words encouraged me. He said, "The goal of life is to make your heartbeat match the beat of the universe, to match your nature with Nature." Plenty of unripe fruit remained in my soul, but there were some real beauties ready for the picking and I was ready to experience the natural blooming and cultivation of Daffy Dave. I started to hit my stride.

I have accomplished so much since that time, overcoming numerous difficulties along the way, but hardship and pain were no match for the momentum I developed during my first six years of developing Daffy Dave. The disease of addiction remained a part of who I am, as it will always be, and financial instability from my years as a "dirty clown" continued into my clean years. It took some time to clean up the mess. But when

Daffy Dave finally became a "clean clown" in 1998, he was shot from a slingshot into the world.

Even after the terrorist attacks of September 11, 2001, when a dark pall covered the land, my spirit continued to move forward. The Divine Spirit likewise moved through my spirit, enabling me to bring joy and laughter to kids, even during that troubled time. I was the silly, innocent "big kid who loves kids" and I brought that aspect of myself to every show I did. Again Joseph Campbell's words encouraged me. "Participate joyfully in the sorrows of the world," he wrote. "We cannot cure the world of sorrows, but we can choose to live in joy." Living in joy is a daily choice and I don't do it perfectly, but my foundation of recovery and daily spiritual practice, my family, the Twelve Steps, my recovery sponsor, and my close soul and support friends all assist me in joyful living. Especially, a lavish loving Presence in all of my life continuously encourages me to dust myself off and get back on the horse of joy over and over again.

On September 12, 2001, or maybe it was a few days after--that whole week was a blur--I had scheduled "the posse" to come to Scotty Smith's recording studio, the Tree Fort in Sunnyvale, California. "The posse" was the affectionate name for a close-knit group of moms and kids who were big fans of Daffy Dave, most of whom lived in Palo Alto where I shared an apartment with my good friend Steve Koehler, who also just happens to be a family entertainer known as "Mr. Horsefeathers." Scotty and I had organized this group of about twenty kids to come down to the studio to sing choral parts for my second album, *Get Down with the Clown*. I had managed to save up about eight thousand dollars for the production costs, and I wanted to create a full-band sound for a rock 'n' roll album for kids. The album contains several parodies of classic rock tunes, and I had also hired some talented local musicians.

Some of the tunes on *Get Down with the Clown* are "That's My Bike, (Uh Huh Uh Huh) I Ride It!" and "StairMaster to 7-Eleven," funny spoofs with a full-band sound. They remind me of the work of Weird Al Yankovich, but with lyrics written for a younger audience. Scotty Smith, musical genius, produced it and made it sound very professional. I was proud to be associated with Scotty and his work; he played drums for the band Giraffe with the late Kevin Gilbert and has worked with some of the top names in the music business. I was really looking forward to recording this album in Scotty's studio, but the country's somber mood after the September 11, 2001, tragedies had me feeling concerned about how our final touches were going to go with the kids' parts.

Sure enough, when the posse arrived, one of the moms was still particularly upset about the tragedy. As the group gathered in the front of the studio to go over the recording agenda for the session, that mom looked at me and said, "Daffy Dave, I'm so glad we're doing this today. We really need it." My heart was so moved by that, and I felt myself start to shake off the disquiet of that dark time.

The kids were very excited, and I chose to join them in their excitement, choosing to be joyful in the midst of the darkness. I joked around with the kids, gave them my silly slapstick high fives, and led everyone into the studio. I made eye contact with each child as I explained their singing parts to them. Another of the moms took pictures from the day and later gave me a framed montage of the photographs from that wonderfully healing recording session. The album release party was held at Saint Mark's Episcopal Church in Palo Alto on my birthday, and it completely sold out. The little girls from the posse dressed up as the "Daffettes" and danced to some of the songs from the album. One of the moms gave me a cake, and the earliest configuration of the Daffy Dave Band rocked out for everyone in that packed fellowship hall. The party happened at the time of George Harrison's death, and we played "Money Can't Buy Me Love" in his honor.

It was truly an unforgettable evening for me. So many disparate parts of my soul came together in that event as the minister joined forces with the clown and the rock star. The party left me wondering how to propel all of this forward. How, I wondered, could I keep the momentum going? How could I market my albums? I had lots of local fans at that point, a website, a fan club, and even a wonderfully fun and positive assistant, Amy Shapas. Amy organized the release party, developed the fan club, and did all the marketing I wasn't able to handle.

Marketing at that point consisted of putting my CD's in local record stores on consignment, selling them at my Daffy Dave shows and occasional concerts, and selling them online at CD Baby.com. Bookings for my shows were being made one to two months in advance and my income was increasing. I had paid off all my student loans and other debts and had even started saving for retirement. I was becoming popular locally, but I dreamed of more. I wanted to expand Daffy Dave's popularity to a national scale. How, I wondered, could I "bottle" Daffy Dave and make it big time?

~.~

The year before I released *Get Down with the Clown* was an amazing watershed of abundance for me. My second anniversary of being free of drugs was on February 1, 2000, and I celebrated by attaining one of my long-lost dreams, that of traveling internationally with a trip to Costa Rica. It's no secret that when you stop spending money on drugs, you can actually save money to do the things drugs prevented you from doing.

As the date for my travel approached, I was both excited and nervous. I studied the travel guides and brushed up on speaking Spanish. I got to travel for two weeks through that lush and friendly country, traversing twenty-two different micro-climates. I delighted in the colorful birds and butterflies, none of which I had ever seen before. I laughed at the monkeys who tried to steal food out of my backpack at Manuel Antonio beach. I saw crocodiles, swam in warm ocean water, and hiked through jungles, where I saw scarlet macaws and toucans. I watched lava streaming down the sides of Volcán Arenal. I rode on local buses, made animal balloons for the local kids, stayed in a grass shack in Dominical, and had the most wonderful, relaxing time in the hot springs at Tabacón near Volcán Arenal. There, after a lava mud treatment and a massage, a hot waterfall thrummed the last of the tension out of my back and shoulders. When I tired of that pleasure, I drifted down a hot river away from the falls and slid down a man-made water slide into a large hot pool. There a fruit drink bar awaited at the far end of the pool, and I floated toward it. I sat on a bar stool submerged in the hot water and drank a delicious fruit drink made from a tropical fruit I had never before tasted--guana-bana. Even having grown up on Kauai, I had never tasted that delectable exotic fruit before.

Of course, it wasn't just my lack of money as an active addict that kept my dreams from coming true before, but also my lack of energy and motivation to save, plan, and have the courage to leave the security of my shrunken world. As an active addict, all I had was the miserable solitude of using drugs alone in my room. Using left me a withered soul with a diminutive life. Getting clean allowed my spirit to fly free out into the big wide world again.

I had been working toward cleaning up my debt even before I got clean and had even saved a little for retirement, but when I got clean, I was able to start a travel fund, too, by saving just a little each week, sometimes twenty-five dollars, sometimes fifty. In a good week, as much as a hundred dollars from income from my shows might go into my travel account. Two years of saving gave me enough money to take my first trip abroad, so I got my passport and went to Costa Rica.

I had such a great time in Costa Rica that I immediately started saving for a much bigger trip as soon as I got home, and I managed to save enough to travel to Europe in September of that same year. I performed more shows than I had ever done before during that summer, hitting a record of sixty-five shows during the month of June. It nearly killed me, and I vowed never to do that to myself again. But when it was time for me to travel again, even though the trip to Europe required about eight thousand dollars, I had enough for the trip when the time came. I got to spend an entire month traveling that continent and decided once I was there that it had all been worth the effort. I backpacked with a rail pass throughout Europe and

visited my old college friends Kirk Chilton and his wife, Katarina Eskilsson, and their two fun kids Kyle and Miranda at their
home in Belgium.

One of my later visits coincided with their son Kyle's
sixth birthday, and, having been informed of this important
fact before I left home, I brought along some of my clown gear.
Kirk said he wanted to be my clown assistant when it was time
for the birthday show, and I asked him what his clown name
would be. "Kirk the Jerk," he said. That made sense to me and I
giggled. Kirk definitely has the coyote spirit! We came up with
a funny skit in which he proceeded to nonchalantly vacuum the
living room right in the middle of my introduction for the skit.
Each time I would tell him to stop, he'd turn off the vacuum, but
then he would turn it back on in only a few moments. Everyone
was in stitches when we performed this routine, and Kirk and
I had to really try hard not to laugh ourselves. The bit ended
with Kirk vacuuming my entire body until my hair got stuck
in the hose and he and I struggled to remove the hose from my
head. The kids laughed so hard they were in tears.

When I was a student at Augustana I hadn't been able
to afford studying for a quarter in Europe, and I was overjoyed with my opportunity to travel as an adult. I made a
point of seeing all the great art I could, and I wept when I saw
Michaelangelo's David in Florence. I boated on the canals of
Venice, and I climbed to the top of the Eiffel Tower and peered
out over Paris. I adored the Mona Lisa at the Louvre, watched a
play of Shakespeare's at the Globe in London, and swam in the
Ligurian Sea along the Italian Riviera in Cinque Terre, where
Rick Steves just happened to be filming one of his travel shows
at the time. I pondered the mysterious Stonehenge in England
and marveled at the many languages, customs, and foods in the
cities on my itinerary: Rome, Paris, London, and Brussels. I was
in seventh heaven. I performed as Daffy Dave at the hostel in
Gimmelwald, Switzerland, in exchange for five nights of lodg-
ing there.

As I journeyed, I was keenly aware that I could never
have had such a trip without being clean and in recovery, and I

kept up my work in recovery as I traveled. On both of my trips that year, in Costa Rica and all over Europe, I found Twelve Step meetings wherever I went. I wrote on my Fourth Step--I was working on my second time of going through the Steps-- while I rode the trains in Europe. I have learned that the disease of addiction doesn't take a vacation, so I pack my recovery with me when I travel. I have friends all around the world because of Twelve Step fellowships. Meetings in Italy, in Denmark, in Costa Rica or anywhere else on earth give me immediate friend- ships in all those places. People in the meetings have offered their hands to me, translated for me, and taken me out to lunch or dinner after the meeting. We know each other as addicts in recovery, and we identify with each other on deep levels. We care and help each other out. It was the gift of the rooms of recovery that made my world travels so fun and friendly. I am never alone in this world because of them. Then, too, I have grown spiritually since getting clean. The Divine is alive in all life, and I have learned to love the company of my own soul.

During that European adventure, one of my friends, Col- leen Huston, and her mom joined me in Rome and Florence for part of the time I was there. Together we toured the Forum and other sites. When we met near the Forum as we had agreed beforehand, Colleen handed me a copy of the *Palo Alto Weekly*. Right there on the cover of that little newspaper was a picture of Daffy Dave, in costume, holding a balloon flower and squeezing a clown horn with my arm curved over my head backward like my college buddy Kirk Chilton used to do when he answered the phone. The story that accompanied the photo was entitled "The Ministry of Laughter," and it was about the release of my first album. It described my local success as Daffy Dave and my history of leaving the ministry to become a clown.

A similar article followed that one in the *San Francisco Chronicle*. My songs got airplay on the nationally syndicated *Doctor Demento* radio show and the *NBC Today Show*, and I even earned some royalties with that one. Positive reviews in national publications, including *School Library Journal*, came soon after. One thing led to another, and I won a Children's

Music Web Award for Best Children's Album for my CD *Get Down with the Clown*. After that, I was awarded Best of the Best Children's Entertainer by *Peninsula Parent Magazine* for nine years in a row.

As my success continued, I continued to travel, too, and I have taken three more trips to Europe. When I wasn't traveling, I created a local television show, *Daffy Dave's Tree Fort*. I made a movie called *The Silly Adventures of Daffy Dave*. I made a YouTube channel that now has more than one hundred videos on it, and I continue to earn revenue from advertising placed on those clips. During this period of my life, I performed some lucrative concerts with the Daffy Dave Band and recorded a total of nine children's music albums. From this time, I have well more than one hundred songs on iTunes. I have done so well financially that I was able to purchase a mobile home in south San Jose, California, where I now live.

~.~

A well known Seattle composer, Carol Sams, created a classical choral piece called "Daffy Dave" during this time, too, based on my dad's poem by the same name. I found out about her composition as I sat in a pew at Prospect Congregational Church in Seattle, where I had once been a youth pastor. Dad was retired by this time, but Mom was still a member of the choir. When I realized the choir was singing about Daffy Dave I almost fell out of the pew! I was speechless and humbled beyond belief. Here are the words the choir sang that day:

Daffy Dave
--Arthur George Mampel
from *Winter Wheat*, Copyright 2005

At thirty-one my only son
Set out with verve and zest
To find his way under the sun
To manage every test.

He had his share of ups and downs

His way had many hits and lows
But when he chose to be a clown
A hearty wind began to blow

And what was once a cloudy day
Turned into blue and sunny ways.

My son was lost, but now he's found
The day he chose to be a clown.
The heavens blessed him on his way
When he was knighted "Daffy Dave."

~.~

The magic formula for "bottling" Daffy Dave and going big time continued to elude me. In fact, I didn't even know what I meant by "big time" or if I really even wanted that life anyway. I met with venture capitalists in the Silicon Valley who talked with me about obtaining funding for my television show, but nothing ever came of it. A script writer from Los Angeles consulted with me to write a screenplay based on Daffy Dave, but that never went anywhere, either. My CD's and DVD's are loved by lots of kids and I still sell them, but I'm not as popular as the Wiggles or Sesame Street. This was during the time when I was filming episodes for my television show *Daffy Dave's Tree Fort* and the movie *The Silly Adventures of Daffy Dave*. I had ideas about creating a media company for my CD's and DVD's, touring the country with the Daffy Dave Band, and having my own kids' television show in Los Angeles.

At the same time, because I still needed to pay the bills and keep up with my rent, I was also performing small and simple live shows around the Bay Area. I began to notice that I loved the intimacy of live entertainment, while I hated the long waits between shots as we filmed the movie and the episodes for the television show. The live shows seemed more natural and organic to me, and I felt more love connection with the audience during live shows. I began to wonder just why it was that I would want to be popular nationally.

I began to get a glimmer that maybe going big time was

not all that desirable, for me anyway, what with all the stressors and pressures. That goal seemed elusive for me. I didn't know how to do it, and I had no one to teach me. Besides, I gradually came to realize that I loved living under the radar. I loved having lots of free time to create, to enjoy life, and spend time with my friends and on my garden and hobbies. Not only that, but the burst in popularity of my local shows, combined with travel, schlepping my equipment, and adrenalin burn-out, took a toll on my body. I had problems with my back, and I had kidney stones four separate times. I developed a hernia; I had surgery to remove my gall bladder; and I had surgery on one of my feet. Then, in June 2001 something happened that prompted me to give up my dreams of the big time once and for all. I had a heart attack.

~.~

I was lying in bed at Stanford Hospital when someone told me what a dad of one of the posse kids said: "The town clown is down." Of course, I had to laugh. The posse brought food to me and gave my mom a place to stay when she came to visit me. I am so grateful for them, and I'm reminded once again that it takes a whole village to support your local clown. As it turned out, my heart attack was apparently caused by an allergy to a statin drug I was taking to reduce cholesterol. When I weaned myself off that drug muscle spasms I'd been having in my legs subsided. I am still searching with my doctors to find the right cholesterol-reducing medication for me.

My health problems did not happen all at once, but I have had a health crisis once or twice a year over the course of the ensuing years, continuing until the present day. I still enjoyed performing as Daffy Dave as these health issues surfaced, but I could see the writing on the wall. I knew I needed to cut back on performing and bring more balance to my life. Today I practice yoga and meditation, and I have hobbies that have nothing to do with creating professional comedy material. I have also started to think about how to move gradually out of doing Daffy Dave and plan for retirement and aging. I'm not in a rush to retire Daffy Dave, but I know now that I want to move into the life of a writer and artist in my later years. This transition has barely begun as I write this book in 2013. I will likely continue to do some form of Daffy Dave as I grow older, but I am also working on developing more online revenue streams from my extensive library of video and music content. To that end, I've hired computer and marketing wizard, my friend Rob Bartz, to help me do that. It's exciting to see this aspect of my business begin to take shape now and to see the possibilities for drawing some more income from my years of relentless creative work and financial investment. To paraphrase the New Testament, I am feeding the ox that pulls the plow.

During a time when I was experiencing health issues, I was asked to visit sick kids in hospitals and perform my funny routines for kids who had life-threatening illnesses. I felt like Reverend Daffy Dave. My experience as a hospital and hospice chaplain came back to me and those qualities ascended in my soul again. I tempered my clown antics for those sensitive hospital environments and brought a kinder, more compassionate version of Daffy Dave to those kids, but the clueless clown kept them laughing anyway. I was so gratified to realize that laughter had a positive effect on their recovery. In one case, I visited one of the kids in the posse, Elle Billman. Elle was quite young at the time and her diagnosis of cancer shook everyone in the posse, including me. I went to see her at Stanford Children's Hospital as soon as I heard she was ill and sang Daffy Dave songs to her. I did some gentle, silly antics and had her laughing and smiling, bringing grateful tears to the eyes of her mom, Dawn Billman. Elle eventually recovered and is now cancer-free, thanks to the combined miracles of science and love. In another case, a friend, Mary Moran, asked me to visit her daughter, River, at Stanford Hospital. Her doctors were concerned because the oxygen levels in her blood were very low. After a bunch of silly Daffy Dave antics that had River, Mary, and Mary's doctors and nurses cracking up, Mary looked over at one of the monitors near River's bed and noticed that her daughter's oxygen levels had shot up, most likely because of her laughter. Laughter really is the best medicine.

~.~

After about fifteen years of performing as Daffy Dave, I became disillusioned, burnt-out. I tried everything I could think of to renew my interest in clowning. I remembered that when the late Marcel Marceau was asked how he was able to perform as a mime his whole life, he answered, "I take a lot of vacations!" That reminded me that in one of my busiest years, the year I was a "six-figure" clown, I took ten weeks of vacation. So, yep, I had tried that. I added new tricks to my show, wrote some new songs, and took lots of breaks. I started gardening and did more journaling. I boosted my meditation practice. I was willing to do whatever it took, but the feeling of burnout persisted. I was scared. I didn't know what new career might await me if I couldn't renew myself as Daffy Dave. I didn't think Depresso the Clown would get many birthday party gigs.

It got to the point where I knew I could no longer foist my jaded, disgruntled state on my fans. But what was I to do? It had taken me the first thirty years of my life to realize I was a clown, and about another ten more to actually accept that I was a clown. Why was I now getting tired of being a clown? I had put too much time and energy--too much of myself--into becoming a very good professional clown. I couldn't just let it go.

I talked things over with a friend whose pithy response was that if I were to stop being Daffy Dave I would get a ton of hate mail. I knew he was teasing, and we both laughed, but this was really serious for me. In my heart of hearts, I still loved being a clown and I couldn't understand, nor did I know what to do, about that nagging feeling of being burnt out.

I realized that a big part of my problem was that I was disappointed that my dreams of making it to the big time had not manifested. I had arrived at an intellectual understanding that perhaps the big time was simply not right for me and I had made a conscious choice not to pursue those dreams any longer, but the feeling of disappointment still lingered. Then, too, I wondered if there might be a deeper disturbance my soul was trying to communicate to me.

Chapter Eighteen:
Beyond the Comfort Zone

"Comedians tend to find a comfort zone and stay there
and do lamer versions of themselves for the rest of their
lives."
--Chris Rock
"To step out of the comfort zone raises the anxiety level,
engendering a stress response, the result of which is an
enhanced level of concentration and focus."
--Wikipedia

I decided to work the Twelve Steps around my vocational life
as a clown in order to discern what was going on with me. I
knew that if I failed to deal with this issue in a timely fashion,
drugs would start sounding like a good idea to this addict again
and my recovery would go down the drain. I remembered that
the Twelve Steps had freed me from active addiction and the
obsession to use drugs, and I believed that working another
round of the Steps would help me resolve my vocational burn
out as Daffy Dave. It's true that faith grows in hindsight.

I had just finished working the Twelve Step process
around some still-lingering resentments I had toward my parents. I have heard it said by my friends in recovery, "Expectations are pre-meditated resentments." Resentments take us
out of acceptance, gratitude, and contentment, and eventually
they can lead an addict back to a life of using drugs if they are
not identified and released. The resentments I still held toward
my parents were based on unrealistic expectations, wanting my
mom and dad to be people they were not. Even with all the
therapy and recovery work I had already done, those unrealistic expectations still remained. I was surprised to discover how
much work I still had left to do in that area.

Before I could even begin, I had to become aware of my resentments and accept that I was still having them. I had to allow myself to see that I was repeatedly setting myself up for anger and hurt every time my parents did or said something that didn't fit my expectations. For instance, if I went home for a visit and noticed that Dad didn't help Mom out around the house the way I expected he should, I would get angry with him for that. Or, I would get angry with Mom for doing all the cleaning without asking Dad to help. These expectations created resentments over and over again; that is, I continued to feel the same anger and disgust over and over again as I rehearsed in my mind the events that had triggered the original feelings. I continued to "re-feel" the same feelings again and again, and it was making me miserable.

When I became aware of this wretched cycle by talking about it with my sponsor, he suggested I work the Twelve Steps around my relationships with my mom and dad. I was angry at first that he would even suggest such a thing. "I've already done so much therapy and recovery work on my relationships with my parents!" I complained.

"Well, obviously you need to do more since you're still having resentments toward them when you go home," he replied.

"Okay," I said grudgingly. "I'll consider it."

A few days later, after some earnest prayer and reflection, I realized I had been in a state of denial about my resentments, and my sponsor's observation had broken the spell of denial. This is why we have sponsors in recovery: you can't see your own self-deception! Addicts in recovery know we can't recover alone. A sponsor, really just another recovering addict who is a trusted friend in recovery, can see our blind spots for us, and a good sponsor will point them out, even if it makes us both uncomfortable to do that. That's why we call our program a "we program."

The Steps helped me to see for myself the part I played in creating my resentments. In the process of working the Steps around those resentments, eventually I was able to let them go.

Einstein said, "We cannot solve our problems with the same thinking we used when we created them." I had to change my thinking, and the process of working the Steps allowed me to do that. First, I became aware of my resentments. I think of that awareness as my Higher Power at work in my life. Awareness led to acceptance, which helped me to let those fantasies about my parents go, leaving me able to live in peace with the people my parents really are.

I reached a point where I was able to see that my own unmet needs for love and acceptance were at the heart of my problem. All of the angst was coming from my wounded self. That traumatized inner child was still stuck in the past and continued to create unrealistic, even childish expectations of my mom and dad. My own unresolved emotional needs, stemming from the trauma of my dad's accident, were flaring up again in the present. As an adult I was able to see that those unmet needs were my own mental and emotional reactions forming distortions in my personality, or as we say in Twelve Step lingo, character defects. My core defects came from a self-centered fear of abandonment and shame or unworthiness. I acted out by trying to control others or rescue and fix them. Not only had those people not asked for my help, I was trying to help them at the expense of taking care of myself. Serenity and authentic intimacy with everyone in my life were sacrificed in the process. I came to see that only awareness, acceptance, and grace could fill the "God-sized" hole in my soul. Saint Augustine said of grace, "...our heart is restless until it rests in you." Today my relationships with each of my parents has been healed because of the Twelve Step process. We are truly good friends now because I accept and love them just as they are, and I have peace within myself as a result.

In similar fashion, when the pain of my recurring burnout as Daffy Dave became too much to bear, I surrendered the notion that I could fix things on my own and sought help. The same process of personal transformation that had occurred when I left the ministry took place again. Yes, I was afraid of change this time, too, but the pain of remaining the same was greater than my fear. I was that desperate. I have learned that the state of desperation is the ideal state for me to be in if I truly want to change something about myself. I didn't leave the parish ministry because I was happy. I was absolutely miserable, but misery was just the gift I needed in order to change. The same dynamic occurred when I finally surrendered to the fact that I was an addict and consequently sought help to get clean. When I let go of my resentments toward my parents the same thing happened again. Most change in life happens in this way, and I suspect evolution occurs in nature this way, too. An organism experiences stress and learns to adapt and evolve in order to survive. In recovery programs, we say, "Work the Steps or die," which could refer to spiritual death, although the threat of actual physical death from the disease of addiction is all too real. Here is another way I've heard the same thing said: "If you don't have goals or something to look forward to, you're already dead."

~.~

As I started working the Steps around performing as Daffy Dave, my biggest fear was that I would discover that it was time for me to leave clowning behind and transition to another career. The thought really scared me. I didn't want to lose my wonderful, free-spirited life as a clown, my flexible schedule, my lucrative and fun ways of making a living, and all the joy I had been having and giving away as a variety comic performer. I was afraid of losing my vacations and the lifestyle I had built that made it possible for me to travel abroad and have so much fun in my life. On the other hand, I wasn't getting any younger and I was finding it harder to perform slapstick and other physical clowning. Schlepping around the heavy equipment was more difficult, too, even though I exercised regularly to stay in shape. How, I wondered, could I keep doing Daffy Dave as I aged? Would it be possible for me to perform fewer Daffy Dave shows and still make enough money to survive?

I've paid for my own health insurance all these years. Every quarter, I pay what seem like vast sums for self-employment taxes, and I pay as much as I can afford into my retirement fund. When I considered these expenses, a "normal" job with benefits looked fairly attractive. As Daffy Dave, I live month-to-month and gig-to-gig. Maybe I needed a quieter job, I thought, a job with a library or something. My debts were paid off, and I had a modest retirement fund. What would it be like to retire as Daffy Dave and change careers in midstream? Would I have to go back to school? Could I train in another profession? How would I be able to pull that off? Might it be possible to reinvent Daffy Dave as a somewhat less active character, or maybe another character altogether, but who? That would mean starting over with my business, wouldn't it? My fans all over the Bay Area know me as my current version of Daffy Dave. How could I start all over again with a new character at my age? As it was, my advertising costs were at a minimum, since Daffy Dave was so popular and well known. Would I then need to come up with new ads for a new character and start all over again?

On and on the questions tumbled through my mind. My sponsor and other addicts in the program reminded me to stay in the moment and not to look too far into the future. When I took their advice I could see that I was living in fear, not in faith. My dear friends reminded me that my loving, greater, helpful Higher Power didn't take me this far in life to drop me on my head! These wonderful recovering friends said that they, too, had similar fears. By working their program they had been led to see that their fears were all in their heads and had little to do with reality. I was told that I just needed trust the process. I needed to remember how everything worked out even better than I ever dreamed it would when I worked the Steps each time before. If I allowed them to, the Steps would help me again.

Even if I did decide it was time to leave Daffy Dave behind, I didn't have to do it all at once. I could make the changes with care and gradually over time. No one was putting a gun to my head! If I did decide to change careers, I could choose to do it in a way that would support me and not leave me stranded, broke, and homeless. Another helpful thing my sponsor said is that it's torture to think I have to do Daffy Dave. If I remember I have a choice to be a clown, I am freed up.

Ah! I relaxed. When I can choose to be Daffy Dave, rather than feel that I am being forced to be a clown by life, circumstances, precedent, or whatever, my sense of freedom grows. I have a feeling of spaciousness that allows me to live freely. I could choose on any given day not to show up for a gig. Of course, I would have to accept the natural consequences of that choice. Or, I could choose to show up for the gig, because I also choose to pay my bills. I have that choice, too. Knowing it is my choice either way, knowing that I am not being forced to do anything creates a sense of personal freedom. I no longer feel trapped by my own perceptions.

~.~

Years before the time when I worked the Steps around performing as Daffy Dave, I was performing one of my comedy magic and juggling shows for a large crowd of fifth- and sixth-graders at a school event in Sunnyvale, California. The kids were so excited by Daffy Dave's wild antics, and they laughed so hard at the end of the show that the Clap-O-Meter exploded from their cheers. The entire crowd of kids jumped up and ran toward me in a frenzy. I was afraid I would be trampled by these amped-up nine- and ten-year-olds. When the first wave of small humans reached my prop box, they knocked it over, spilling my tricks on the pavement. I summoned every ounce of my voice and spirit to yell "Stop!" at the top of my lungs. Some of the smaller kids were being trampled, and I nearly lost my balance, too. I was livid. "Back off!" I screamed, and the diminutive mob quieted and started to back away. The teachers who were there jumped in and calmed the students down. Gradually, the commotion subsided, and thankfully, no one got hurt.

That stressful incident showed me that I needed to change the ending of my shows so that I calm hysterically laughing kids down just before the end of the show. Adults crack up for a standup comedian, but from what I've seen, most adults have learned how to contain themselves and rarely storm the stage, even if they really like the comedian, but kids still have some developing to do. I pondered group energy and considered how crowds can sometimes go out of control and stampede and trample people to death. We've heard about this happening at huge soccer matches, or on Black Friday shopping. I thought about the times when the Beatles were attacked after their concerts. I wondered how I should handle this problem. I needed not only to protect the kids from themselves, I needed to stay alive and unhurt myself so I could go on to the next show and continue to pay my rent!

I'm not sure how it came to me, but at another show soon after this near-disaster I sensed the kids were about to get up and go for me again, right after the Clap-O-Meter exploded. This time, I quickly yelled, "Who wants a prize?"

Every hand in the audience went up, and every kid shouted, "I do! I do!"

"The first person to lie down and go to sleep will get a prize!" I said, and every kid there plopped down on the lawn and pretended to take a nap. That was a pleasant surprise! The parents who were there cracked up. I grinned at them and went on. As the kids lay there, I intoned in a calm and quiet, golf-announcer voice, "And now, kids, as you hear the sound of my voice, you are sinking deeper and deeper into a hypnotic trance." I paused. "On the count of three, you will wake up and have the strange urge to want to go home, clean up your room, and go to bed early so your parents can stay up and watch David Letterman." And then I stood there, perfectly silent. Cameras clicked and parents were laughing. I just stood there for a while, looked at my watch, and let the kids "sleep" while I whistled a happy tune and put away all my props and sound equipment.

Finally, a kid said, "Hey! You're not counting!"

Without looking up from what I was doing, I took a deep breath and calmly said, "One," drawing the word out with a lengthy exhale. I finished putting my equipment away and walked around to chat with the parents. I passed out a few business cards, and then, "Twooooooo," I said. I walked over to the snack table and munched on some chips. "Two-and-a-half," I continued. I loaded up my props and started heading for the door. "Two-and-three-quarters." When my prop box and equipment were stacked by the door, "Two and peanut butter in your belly button," I said. And finally, I stood in front of the kids again and said, "Three." I paused again, then said, "Okay, wake up, cross your legs pretzel style, hold your hands up above your head, and look wistfully up at me." I looked wistfully out at them to demonstrate what "wistful" meant, and they returned my gaze, calmly. From that point of calm, I passed out prizes, gathered the kids around the cake for the birthday song, and headed out to my next party without losing any blood or being sued for starting a riot.

This was the beginning of my now very much appreciated "bring their energy down" ending of my show. Parents absolutely love it. The kids totally calm down and will do anything I say if a prize is waiting on the other end. I've now expanded this ending to include a series of affirmations the kids have to repeat before I hand out the prizes: "I get what I get. I want what I get. The color doesn't matter. I will be happy with anything the clown gives me. And, I will fake it till I make it. Daffy Dave is a marketing genius. I will like the Daffy Dave Facebook page. I will download Daffy Dave on iTunes. I don't really need this prize to enjoy life right now. I'm okay; you're okay, and that's beautiful!" Then I'll ask, "Did you like your prize?"

It never fails that some kid will protest, "But we don't have a prize!"

I'll hold my hand over my heart and say, "Oh, it's an inside-your-heart, self-esteem kind of prize. Those are the ones that last forever." As soon as the kids protest, and they always do, I'll act disgusted and say, "Okay, who wants a temporary, materialistic prize instead?"

I used to think I was manipulating kids with this bit, but now I see it as a kind of incentive program. In fact, I now see that this whole routine comes from my past experience with

Aunt Jeanne when, as kids, we were too excited to go to sleep the night before our first trip to Disneyland. That night, Aunt Jeanne said she'd give fifty cents to the first kid who went to sleep, and we all quieted down and drifted off right away. I remembered that I didn't feel manipulated, I just felt fifty cents richer, because we all got fifty cents the next morning. I suppose it's the same thing for an adult who works at a crummy job just so they can get a paycheck at the end of the week. Maybe I'm just preparing kids to be ready for the real world.

All kidding aside, this is what I now call "clown evolution." My clown organism was so stressed by an amped-up kid environment during that near-trampling at the grade school that it opened up new channels of focus and concentration in my brain to create that spontaneous spectacular ending for my show, thus allowing me to continue to pay my rent and survive another day. Inadvertently, in the process I created new Daffy Dave comedy material. I could have stayed in my comfort zone and continued to use the same old ending even though it had proven to be dangerous, but that would have been lame and being lame makes a clown vulnerable to attack from overwrought nine-year-olds.

In my Twelve Step examination of my character Daffy Dave, I identified my unrealistic expectations and resentments around success, money, the Internal Revenue Service, the "big time," agents, clients, colleagues, and stage conditions. I realized that I thought I always had to have a great show, and I discovered that I had been afraid to create new material for Daffy Dave because I feared new material might not work. I was stuck in doing the same old show, the same old tricks over and over again because what I had been doing had been so successful for so long. I feared that new material would throw off my timing, break my focus, and cause me to step out of character. I was afraid that introducing anything new into my show would ruin the good run I had had for so long. My show had gone stale for me. Kids and parents were still laughing, but I wasn't growing as a performer, and that was depressing, whether I consciously realized it or not.

My work on the Steps helped me to identify my fears and let them go. I consciously chose to resume my reliance on faith, as I had when performing was new to me. I started to create again, and my old chutzpah gradually began to return. I hired Leonard Pitt, the Berkeley-based protégé of French mime artist Étienne Decroux, to study and direct my show, and I rededicated myself to my craft. I rehearsed; I tried out new material at farmers' markets; and I hired another teacher of mime to further perfect my performances. I attended live performances of clowns I admired and considered masterful, Avner the Eccentric, Bill Irwin, and Geoff Hoyle. I studied films of Buster Keaton, Charlie Chaplin, and other great physical comedians. I discovered that when I admired a particular move, gesture, vocalization, stunt, or trick from these performers, I expressed that bit naturally in my own performance, but in my own unique way. Truly, we do become what we admire.

One of the things I learned during this Daffy Dave renaissance was the value of "reporting to the audience," a technique in which the performer looks at the audience and "reports," by means of a facial expression or physical gesture, his or her reaction to what's going on. When a performer reports to the audience, members of the audience can connect with the performer's world and better experience what the artist on stage is experiencing. I also learned to express more by doing less. In other words, I eliminated wasted movements. I learned to continuously scan the audience, make eye contact, and play to the back row. I gained some skill in making movement lead back to stillness and performing with more dynamics so that the audience could catch their breath. For instance, I now intersperse bold, hilarious antics with quiet, mysterious magic followed by loud, uproarious physical comedy, complete with spinning plates and juggling clubs and exploding Clap-O-Meter.

I learned to be okay with an audience's apparent boredom or lack of response during a show. I've learned to be more full-hearted on stage. Now I improvise more and play off audience members who are responding to my act, and when necessary, I've learned not to depend on obtaining any response but just to continue performing as Daffy Dave. I learned to commit in the moment to each choice I make onstage with words, movements, voices, and attitudes. For example, the old Daffy would sometimes hesitate about whether to be outrageous or clueless in a particular moment and would lose energy in that hesitant moment. I became more conscious of my breathing, and that allows the audience to breathe, too, giving a pause for laughter and even applause to rise up before the next bit. This practice is called "protecting the audience." In other words, if I don't honor the audience's laughter and applause by being still and accepting their response, they will become less inclined to laugh and applaud. I learned how to engage my lower body more so as to ground my energy. When I perform today, I bend my knees more and I use my legs more expressively. I use my entire body, not just my face, arms, and voice. I became bolder and tried out new character voices in my show, new accents, new pitches and lines.

I gained so much performing wisdom at this time. I learned how to conserve energy on stage so as not to end each show feeling drained. I began taking herbal supplements, in particular holy leaf basil, which is said to restore the adrenal glands after an adrenalin rush, such as happens when a clown performs a series of shows in a single day. I started getting more physical exercise on a regular basis, and I bumped up my yoga and meditation practices. I took up some new hobbies to give myself mental breaks from performing. I became an avid organic gardener and a gourmet cook. Today, I've expanded these avocations to include working on my house, painting, and art I create using sea glass and drawing with pastels. But I believe the single most important factor in regaining my mojo was the fact that I found the courage to try new material again and risk bombing a show or two.

~.~

As my momentum increased with my new performing skills, I started having fun again. I saved up twelve thousand dollars for the biggest adventure so far in my lifetime, another trip to Europe. This was in 2009. During that trip, I attended a convention for recovering addicts in Barcelona, Spain, and then traveled to ten European countries in thirty-four days. This trip confirmed for me that magic happens when I take the risk of going outside my comfort zone. The entire trip occurred as a seesaw of fearful, uncomfortable events each followed immediately by ecstasy followed by more discomfort followed by ecstasy again.

I had insomnia for the first two weeks, along with pain in one of my feet and a kidney stone. I missed one of my trains in Germany, and I had other mishaps. Each time misfortune threatened to ruin my trip, I consciously made the choice to cut my losses and move on. Instead of focusing on whatever I was unhappy about, I chose instead to focus on the beautiful scenery, listen to some live music, eat some delicious food, enjoy some exalted works of art, and have fun. I told myself I had worked hard to save up all that money so I could take the time to come all the way to Europe, and I would be damned if I was going to let a little discomfort rob me of joy! I had learned a long time earlier that depending on comfort in order to be okay and have fun was a trap, and my trip reminded me of that lesson. I let go of thinking I had to have my meals at customary times, or that my bed had to be just right, or that I needed to be pain-free. As I let go, the pains and discomforts subsided, and I ended up wandering through Europe in blissful joy.

When I got back to Palo Alto after that pilgrimage, my shared apartment felt cramped. Not only had I outgrown my older version of Daffy Dave, I had outgrown living with a roommate, too. I had lived with roommates since 1992, when I first moved to California, and I was now ready to live in a place of my own. I made a list of everything I wanted in my new solo place and started looking for it. When after about eight months I hadn't turned up anything that worked for me, I stopped looking. As soon as I did, Scotty Smith (alias Dusty Buckles) called and asked if I wanted to buy his mobile home in south San Jose. I had been looking for a cottage or solo apartment in Palo Alto to rent, and the thought of actually buying a home hadn't even crossed my mind. I had had a mobile home before when I was a minister in Idaho but lost it when I left the ministry. Truth be told, I also considered that in large part I lost that home because of my active addiction. I never imagined I'd ever have enough money to actually buy another mobile home, especially in the over-priced Bay Area. I was surprised at this turn of events but kept an open mind.

Scotty said, "Well, you don't have to do it, but why not just come down and take a look." I asked him how much he wanted and he told me fifty grand. I could hardly believe it. I quickly rethought my vision and goals from a brand-new perspective. Fifty grand for a one-thousand-square-foot home of my own was a really good deal. I realized my loving Higher Power was far more lavish than I had thought, and I smiled. Where I had only been visualizing a rental for my new living quarters, I was being led to have a chance to buy a home of my own. Again, the abundant universe stepped in to shower me with blessings once I took a single step outside my comfort zone. I know for sure I am not the only one this principle works for. It can work for anyone who tries it. Keep following your bliss, even as that inspiration changes shape and form, and you--and the world-- will be blessed by it.

I thought, "Wow, I'm turning fifty this year. That sounds synchronous. I could buy a place for fifty Gs on my fiftieth BD." I would need to consider the space rent, but there would be no property taxes on a mobile home of that vintage. And when I went to see Scotty's mobile home, I fell in love it. It was roomy and comfortable, and I could see myself living there. I would have more privacy to create, rehearse, work on new material, and grow. It would be a risk, but I had learned in recovery that when I took risks that I believed were in accord with my Higher Power's will for me, I grew each time, even when I stumbled. This kind of risk is not to be confused with the "risky behavior" I had indulged in as an active addict. This time, I was taking a risk to grow again by accepting the opportunity to have a second chance in life to own my own home.

One thing led to another and by June 1, 2011, I had purchased my mobile home and moved in. I now own my own home again, albeit a mobile one, better known as the "clown lair." It's a home on the fringes of the American Dream, as my friend Mick says, and owning it is something that never would have been possible had I not stayed clean and continued working my program of recovery. Because I worked the Steps again around my need to grow as a performer, I also took other risks in life, including taking an extended vacation in Europe and purchasing my mobile home. Without my program of recovery I would never have had the experience, courage, and faith to take any of these risks. I know that more risks, more growth await me in my life. As we say in recovery, "More will be revealed."

Chapter Nineteen: Reverend Satellite, Minister in Disguise

"Sometimes, when we lose ourselves in fear and despair, in routine and constancy, in hopelessness and tragedy, we can thank God for Bavarian sugar cookies. And, fortunately, when there aren't any cookies, we can still find reassurance in a familiar hand on our skin, or a kind and loving gesture, or subtle encouragement, or a loving embrace, or an offer of comfort, not to mention hospital gurneys and nose plugs, an uneaten Danish, soft-spoken secrets, and Fender Stratocasters, and maybe the occasional piece of fiction. And we must remember that all these things, the nuances, the anomalies, the subtleties, which we assume only accessorize our days, are effective for a much larger and nobler cause. They are here to save our lives. I know the idea seems strange, but I also know that it just so happens to be true."
--Zach Helm, from the shooting script for
Stranger than Fiction

It wasn't too long after our family moved from Kauai to Seattle in 1978 that my dad discovered an unassuming little tavern with a fireplace. Every now and then, he would hop into his Model A and putter down toward Lake Washington to an area known as Madison Park. The tavern, called the Red Onion, played host to an assortment of friendly folks, and Pops would go there to sip wine and read and write poetry, watch a Mariners game on television, or chat with the locals. After he had been going there for about five years, he was sitting by the fireplace reading a book of poems by the late Theodore Roethke, and the proprietor noticed the book. "I knew that guy," he said.

Dad looked up. "This guy?" He pointed to Roethke's

name on the cover.

The tavern owner nodded. "He used to hang out at my place when it was a few doors down."

"What? Really?" Excited, Dad sat up straighter. "You've got to tell me anything you can remember about him. What was he like?"

"He looked like some Mafioso," said the owner.

"Anything else?"

"Nah. I didn't know him that well. He was just a customer."

It wasn't much, but it was enough for Dad. "I'm going to make this my hangout," he said to himself, and he's been going there ever since. When I'm visiting my family in Seattle and Dad's not around, whether it's lunchtime or late afternoon, chances are he's at the Red Onion, sitting by the fireplace, scribbling a poem, sipping wine, eating a bowl of chili, or chatting with the locals, some of whom might even have known Mr. Roethke from the times when he frequented the tavern, back in the 1950's. I once asked my dad why he likes to go to the Red Onion so much and he said, "It's my satellite church." Half-jokingly, he compared himself to Graham Greene's "whiskey priest" in his 1940 novel, *The Power and the Glory*. Dad retired from his ministry at Beacon Avenue United Church of Christ in 1998, but even before his retirement, when he wasn't attending to his flock up on Beacon Hill, he was a minister in disguise down by the lake at the Red Onion. He published a poem about the tavern that now hangs on the wall there:

Red Onion
--Arthur George Mampel
from *Antlers in the Treetop*, Copyright 2000

Red Onion, what a place to be!
How fond your pleasant company
when night-time fingers slowly creep,
descending on you like a thief,
comes stealing o'er the dreamy heart
at rest beside the brazen hearth.

Your rousing mood brings cheer to all
who share the embrace of your walls.
At eve our hobbit thoughts pursue
the drinking of your magic brew.

We raise our glasses to be filled
with an alchemy distilled,
that works upon the soul's climb,
as tales told in eerie rhyme.

Sweet Tavern near the Puget Sound,
safe haven from the blight of town,
soft messenger with lyric style
invites us come and rest awhile.

~.~

One morning in Palo Alto when I was in early recovery from addiction, I noticed that the birds were singing and I felt with delight the warmth of sunlight on my face. I smiled, I walked out to the back patio, sat down in a chair, and watched the breezes move the leafy shadows from the swaying birch trees above me, transfixed by the simple beauty around me. Active addiction had robbed me of the ability to appreciate such nuances, but active recovery restored my ability to appreciate them again. Later that day, I stood up and spoke about this ordinary but profound experience and found myself moved to tears.

Fourteen years later, when I worked the Twelve Steps around my vocational dissatisfaction, another level of nuances revealed themselves to me, and I felt perhaps even more passion and conviction about this new level of awareness. This time, though, along with working the Twelve Steps with my sponsor, the avocations I had developed in recent years also played a part in bringing to light my new level of awareness. Writing poetry, gardening, painting, and other hobbies I had returned to as I continued in my recovery further opened my senses and my soul to the beauty of small, particular wonders all around and within me.

263

Recovery fellowships certainly don't have a monopoly on spiritual principles, but they are such a wonderfully effective path for remembering and engaging with these principles in daily life, especially if you are an addict of any kind. Recovery work helped me to let go of foolish aspirations for the "big time." While all along I had known my ambitions might lead me away from the path that was truly mine, the Steps clarified the issues for me and allowed me not only to see but to feel how distracting, painful, and harmful to my spirit was my pursuit of fame and fortune. Not that there is anything inherently wrong in fame and fortune, but I had been postponing my joy until Daffy Dave hit the big time. I was distracted and blind to the miracles of life already happening around me, in small, everyday events and nuances. I learned, this time through the Steps, that not only can the Twelve Steps free me from active addiction to drugs, but they can continue to free me from the ways in which my personality became distorted during my drug-using days, distortions that rob me of the ability to live life fully and in the moment. Thanks to recovery and the Twelve Steps, I now live with daily contentment and occasional wild joy.

I suppose aging, in particular hitting that milestone birthday of fifty years, also helped me to appreciate the little things in life more, too. Statistically speaking, I'm closer to the grave, and that knowledge creates a sense of urgency in me to live life with more gusto. Dad likes to say, "Life begins in earnest at fifty."

As the fires of my ambition for the big time died down to mere smoldering embers, my passion for performing as Daffy Dave returned. I experienced a rebirth of creativity and along with it a renewed enthusiasm for my other interests in life. As I continued taking risks and stepping outside of my comfort zone, my spirit came alive and inspiration flowed into me, and abundance flowed my way, too.

Abundance is tricky, though. I try to remember that it's all transitory and be grateful for it, however it manifests, in the here and now. For example, when I moved into my new mobile home in San Jose, I was amused that the word "mobile" described my home. I thought of myself as a hermit crab who had outgrown one shell and was trading it for another. When I'm alone in my home these days, it feels to me like one of the old clubhouses I used to build when I was a kid, or maybe, I think, it's a houseboat shipwrecked in a mobile home park. The word "mobile" reminds me that all life is transitory and I'm just a pilgrim passing through the shadows of life. Despite the fact that my mobile home is transitory, I care for it and decorate it as a kind of friendly temple. It is neat, clean, and uncluttered so that chi, the life energy in all things, can flow and I can have room to create and grow. In the Eastern tradition of Shambhala this is known as "raising the wind horse." It doesn't matter where you live, even if it's a mud hut, the care and cleanliness you bring to your home, the respect and creativity you apply toward it, can lift your spirits and boost your soulfulness.

The transitory nature of my home also reminds me that, like Steinbeck in *Travels with Charlie,* I am a "vacilando," a Spanish word that Steinbeck used to mean someone for whom the experience of travel is more important than reaching a specific destination. My dad, my Uncle Ed, and I once took a road trip on Route 66, and on that trip we called ourselves "the three vacilanders." Believe me, traveling with those two clowns, it's a good thing our destination wasn't very important because we repeatedly got lost!

Moving was stressful, of course, as moving nearly always is. My new place needed lots of repairs, and I felt lonesome for my old friends, most of whom belonged to the recovery community back in Palo Alto. I also experienced a certain amount of buyer's remorse when I became aware of the almost-constant noise from the freeway about a half-mile away. Then, too, the necessary repairs were expensive at first. My new home needed a new water heater and a new toilet. It had a kitchen faucet that dripped continuously and a leak in the roof. I made a costly error on the taxes for my new home and had to come up with ten thousand dollars that I hadn't planned to spend. I really thought I had made a mistake at first.

The streets in my new neighborhood were quietly spacious and there were hardly any cars going by. The quietness left me feeling lonelier than ever. I was homesick, pure and simple. My new home was nestled out in the country, and from my new front porch I could see the Coyote Creek hills and Mount Hamilton in the distance. With the rains of winter and spring, they turn bright green, fading into a beautiful gold in the drier months. Still, I missed the cafés of Palo Alto and the cultural stimulation I was accustomed to on the Peninsula. My soul had intermingled with Palo Alto for so long, and I was still attached.

In recovery meetings, I felt like a newcomer again. That old feeling that I didn't belong anywhere, that feeling of being on the fringe, returned to haunt me. In our recovery fellowship, though, it is suggested that when you're new to an area, you make yourself known. It's a way of asking for help. I was new to the San Jose recovery community, so I took that suggestion. I announced myself as new to the area at every meeting and went out for dinner with other members after the meetings. I came early to meetings and stuck around afterwards to talk with people, and I took on service commitments as soon as the opportunities arose. I threw myself into my recovery with passion and went to different meetings in San Jose even when I didn't feel like it. That dedication to get involved right away really paid off. Now, two-and-a-half years later, I am known in the San Jose recovery community. I have friends and close support here, and I feel like I belong.

It was summer when I first moved into my new home, so I was performing nearly every day as Daffy Dave. After a day of performing I would come home and go to work fixing something on my house. I hired a local handyman to help me with repairs, and gradually I grew to enjoy living here. Over time, the freeway noises receded from my awareness, and I became more comfortable in my home. I keep it clean and I have decorated it with my favorite art and simple elegant furniture. I added some landscaping and even have a small garden. I have gotten to know my neighbors and I love them. We watch out for each other; we joke and share stories; and we share produce we've grown in the summer and soups and casseroles in the cooler months. Sometimes, I play basketball with the kids who live near me or toss around a football with them in our nearly empty streets. I added a patio area behind my home to make space for a dog and a cat I hope to welcome into my life soon. I am comforted when I realize that every piece of art in my home and every plant that graces my outdoor living space is reflective of my life's journey, the travels I've taken, other places where I've lived, and values I hold dear.

Just as I had envisioned and imagined, as I continued to refurbish my new home and it grew more beautiful and uncluttered, my soul expanded into its private space and my creativity expanded, too. It took about four months, but I started feeling somewhat settled at that point, and I resumed creating different magic and comedy routines for Daffy Dave. Some of the new characterizations and voices I had been experimenting with in my old home in Palo Alto now turned into actual new characters who occasionally make appearances in my shows. Two of my favorites are Foolia Child, the French-fried chef, and Jacques, the arrogant juggler. I've created new videos for my YouTube channel in my new home and written ten new poems. I've written some new stories and devised some new magic routines. With Scotty Smith's help, my ninth Daffy Dave album, *Clown Record*, was released in January 2014. I've started working on a new puppet character, "Little Big Foot," a sloth-like puppet kids adore. Little Big Foot gets hungry and tries to eat my hat, my finger, and my nose. He makes mistakes when he tries to recite the alphabet, sending little kids into delirious laughter. I also started working on some standup comedy routines for adults, practicing and videotaping in my living room. Going beyond my comfort zone, I did my first five-minute adult standup routine for a comedy showcase on Channel 27 in San Jose. That experience gave me confidence and opened up opportunities to look into the possibility of being a public speaker sometime soon. This book, too, took on a life of its own after I moved to my new place. I may return to developing more standup comedy material later, but just trying it gave me more poise and confidence. It expanded my comic vocabulary and enhanced what I think of as the "two-level" approach to my family shows: I create one level for kids and another for adults, just as the cartoons I grew up with did and as modern Disney films do.

I have started over with working the Twelve Steps again. This time around, my efforts are focused on romantic relationships, and once again, I am going beyond my comfort zone. I realized with the Twelve Step work I was doing this time that I had been contentedly single for the past twelve years, but the thought continues to occur to me that perhaps it is time for me to explore dating again. I don't even know for sure whether I even want to have a female companion in my life, or whether I'll choose to remain single. My writings this time through reveal many unresolved emotional patterns that I need to work through.

For instance, I have a long history of being attracted to unavailable women. This relates to the time when I unconsciously became the man of the family after my dad's accident. Mothers provide us with our first experiences with intimacy and bonding. In my little-boy mind, my mom became unavailable to me, because I was her little boy and not her husband. I tell you, the workings of my mind are a real treasure trove for psychotherapists! I'm now slowly, in fits and starts, learning to move beyond desiring women who are unavailable to me. I am learning to date available women without acting out and projecting my fantasies onto the women I go out with. It's difficult work for me, but there are glimpses of freedom for me now and then. I'm making progress and trust I will grow from this process of introspective Twelve Step recovery work and learn to be more content, with or without a date, a partner, or companion of some kind. I trust this process because over the past fifteen years, the same process gave me a miraculous freedom from drugs, allowed me to let go of my resentments with my parents, and helped me overcome vocational burnout.

My trauma from Dad's accident left a longstanding wound which still hinders my efforts to be intimate with others and, at the same time, also inspires immense creativity and empathy in my soul. I'm sure these issues--in addition to the fact that the coyote spirit reigns in me--are the reason why I am just now ready to deal with healthier dating and romance, at the age of fifty-two. That wild coyote spirit has so many competing desires that it takes us coyotes longer to develop and find our niche in everyday society. Coyote spirits are on the fringe of the tribe, as they must be in order to mirror, through comedy and outrageous creative acts, the everyday life of the tribe. I'm not sure my soul could be balanced enough to be in a relationship with a woman. The verdict is still out as I explore and test the waters again.

~.~

I am also beginning to go through some kind of vocational transition. I still want to do my Daffy Dave shows but gradually scale back and become a full-time writer, speaker, and artist. I always imagined that I would mature into a writer toward the end of my life and that has started to happen. I've started writing a novel with the working title of *Alchemy Rising* about a talented but struggling young photographer who goes to visit his dying grandfather in Bologna, Italy. The grandfather is from a long line of alchemists who were rumored to have been the only alchemists with true esoteric information about how to change mercury into gold. There is a corrupt wing of a secret society whose members want to get their hands on this information, and Nick, the novel's protagonist, stumbles into intrigue that brings him by twists and turns to a surprise ending. I am also designing an artist's studio and writer's cabin behind my mobile home and I'm starting to paint again. I continue to be very involved with my entertainment business and have recently hired my friend Robert Bartz to upgrade my online presence by streamlining my computer setup, upgrading my website, and expanding my Daffy Dave music distribution to include airplay on Pandora Radio. This is exciting to me, as Robert is enhancing my website to facilitate user downloads and monetize more of my videos and media materials.

The more my recovery Step work and avocations like gardening, poetry and art help me to let go of the worldly ambitions I never really wanted in the first place, the more I fall in love with the heart and soul of Daffy Dave all over again. Today, I not only love the character and my show, but increasingly, I've fallen in love with my fans and friends, with all the cute, spontaneous moments, all the gestures and words of the kids and sometimes the parents at my shows. I've been collecting and posting these sweet moments on my Daffy Dave Facebook page over the past few years so I can share them with my fans because they delight me so much and because it is a wonderful and fun way to connect with people and let the love and joy flow through me.

This is the real "big time" for me now. My pantheistic spirituality resonates with these delightful moments and all the other little everyday nuances of life. These are the subtle ways the Divine speaks to me and touches my heart. Now I know why Native Americans say the trees talk to them and that even the rocks are alive. If we pay attention, all of life speaks to us. Since everything is a part of everything else and everything is connected with everything, God, the Divine life force, flows around and through it all.

~.~

Recently I performed a show in Marin at a preschool Halloween event. When the show was over, I closed the stage curtains to put away my props and sound system. As I was packing up, I heard a little girl on the other side of the curtain ask an older girl, "Why did Daffy Dave go behind the curtains?"

The older girl replied, "Because that's where Daffy Dave lives."

~.~

A few Halloweens ago, a mom sent me a picture of her son dressed up as Daffy Dave for trick-or-treating. I loved that. And just as I was putting the final touches on this book, a note came to me on the Daffy Dave Facebook page that made my heart swell with love and satisfaction and reaffirmed my love of clowning and performing:

"Dear Daffy Dave,

"I know you won't remember me. My name is Elizabeth Donovan. I am thirteen years old now but I still remember you [for] how you created a positive outlook on my life. I looked up to you; you were my role model for a very long time. I still am shocked at how my friends didn't get the Daffy Dave experience as a little kid. (My best friend is actually from South Africa, so she missed out on a lot more than just you.) I had just always assumed that you were the most famous comedian in the world. I'm probably sending this to the wrong place, but I hope this will make its way to you one way or another.

"From your biggest fan,
Elizabeth Donovan"

That note validated for me that I was right to continue trying to pass on to others what I have been given, especially now, in the "sage phase" of my life. Whatever wisdom I've distilled from experience and learned from others I need to give, however I am able. I know that leading by example is the best way to teach. As Dad told me many times, "If you want your kids to read, you must love to read and do so yourself." Passing wisdom on to the next generation is what the phrase, "Spare the rod, spoil the child," really means. The "rod" symbolizes tribal traditions and values. If you spare the rod, in other words, if you don't pass along the tribe's traditions and values to children, you truly spoil them, and the next generation is left lacking.

And, then, this comment came from a parent regarding the letter that Elizabeth Donovan posted:

"On behalf of parents everywhere, thank you for entertaining our children in your gentle, inclusive (and hilarious) way... and for teaching us how to be silly with them at the same time. I'm sure there are thousands of unwritten versions of this letter out there.

"Sara Niendorf Fotakis"

~.~

I have to say, though, that the spontaneous, loving hugs I get from kids are my favorite reward. I love to hear about kids who want to be clowns like me when they grow up, and I feel such happiness when kids and parents tell me, over and over, "Daffy Dave, we love you." I love to see kids rolling on the floor in hysterical laughter, and when they laugh so hard they just can't help but pee in their pants, it's like a standing ovation to me. I live for those moments when moms come up to me after my show with tears in their eyes from laughing so hard, when dads play along with me when I wrap my long clown socks around their heads with the innocent comment that my socks would make a great Ninja Turtle head band. My ambition for fame and fortune of the Hollywood variety almost made me lose sight of those beautiful innocent moments and made me feel discontented. That kind of ambition has receded into the background because that's not who I am in my true soul. So much grace, so many people and events, and so much hard work have led me to emerge from discontentment and be in tune with my life, just as it is. I love living under the radar, close to people, my garden, animals, wild nature, and real life. I don't want to be chewed up and spit out by some corporate Hollywood monster. I see myself now as a minister disguised in a clown suit. The everyday world is my satellite church. And, like Harold Crick in *Stranger than Fiction*, this is possible because I woke up one day, stopped counting, and started to live my life. Once we decide to live our lives, our lives come into alignment with Life itself. The perfect level of abundance begins to flow for us, and we become the gifts we were intended to be by the Breath Maker of all creation.

Epilogue

It's January 2014 and I'm sitting in the Edelweiss Hotel in Leavenworth, Washington, with the entire Mampel clan. We've all gathered together in a single room even though we have rented four rooms. The clan includes my elderly mom and dad, my sisters and their husbands and children, three small dogs, and me. We have come for our annual winter retreat, the family highlight of the year, to this kitschy Bavarian town. We chose this year to eschew our usual fancy ski lodge in favor of coming to where we can go sledding with the younger side of the clan. There's a slight hitch: There is no snow here for the first time in years. Some in the clan are disappointed, but most of us don't really care. We just love being together.

My sister Sara plays "You Can Ring My Bell" on her smart phone, and we laugh and joke and reminisce about the disco days. In the crowded room, we make the funny dance moves we used to make in high school. "I hear an alarm!" shouts my niece Kelly Swanson over the din.

"No, Kelly," a mature adult answers, "it's just the whistle part in the song." Nonetheless, the sound of the alarm grows louder. Someone opens the door and we can see strobe lights blinking in the hallway. The obnoxious klaxons can no longer be ignored. We run en masse into the hallway and see smoke billowing out of a room a couple of doors down. My brother-in-law emerges from the smoke-filled room, looking chagrined.

"I burnt some popcorn in the microwave," he says apologetically. Someone scrambles to call the authorities. The fire department arrives, bringing with them a gas-powered industrial fan, the largest, loudest fan we've ever heard, and they set it up to blow the thick gray smoke out of the grungy hallways.

My sister Colette dares to suggest to the fire fighters that they place the fan in the middle of the hall and not by the window. The captain says, "No ma'am! It's gas-powered and needs to be near an open window." No one can figure out how to shut off the alarm and there is no management around. When we first arrived for our stay in the Edelweiss, we found a note stating that the hotel was a self-service European-style hotel and we were on our own for the next few days. It was the week after Christmas, after all. Somehow this feature failed to impress us when we booked our rooms the previous summer, not to mention the fact that our poor mother was forced, with no cartilage in her hip, to walk up forty wooden steps to get to our rooms. Other "European" features included a lack of bathrooms in some of the rooms and drunken youths, according to another guest, who had been running up and down the halls the night before we arrived, pouring beer all over the beds.

The three little dogs try to bark over the horrible racket of the alarms and the jet-engine roar of the enormous fan while fire fighters shout orders to each other like the Keystone Cops. We Mampels don't mind. We are laughing so hard that tears stream down our cheeks, and not just from the smoke. Our reunions usually have a comical episode or two, but we all agree this one tops them all. We have already started telling and retelling the story to each other even while it is still going on. This is how I grew up, this is how I live, and this is how I'm going out.

There are no phones in these rooms, so I hereby establish the last sentence of this book to be my last will and testament: I bequeath everything I own to my future dog which I don't have yet.

###

Thank you for reading this book. If you have enjoyed it, won't you please take a moment to leave a review at your favorite retailer?

Thanks!

Dave

Acknowledgements

More than four years ago, my friend Mick Wells read the first rough draft for this book. Mick, ever astute and engaging, had some criticisms about my work that I didn't want to hear back then, but I knew right away that I would need to address his concerns if this book were ever to see the light of day. Discouraged, I put the manuscript away for a full two years while I pondered his comments. In the meantime, Mick helped me make the move from apartment living when I became the proud owner of a mobile home. He has over and over proved himself to be a true friend in plenty of other ways. When I finally picked this manuscript back up again, I took Mick's suggestions and made some deep revisions, added dialogue, fleshed out the story, and worked on inviting the reader into the moment. I am forever grateful that Mick chose to be a true friend by being unfailingly honest with me.

During those years when this book was in dark and quiet gestation, I met Carrol Strain, who agreed to work with me to edit and publish the ebook versions of my book. I send a big thank you to Cinde Anderson for her eagle-eye proofreading and a hearty mahalo to Jan Sueoka for her assistance with correcting the spellings of some of the Hawaiian words and place names. I am grateful to Mary Jo Gorney-Moreno for her valuable insights and suggestions and to Robert Bartz for his advice about ways in which to promote this book.

Many thanks to Scotty Vincent for an awesome cover design. The photographs on the cover of me as Daffy Dave were taken by Dave Lepori. Bruce Carlson took the picture of me as a child hanging upside down from the monkey bars. Sara and Mike Greshock gave permission to use their picture of me in my minister days in the split shot, and the other picture of me from those days is from a family collection.

Every single person mentioned in this book could also be rightfully named in this section, as each person is included in this book as an acknowledgement of the life energy and influence he or she gave to me as I grew and my life unfolded. Thank you, every one of you, for giving me such an interesting story.

Finally, I must thank my parents, without whom, of course, I simply wouldn't be here, and because they, too, believed in this book as it developed and helped me to bring it to completion in a form that makes me feel proud.

To my father, the accomplished poet A.G. Mampel, I offer warm gratitude not only for his allowing me to include several of his poems but also because of his gracious acquiescence to my sharing of a number of intimate stories about the relationship he and I share. His insights during the revision process were invaluable and led to a work that is eminently more literary, humorous, honest, engaging, and readable than it was in its earlier forms. He took great pains to critique the nearly final manuscript objectively, trying and yet failing to forget during his scrutiny of the manuscript that he was reading about his relationship with me from my point of view. When this erudite published poet and gifted writer confessed to me that he admired my writing style, I felt acknowledged in ways that I have yet to fully comprehend. Best of all, while he and I were working together on the final versions of this book, we grew ever closer in spirit and have vowed to work together in the future on other writing projects.

I must admit that I found his suggestion to interject humor into the accounts of my out-of-body experiences jarring. Those episodes seemed so serious to me, and the infusion of humor into my telling of them seemed to belittle those experiences. I tried to take his advice, however, and found myself thereby filled with inspiration and a joyful release. Events I once thought of as strange and disturbing now occur to me in the light of bold, even profane, jocularity.

My mother, Jackie Mampel, helped me remember some very important parts of my childhood. When she read one of the later drafts, her insightful understanding of those early events in my life helped me to revise those sections in order to include essential aspects. She was also the first person to encourage me to bring this project to full completion. For her faith in this book and in me and I will be forever grateful.

Others whose support and encouragement were pivotal in bringing this book to fruition include my brothers-in-law Mike Greshock and Craig Swanson, my niece Kara, and my sisters Colette Olsen, Sara Greshock, and Jeanie Swanson. My loving heart thanks every one of you.

About the Author

Dave Mampel, known by kids all around the San Francisco Bay Area as Daffy Dave, lives on the fringes of the American Dream in a mobile home park near the outskirts of San Jose, California, with his adopted dog Poppy. When he's not performing as a professional clown or throwing a frisbee for Poppy, he's writing his next book, a novel called *Alchemy Rising*. Find Dave online at http://www.daffydave.com.

About the Publisher

This book was published by Sturdy Grace Services, a full-service book-creation company offering ghostwriting, editing, proofreading, and ebook publishing assistance. Find Sturdy Grace Services at https://sites.google.com/site/sturdygrace/.

Endorsements

"History is best revealed not through the life stories of public figures--the generals, the popes, those with self interests to promote--but by the often-lost stories of the unsung--the grunts in wars, the parishioners, the ordinary individuals whose lives are often the least noticed. David Mampel's memoir brings to light the joy and the anguish of growing up in an America where Ozzie Nelson and Timothy Leary lived on the same street. Mampel went from drugs to the pulpit, from the United States mainland to Hawaii and back again. Now, he is a popular clown, a poet, and an explorer of life. He is several of Shakespeare's characters in one human being, with wit and wisdom that are sure to be applauded by a large audience with the release of this book."
--**Steve Glauber**, award-winning producer of CBS News' *60 Minutes*

"Everyone has a life story filled with personal adventure but writing it requires an artistic gift. Reading *Coyote Spirit* was like witnessing someone's family album come to life. Dave Mampel has that rare gift of using words like an artist uses a paint brush to bring his creative process alive. The most prized feedback an author can receive is to be told his book is a page turner and that the reader couldn't put it down. Dave's writing will invite you in and take you on his own personal journey of growth. It is more than a memoir. His life is a backdrop for spiritual insights and teachings interwoven throughout the whole book. You will not only come to know and love this multifaceted man intimately, but by the end of the book you will be compelled to hang out with him. Dave Mampel's *Coyote Spirit* will touch your heart and awaken your spirit."
--**Tom Catton**, author of *The Mindful Addict: A Memoir of the Awakening of a Spirit* and *May I Sit with You: A Simple Approach to Meditation.*

For More Information

To learn more about how a Twelve Step program can help people who have a problem with drugs, visit http://www.na.org.

Made in the USA
San Bernardino, CA
30 March 2016